PRESCRIPTION FOR PROFITS

How the Pharmaceutical Industry
Bankrolled the Unholy Marriage
Between Science and Business

LINDA MARSA

SCRIBNER

SCRIBNER
1230 Avenue of the Americas
New York, NY 10020

Unless otherwise noted, all quotes are from interviews I conducted in the past four years while I researched this book and for the series of articles that led to the writing of this book.

DESIGNED BY ERICH HOBBING

Text set in Caledonia

Manufactured in the United States of America

1   3   5   7   9   10   8   6   4   2

Library of Congress Cataloging-in-Publication Data
Marsa, Linda.
Prescription for profits: how the pharmaceutical industry bankrolled the unholy marriage
between science and business/Linda Marsa.
p. cm.
Includes bibliographical references and index.
1. Pharmaceutical industry—United States. 2. Pharmacy—Research—United States—Finance.
3. Drugs—Research—United States—Finance. 4. Pharmaceutical policy—United States.
5. Science and state—United States. I. Title.
HD9666.5.M377   1997
338.4'76151'0973—dc21   96–48440   CIP

ISBN 0-684-80002-0 (alk. paper)

CONTENTS

FOREWORD

I've done investigative stories about medicine for a variety of magazines for more than a decade. In the course of doing several stories on AIDS research, I came to an unsettling realization. The search for a cure, for an effective vaccine, even for treatments to ease the symptoms of this deadly disease, was hobbled by the dominance of a tiny network of friends and colleagues at major research universities, and at the National Institutes of Health. What was even more disturbing was that many scientists in the AIDS inner circle had become rich off the epidemic, through patent royalties, corporate consulting contracts from drugmakers, and stocks in biotech firms. This was not only a serious conflict of interest; it also meant that the pharmaceutical industry was setting the taxpayer-supported research agenda.

I discovered this pattern was a trend in science: AIDS was merely a paradigm for what had occurred in biomedical research through the 1980s. Under the guise of speeding the commercial development of new discoveries made in academic laboratories, the Reagan White House encouraged government researchers to forge ties with industry, which transformed the once pristine laboratory into a hotbed of commerce. A decade and a half later, the unexpected legacy of these policies is that the serpent has entered the garden: the quest for profits has poisoned science, while the government oversight agencies that should have been monitoring these deals were gutted and politicized during the probusiness, antiregulatory Reagan-Bush administrations. The scientific culture is now so steeped in business that research is governed by the whims of the marketplace, not by good science. Little wonder medical science, despite billions of taxpayer dollars being poured into research, hasn't made much headway taming the chronic ills like heart disease and cancer that kill most Americans. The commercial juggernaut, in short, has so sullied the research process that it now threatens public health.

As someone who grew up in a family that revered science and its power to transform society, I found this change profoundly disturbing. Much of this story hasn't been told before because of the complexity of the science and the inherent problems of beat reporting. Journalists are dependent on their sources, and if key people stop returning their phone calls, they might as well look into another line of work. And the scientific establishment can be particularly punitive. "Journalists who make too many mistakes, or who are sloppy," warned Anthony Fauci, head of the National Institute of Allergy and Infectious Diseases, in a thinly veiled threat, "are going to find that their access to scientists may diminish."

To graphically illuminate what happened in a way that's accessible to the average reader, I focused upon two separate but intertwined stories: medicine's quest to conquer AIDS, tracing its development from President Nixon's War on Cancer to the fatally flawed assault on AIDS; and the simultaneous rise of biotechnology, which was best exemplified by Genentech, the first and the foremost of the biotech companies, starting with its birth in the academic laboratories of Herbert Boyer at the University of California at San Francisco through the development of its flagship heart medication, Activase, to its current incarnation as a subsidiary of Hoffmann-La Roche, a giant Swiss pharmaceutical company. But these two stories are really branches of the same scientific tree: molecular biology, the study of the basic building blocks of life, which is the foundation of virtually all medical research in the world. In the late 1960s and early 1970s, molecular biology split off into two distinct yet overlapping disciplines: tumor virology, the inquiry into the role viruses play in cancer, which evolved from cancer research to AIDS; and genetic engineering, the stunning feat of biological legerdemain in which genes from one organism are patched into the DNA of another, which spawned the biotechnology industry.

Some of the material may seem familiar, particularly the sections dealing with former National Cancer Institute scientist Robert Gallo and his bitter battle with French scientists over the discovery of the AIDS virus, which has generated a lot of media attention. What hasn't been revealed up until now, however, is the machinations behind the scenes at the National Institutes of Health: the participation of top government officials in the campaign to protect Robert Gallo and the millions of dollars in patent royalties stemming from his supposed discovery of the AIDS virus, and the pressure exerted on honorable scientists to remain silent. Putting these shocking new revelations into context with what we already know presents a damning indictment of the unconscionable behavior of public servants in the midst of a deadly epidemic—which is the direct result of infecting the academic research process with the profit motive.

To truly understand the depth of this tectonic shift, however, and the magnitude of the disastrous consequences of this change, it's crucial to know the history of how medical research evolved. This story really begins more than half a century ago, when doctors were driven by an unselfish devotion to easing human suffering, at a moment suspended in time before the outbreak of World War II ushered in an entirely new era. Medicine was emerging from an awkward adolescence, when faith healers and snake-oil salesmen still inhabited the fringes of respectability, and medical science was taking its first, tentative steps into adulthood.

I tried to be fair and accurate in my reporting, and to give the principals involved a chance to tell their side of the story. Most were kind enough to speak with me, but several chose not to do so, including Dr. Robert Gallo and Dr. Eugene Braunwald. On the other hand, the people at Genentech, including current and former employees, were most cooperative. That section is based on government documents and interviews with numerous people who were involved in the development of Genentech's heart drug, Activase, including Drs. Elliott Grossbard, Diane Pennica, Désiré Collen, Burton Sobel, among numerous others, as well as with Genentech's public relations director, Paul Leyland.

Regarding the section dealing with the controversy over the discovery of the AIDS virus and the subsequent patent dispute, I relied on government documents, published reports, interviews with sources who were deeply involved in the lengthy investigation, a report by the Office of the Inspector General, which is the investigative arm of the Department of Health and Human Services, and an exhaustive 267-page report prepared by the staff of the Subcommittee on Oversight and Investigations of the Committee on Energy and

Commerce of the United States House of Representatives. Though the so-called "staff report" was never formally released because the Republicans took over control of Congress in 1994, it has been widely circulated and is available in its entirety on the Internet.

Dr. Robert Gallo only spoke through his attorney, Joseph Onek, who characterized the staff report as the work of unreliable, biased, and discredited investigators. Gallo has continued to maintain his innocence of any wrongdoing, and insists that his alleged "appropriation" of the AIDS virus discovered by the French was the result of an accidental laboratory contamination. Although a probe by the HHS's Office of Research Integrity initially found that Gallo had been less than candid, it later dropped its investigation of Gallo when an appeals board overturned a finding of scientific fraud against his chief lieutenant, Mikulas Popovic.

But the sentiments of many in the scientific community echo what John T. Edsall, a highly respected professor emeritus of biochemistry at Harvard University, wrote in a sharply critical letter to Representative John Dingell, who chaired the committee. "Although the Review Panel, which up to now has been composed entirely of lawyers, has in effect brought about the clearance of Gallo from the legal charges in this case, I believe that the standards of ethical conduct for scientists are, and should be, more demanding than the purely legal rules . . . grave questions remain concerning the allocation of the patents, and what appears, to a great many scientists and others, as a violation of the rights of the French investigators and the French government."

The process of writing a book, especially a first book, is daunting, and the learning curve, at times, felt nearly vertical. What made this task immeasurably easier was the generous and unstinting assistance of friends, colleagues, and sources. There are numerous people deserving of special thanks, among them reporters Tinker Ready of the *Charlotte News-Observer,* Richard Sia of the Center for Investigative Journalism, and, most especially, Larry Husten. Thanks, too, to the gang at *Omni,* and in particular, the late Kevin McKinney and the late Murray Cox, both of whom are sorely missed by those of us who loved them. Thanks also to my *Omni* editor and friend, Beth Howard, who got me started on the cycle of stories that led to this book. I owe an incredible debt of gratitude, which I can never repay, to my friend and longtime mentor, Patrice Adcroft, Omni's former editor-in-chief. I am also greatly indebted to my agent, Bonnie Nadell, who nurtured this book from its inception. At Scribner, my editor Hamilton Cain's wise counsel and unflagging encouragement kept me going throughout this long process. His assistant, Jennifer Chen, was also helpful. I am also grateful to copy editors John P. Lynch and Angella J. Baker and proof-reader Estelle Laurence for their dilligence. I would also like to thank Leslie E. Jones for her guidance.

There were dozens of sources who generously shared their time and insights, and without them this book would not have been possible. Especially helpful were Peter Arno, Gunther Stent, Frederic Richards, Victor Marder, Charles Hennekens, Diane Pennica, Elliott Grossbard, Désiré Collen, Burton Sobel, Zaki Salahuddin, Robert Gallagher, Jonathan King, Sheldon Krimsky, Walter Stewart, Ned Feder, Suzanne Hadley, Peter Duesberg, Peter Vogt, William Bell, Stanley Falkow, Peter Rentrop, Michael Lange, Pamela Mellon, Susan Wright, Steve Jenning, Peter Stockton, James Love, and Al Meyerhoff and the staff at the Natural Resources Defense Council. I'd also like to thank Helen Willa Samuels, Elizabeth Andrews, and Margaret Martin-Heaton, archivists of the MIT Oral History Program, who were most helpful, and MIT's Charles Weiner for having the foresight to assemble the Recombinant DNA History Project, an absolutely invaluable resource which is housed in the Institute Archives and Special Collections of the MIT libraries.

And finally, I'm blessed with a multitude of friends and family who supported this project, including Alicia Goldstein, Michael Syberg, George and Helen Veneziano, Kathy Seal, Celia Farber, Susan Golant, David Cay Johnston, Frank Rothschild, Brenda Goodwin, Greg Sarris, and Scott Lyness, who dutifully read every word of my initial drafts. I'm sure there are people I've forgotten and I hope they'll forgive the oversight.

PRESCRIPTION FOR PROFITS

CHAPTER 1

An Aristocracy
of Excellence

No art or popular entertainment is so carefully built as is science upon the individual talents, preferences, and habits of its leaders.[1]

—*The Eighth Day of Creation*
by HORACE FREELAND JUDSON

The modern age of medicine began in 1928 when Alexander Fleming discovered penicillin. Working in a cramped laboratory in a London charity hospital, the Scottish microbiologist had been searching since World War I—when more lives were lost from infections than on the battlefields—for a therapeutic agent that would selectively kill bacteria without harming the tissue of the host. While Fleming was on vacation, a green mold had drifted in through the window of his laboratory at St. Mary's Hospital in downtown London, contaminating a culture growing in one of his petri dishes. Fleming was startled to discover that microbes on the mold were sucking up the once thriving colony of bacteria. Fleming was elated. Penicillin, as Fleming named the germ-fighting contaminant, held out the promise of being a magic bullet to stop these pathogens.

But coaxing the mold to produce penicillin was unexpectedly tricky—the compound turned out to be delicate and unstable. Scientists had trouble growing the mold, extracting the active ingredient was even more difficult, and purifying enough of it to perform experiments was nearly impossible. "The mold is as temperamental as an

15

opera singer," a drugmaker would say later. "The yields are low, the isolation is difficult, the extraction is murder, the purification invites disaster and the assay is unsatisfactory."[2]

So Fleming was never able to find a chemist who could or would purify enough of this substance so he could demonstrate its practical use in human beings. In 1935 a disheartened Fleming attended a lecture at the Royal Society of Medicine that extolled the wonders of Prontosil, a recently discovered sulfa drug that could stop deadly bacterial infections. After the talk, he confided to a fellow scientist, "I've got something much better than Prontosil, but no one will listen to me. I can't get anyone interested in it. No chemist will extract it for me." Penicillin was forgotten, dismissed as a laboratory curiosity.

Penicillin's eventual rescue from obscurity and transformation into a miracle drug was a landmark in scientific history, and ushered in a new age in therapeutics. The story of the discovery of penicillin also illuminates the culture of science in that more innocent era, when researchers were driven by an uncynical devotion to the betterment of humanity, and a powerful reminder of how much that culture has changed. Long after Fleming had given up in frustration, a handful of researchers on both sides of the Atlantic continued to experiment with penicillin. Like Fleming, they were convinced it could be a lifesaving elixir that could cure often fatal ills like scarlet fever, rheumatic fever, bacterial infections, pneumonia, and septicemia (so-called blood poisoning) that had previously defied treatment. One of these scientists was Max Tishler, who headed a small research team at Merck. He would later play a pivotal role in devising a method of mass producing penicillin.

Max Tishler was a close relative of mine and was—and still remains—one of my great heroes. He was a leader of the generation who launched the golden age of American science, when Europe lay in ruins and the United States was a beacon of innovation in the decades following World War II. Max was also one of the first generation of Jews who came to dominate the upper strata of science in the postwar era, compelled by the atrocities of the Holocaust to prove their moral and intellectual superiority. Some of them were refugees who had fled from Hitler in the 1930s while others, like Tishler or Jonas Salk, who was born in an East Harlem tenement, were the offspring of immigrants who rose out of poverty.

Medical research in the years preceding and following the war certainly had its share of titanic egos and fractious rivalries surpassing anything in Shakespeare. But, mostly, science was a priesthood, an aristocracy of excellence informed by a deep sense of moral obligation. Scientists lived on modest teaching salaries or grants from foundations endowed by the Rockefellers and the Carnegies. They were drawn by the intellectual adventure of solving life's mysteries, of breaking new ground, of being first. For them, the respect, or even envy, of their peers was the lure—not money.

In any hierarchy—and medical science was as stratified as the English class system—those at the top set the tone. Max Tishler embodied the ideals of American science in that era. A small, courtly man with a shock of russet-colored hair, a thick mustache, and horn-rimmed glasses, Tishler looked like a Depression-era proletarian intellectual who would have been comfortable on a soapbox. But Max was proud to be an American, in the way that only a child of immigrants can be, and his life was the fruition of the American dream.

He was the fifth of six children in a family of Romanian Jews whose father abandoned the family when he was three, the poor boy who made good through a herculean capacity for hard work and a keen intelligence that embraced challenge. And Max practically lived in the laboratory. His car would be the first one in the parking lot in the morning, and the last one there at night, seven days a week. "He was born a Type A," said Lewis Sarett, the scientist who succeeded him at Merck as director of research, "and patience had to be acquired like a foreign language. But he did it."

Even as a child, he helped support his family by delivering newspapers, selling hot rolls, mixing syrups for soda fountains, and packaging drugs for pharmacies. During the 1918 influenza epidemic, he was an errand boy for a pharmacy in the tough section of Boston's Back Bay where he grew up. That job changed his life.

World War I was fought in muddy trenches, which were a breeding ground for germs. The troops returning to the United States from the war brought with them the deadly influenza microbe. The disease swept across the country like a tsunami, killing 500,000 Americans during the fall of 1918 and claiming 21 million lives worldwide. Sensitive and compassionate, Tishler, then twelve, was devastated by the suffering he witnessed. He was also frustrated that the remedies he delivered did little to ease the misery. "I resolved then that I was going to do something in medicine," Max recalled, "whether it be in pharmacy or in practicing medicine, or in some other approach that I didn't understand at the time."[3]

He went on to a life of extraordinary accomplishments. But his crowning achievement would be to midwife the birth of a miracle drug that eradicated once fatal pathogens. Tishler received his doctorate in chemistry from Harvard in 1934, supplementing his scholarships with income from a series of odd jobs and selling his classmates candy bars, which he stored in his locker in the lab. He longed for the life of an academic but he knew he had no future at Harvard, which was then fiercely anti-Semitic. So, in 1937, he took an unusual step for someone with his credentials: he accepted the only job he was offered and went to work for George Merck, who harbored no prejudices against Jewish chemists and was a man whom Max came to admire greatly.

In the 1930s, reputable drug companies still had an unsavory image among the Ivy League elite; the youthful pharmaceutical industry was tainted by the presence of pill pushers peddling worthless nostrums like Wendell's Ambition Pills and William Radam's Microbe Killer. Nonetheless, George Merck dreamed of creating a research laboratory eclipsing anything in academia, and he aggressively courted respected scientists. In him, Tishler found a kindred spirit.

Tishler eventually was appointed Merck's president of research, and instilled the rigorous scientific ethos that made Merck—which was a chemical supplier that hadn't yet formulated a single drug when he joined the company—arguably the world's most innovative pharmaceutical. He led research programs that synthesized drugs for heart disease, hypertension, and arthritis, vaccines for measles, mumps, and German measles, and a process to mass-produce cortisone, the first effective treatment for crippling inflammatory diseases. He held more than 100 patents, including ten of the top-selling drugs in history. A member of the National Academy of Sciences, Tishler served as president of the American Chemical Society, and was awarded the Priestley Medal and the National Medal of Science, among the nation's highest scientific honors.

Despite all the accolades, he remained modest and unassuming, preferring to downplay his natural gifts. "I'm not smarter than anybody else," he liked to say. "I just work harder." Whether that was true or not, what's not in dispute is that he possessed the instincts that separate the truly great scientists from the merely very good ones. He told a subordinate once, "There are a lot of steroids in the body. Find out what they do." That seemingly offhand remark led to the synthesis of cortisone, which initiated a new era in the treatment of inflammatory diseases like arthritis.

Perhaps Tishler's finest hour, though, was leading Merck's penicillin project during World War II. Initially, his team didn't have much luck either in handling the unstable mold. In 1940, however, a group at Oxford University, funded in part by the Rockefeller Foundation, isolated enough penicillin to test it on twenty-five mice which had been injected with lethal doses of streptococci. Its therapeutic effects were miraculous—the untreated mice died within hours, while the treated ones played merrily in their cages, undisturbed. Subsequent tests on patients, who were brought back from the brink of death, confirmed that penicillin was indeed a wonder drug.[4] But Britain was then being ravaged by 50,000 tons of bombs the German Luftwaffe was dropping on London and on key industrial regions during the Blitz. Winston Churchill was locked in a battle not only to save the Empire but to rescue civilization itself from the seemingly invincible Nazi onslaught. There were simply no resources to devote to penicillin.

The world, however, couldn't wait for this miracle cure. So on June 30, 1941, two of the Oxford researchers, Howard Florey and Ernst Chain, boarded a Pan Am Clipper in Lisbon, their lab notebooks and a supply of the precious mold in their luggage. They were on a secret mission to enlist American aid.

Florey and Chain touched down in New York on July 2, in the midst of a torrid heat wave which they feared would destroy their temperamental mold. The mold managed to survive the transatlantic flight and the sweltering weather. But this unlikely sales team spent a discouraging summer tramping through the Midwest and Canada, talking to drugmakers.[5] Just when they had despaired of finding an ally and were ready to return to England, Florey stopped off in August in Philadelphia to visit an old colleague, A. N. Richards, a University of Pennsylvania pharmacologist and administrator. Richards also chaired the Committee on Medical Research (CMR), the medical advisory panel of the Office of Scientific Research and Development (OSRD), which had been established by President Roosevelt that June to mobilize scientists to produce new technologies for a possible war with Germany and Japan.* Richards listened patiently to his friend's concerns and promised to help.

He kept his word.

In early October, Vannevar Bush, FDR's informal science adviser and head of the OSDR, summoned four companies—Merck, Squibb, Pfizer, and Lederle—to Washington for a clandestine meeting at the Carnegie Institution, the de facto headquarters for the OSDR housed in an elegant granite building near the Dupont Circle diplomatic enclave. Bush, former dean of the school of engineering at MIT, president of the august Carnegie Institution, and Roosevelt's trusted confidant, was accustomed to operating at the nexus of power. He impressed on the drug companies the importance of penicillin to the war effort, especially since intelligence reports from Europe suggested Germany's much vaunted chemists were well along on their own penicillin project.

After some initial reluctance, Merck, Squibb, and Pfizer agreed to put aside their competitive differences, and teamed up with Department of Agriculture fermentation experts in a massive, top-secret development program. Merck, which had far superior research capabilities, swiftly pulled away from the pack, driven by an almost frenzied Max Tishler, who pushed his staff mercilessly and seemed bent on bullying the miracle drug into existence through sheer force of will.

Every milligram they produced was hoarded. When one of Max's technicians complained about the minuscule amount of penicillin he was being given for research, Tishler impatiently responded, "Remember, when you are working with those fifty to one hundred milligrams of penicillin, you are working with a human life."[6] By March 1942, Merck scientists had isolated enough penicillin to test it on humans.[7]

The first American to receive penicillin was Anne Miller, the thirty-three-year-old wife of Yale's athletic director, who had developed a

*In an interesting historical footnote, the genesis of the OSRD was the now famous letter written by physicist Leo Szilard and signed by fellow physicists Albert Einstein and Enrico Fermi to Roosevelt in 1939 in which they discussed the military potential of atomic energy. They shared with the President their insight that sustained nuclear fission, a chain reaction, could create a massive explosion; ironically, it was a conceptual breakthrough physicists, many of whom were European intellectuals who had fled the Nazis, hotly debated about keeping secret because they understood only too well its dire consequences. Einstein, a lifelong pacifist, later admitted he had made one great mistake in his life—writing that letter to Roosevelt.

severe streptococcus infection following a miscarriage. For four weeks, she was delirious, devastated by high fevers and life-threatening blood clots. A hysterectomy was performed to stem the infection; she was given six blood transfusions and massive doses of sulfa drugs. She continued to deteriorate, though, and her prognosis was bleak.

On March 14, 1942, however, Miller received her first shot of penicillin. Within twelve hours, her temperature plummeted from 105.5 degrees to 98 degrees. By the second day, her condition had improved dramatically, and she was discharged from the hospital a few weeks later, completely well.[8] But the public knew nothing of this striking demonstration of penicillin's powers. The drug's existence was still a closely guarded military secret; only a select group of doctors around the country were permitted to conduct clandestine tests of the precious elixir. Nor did scientists know how useful the antibiotic would be under battlefield conditions. Sadly, they found out eight months later.

On the evening of November 28, 1942, more than 1,500 revelers from the Boston College–Holy Cross football game jammed into the Cocoanut Grove, Boston's oldest nightclub. When a busboy lit a match and accidentally ignited an artificial palm tree, the packed nightspot was quickly engulfed in flames. In the ensuing panic, hundreds of people were trapped inside. Three hundred people succumbed almost immediately from the intense heat, poisonous fumes, and lack of oxygen. Within two days, the Cocoanut Grove death toll climbed to nearly 500. Another 220 victims clung precariously to life, in agonizing pain from massive burns, their bodies ravaged by infection. Doctors treated the burns with ointments and tannic acid. But they could not halt the infections which kill most burn victims.

Within a half an hour of the start of the blaze, the Red Cross had mobilized what one newspaper called a "Rehearsal for Possible Blitz." Five hundred Red Cross volunteers rushed to their posts, and 150 vehicles were commandeered to transport fire victims to local hospitals. The mayor of Boston imposed martial law. Military officials quickly realized this disaster would provide an excellent natural laboratory to test the effectiveness of their miracle drug in treating the acute traumas of combat. The CMR ordered Merck to dispatch to Boston whatever supplies of penicillin they could spare, and to refine any crude penicillin broth brewing in Merck's fermentation vats. Max Tishler drove his teams in round-the-clock relays, and kept himself awake with black coffee and an endless stream of the cigarettes that would eventually kill him.

Three days later, at about 9 P.M. on December 1, a refrigerated truck containing thirty-two liters of injectable penicillin left Merck's Rahway, New Jersey, plant. Accompanied by a convoy of police escorts through four states, the vehicle drove 365 miles in a steady rain through the night, arriving at Boston's Massachusetts General Hospital shortly before dawn. What happened next went down in the annals of medical history—and dozens of lives were rescued from certain death by this miraculous drug. And the existence of penicillin could no longer be kept a secret from inquisitive reporters and an exultant public. Within fourteen months, penicillin production escalated exponentially, churning out sufficient quantities to save the lives of thousands of soldiers in the Allied armies.[9] By D-Day in 1944, A. N. Richards wrote in *Nature*, "the total penicillin available from American and British sources was enough for the treatment of casualties of the Normandy invasion."

In October 1945, just weeks after the Japanese surrender ended World War II, Alexander Fleming, Howard Florey, and Ernst Chain were awarded the Nobel Prize in medicine. None of them ever earned a dime from their remarkable discovery.

It is impossible to overstate the importance of the discovery of penicillin. Common illnesses like pneumonia and bacterial infections that had often turned deadly now became relatively minor ailments. And the unprecedented collaboration between government and industry to mass-produce penicillin was a spectacular demonstration of what a well-financed, cooperative research effort can accomplish.

The wartime collaboration to concoct penicillin became the catalyst behind a vast paradigm shift in the way medical research is conducted in the United States, a shift that would ultimately dislodge the Rockefellers and the Carnegies as science's chief benefactors. As Florida's Senator Claude Pepper told Congress: "It took a war of catastrophic dimensions to jar enough money out of the national pocket to enable medical research men to conduct their work on an adequate scale."[10] Before World War II, federal funding of medical research was minimal. "Research was not in a position of high visibility or universally accepted value in our country," notes Stephen P. Strickland in *Politics*,

Science, and Dread Disease. "In the universities, soon to house great laboratories often involving large teams of scientists, research before the war was but a fractional part of normal campus activity. It was an activity usually small and personal, often disjointed and sometimes, by some academicians, disdained."[11]

Medical research's primary patrons, by far, were Andrew Carnegie and John D. Rockefeller, two deeply religious Victorian-era robber barons who built their fortunes by monopolizing the raw materials—steel and oil, respectively—that fueled America's industrial expansion. By the turn of the century, these two billionaires, driven by a Calvinist ethic of obligation to the less fortunate, were giving away millions of dollars to worthy causes through scientific, educational, and humanitarian foundations that still bear their names.

In 1904, to cite one early example, the Washington-based Carnegie Institution established the Station for Experimental Evolution at Cold Spring Harbor, a rustic inlet on Long Island's North Shore near the monied estates of Oyster Bay. The field station was the forerunner of the Cold Spring Harbor Laboratory, which is now one of the world's leading independent research centers. And John Rockefeller played an even more pivotal role in the sponsorship of medical research. The oil magnate was depressed by the sorry state of medical practice, which he viewed as based on little more than guesswork and faith healing. Drawing from his vast wealth, he founded New York City's Rockefeller Institute in 1902, an independent medical research center modeled after the Pasteur Institute in Paris, then considered the world's preeminent research facility.

The Rockefeller Institute, which was generously funded by a $65 million endowment, was housed in a cluster of ornate buildings spread over a twenty-eight-acre campus along the East River on Manhattan's swank East Side. There, the nobility of science, unencumbered by teaching duties or the need to scramble for grant money, toiled in splendid isolation pushing forward the frontiers of medical science. In the Institute's gleaming state-of-the-art laboratories, seminal discoveries were made in virology, in genetics, and in infectious diseases that later revolutionized medicine. These breakthroughs rippled like shock waves throughout the cloistered research community, and for nearly four decades, virtually all paths in American medical research emanated from or somehow led back to the Rockefeller.

The scientific community itself operated on a sort of communistic model, where discoveries were freely shared and the practice of patenting inventions was universally condemned. As sociologist Robert Merton noted: "The scientist's claim to 'his' intellectual property was limited to that of recognition and esteem."[12] Scientists tended to be intellectual mavericks who obstinately bridled at the merest hint of regimentation. They preferred the small, elegantly designed projects that could be done with the help of a tiny coterie of colleagues and devoted graduate students, using inexpensive equipment they threw together themselves. If they needed more money, they could tap in to a network of private sources for financial support, which ranged from privately endowed philanthropies like the Commonwealth Fund and the Lasker Foundation, to such publicly supported charities as the National Foundation for Infantile Paralysis, which, through its phenomenally successful March of Dimes, had turned "mass fund raising for medical research . . . into a high art."[13]

But in 1944, with Allied troops steadily advancing across Europe and the defeat of the Third Reich imminent, President Roosevelt asked Vannevar Bush to map out a blueprint for government support of science and research after World War II. Bush convened a panel of scientists to write a report, *Science: The Endless Frontier,* which became the impetus behind an unprecedented outpouring of public support for research. This audacious manifesto, a New Deal for science ironically crafted by the deeply conservative Bush, called for the creation of a national science foundation that would oversee the nation's research needs, endowing pure research programs at universities, colleges, and nonprofit institutes without the unwelcome intrusion of government regulators. The academic community was cast as an idyllic Platonic Republic, an incubator for new ideas and fresh insights that functioned best with a high degree of autonomy and intellectual freedom.

Wise to the ways of Washington, Bush shrewdly positioned this outrageous scheme in a way that aligned science's agenda with the national interest. Despite the apparent remoteness of academic scientists from practical applications of their work, advancements in basic science—like penicillin or the development of radar at MIT—could be useful to industry, smoothing the conversion of the war-inflated economy to a prosperous peace.

"Basic research is the pacemaker of technological progress," Bush wrote. "Basic research leads to new knowledge. It provides scientific capital. It creates the fund from which the practical applications of knowledge must be drawn. New products and new processes do not appear full-grown. They are founded on new principles and new conceptions, which in turn are painstakingly developed by research in the purest realms of science."[14]

In our media-drenched age of the instant news cycle and the pithy sound bite, it is difficult to comprehend the impact of this dry, scholarly tome, which was condensed in *Fortune* and spent weeks on the best-seller list. And Bush, an architect of the A-bomb who was famously photographed in a crisp white lab coat holding a pipe in one hand and gazing raptly at a test tube held aloft in the other, symbolized America's postwar dynamism. The sensational contributions of scientists to the war effort—penicillin, atomic weapons, radar—enhanced the research community's power and prestige. And it exalted men of science like Einstein and Robert Oppenheimer, leader of the Manhattan Project's atomic bomb design team, to the status of celebrated cultural icons.

"The logic of survival in modern warfare," Max Tishler later wrote, "had dragged science from the periphery of our society right into the maelstrom of its center."[15] Whether these inventions actually armed the Allies with a decisive edge in vanquishing Hitler was almost beside the point. Americans were convinced they had, and a grateful nation was ready to show its appreciation.[16]

If it had been up to Roosevelt, a companionable patrician who got along well with Bush, a flinty clergyman's son from Irish working-class roots, this bold manifesto might have been rubber-stamped. But Roosevelt died in April 1945 before the final report was released. His successor, the astringent Harry Truman, was a prairie populist with an ingrained distrust of the Eastern intellectual establishment. He wasn't about to give a bunch of elitist eggheads a blank check, no questions asked.

Truman's longtime ally, Senator Harley M. Kilgore, a New Dealer from West Virginia, was his point man in Congress. Kilgore, like other New Dealers, was alarmed by the growing control "monopolies" exerted over public resources like science. During the war, in fact, a handful of large firms and little more than a dozen of the nation's top private universities consumed the lion's share of defense research dollars; MIT, Vannevar Bush's alma mater, gobbled up $56 million alone, more than a fifth of the $250 million the federal government pumped into university research while the war raged. To ensure that these "giveaways" weren't perpetuated after the war, Kilgore had drafted a science mobilization bill in 1943 that also called for a superagency to coordinate research, but would subject government subsidies to strict congressional oversight and be accountable directly to the President.

Scientists were dismayed, convinced that controls by government officials who knew nothing about the research process would jeopardize scientific progress. "Science flourishes to the greatest degree when it is most free," Bush wrote in a letter to *Science* magazine in 1944.[17] Later, he insisted it was essential to leave "internal control of policy, personnel, and the method and scope of the research to the institutions themselves."[18] Frank Jewett, a former director of AT&T's Bell Laboratories and then head of the National Academy of Sciences, was more to the point. Kilgore's plan, he charged, would make scientists "intellectual slaves of the state."[19]

The issues debated in Congress those first few years after the war resonate even to this day. The outcome revolutionized science. In 1948, Truman vetoed the package put together by Vannevar Bush and his allies, calling it one of the most antidemocratic, elitist pieces of legislation he'd ever seen. But his attention was eventually diverted by the Korean War and the growing Soviet threat. Kilgore's counter-bill met with stiff opposition in the Republican-dominated Congress; however, policies that combined the approaches of both men were gradually adopted. But neither Kilgore nor Bush could ever have imagined what they unleashed.

Huge amounts of public money started to flow into research. The government's largess launched an unprecedented era of achievement in American science. Scientists conquered polio, cracked the genetic code, harnessed the power of the atom, discovered the earth's radiation belt, invented lasers, transistors, microchips, and computers, sent missions beyond Mars, and eventually landed a man on the moon. During this time, federal research budgets skyrocketed, jumping from $920 million in 1946 to $3.45 billion a decade later. But this was the dawn of the Cold War, so nearly eighty percent of this money was funneled to the Department of Defense. Such a gargantuan bureaucracy was created to construct a weapons arsenal that President Dwight Eisenhower, in his 1960 farewell address, felt compelled to warn the nation of the dangerous ascendancy of what he called the military-industrial complex.[20]

In medicine, however, it was a time of unbridled optimism. In 1948, U.S. Secretary of State George Marshall confidently predicted that infectious diseases would soon be wiped off the face of the earth.[21] And by 1950, with health considered a national priority, the basic structures that would administer government-sponsored medical research into the next century were in place as well. This set the stage for the transformation of an inconsequential agency of the Public Health Service into the colossus the National Institutes of Health has become today, the world's flagship research center, unrivaled in size and scope.

Ironically, the NIH's origins were quite humble. It was born in 1887 as the Hygienic Laboratory, a tiny bacteriological laboratory established by a young doctor, Joseph H. Kinyoun, in the Marine Hospital, a Navy facility located on Staten Island in New York City. For the next several decades, the Hygienic Laboratory, which moved to Washington, D.C., in 1891, grew slowly, concentrating on practical public health issues like helping physicians fight outbreaks of disease epidemics and monitoring the production of vaccines, most of which were made in Europe. One of its greatest successes, in fact, was inventing an effective vaccine for Rocky Mountain spotted fever, which is caused by a tick-borne virus.

In 1930, Congress expanded the Hygienic Laboratory and renamed it the National Institutes of Health, in response to pressure from academic scientists to create a government-sponsored laboratory devoted to pure, basic research on the biological underpinnings of disease. In 1937, the National Cancer Institute (NCI), the first specialized institute, was created. By 1950, thanks to the goodwill engendered during World War II, six other institutes had been added, while the agency's overall budget ballooned to more than $46 million annually. Not all of this money stayed at the NIH, however. Nearly half of the NIH's budget was dispensed to academic institutions, whose scientists were recipients of extramural grants awarded through a rigorous peer-review process. The NIH was like a magnanimous mother ship to which medical researchers throughout the United States were tethered.

Despite the vast increase in financial support for medical research, however, the embryonic National Institutes of Health still paled beside its European counterparts like Paris's esteemed Pasteur Institute and the venerable Max Planck Institute in Germany. The NIH's research institutes, as part of the Public Health Service, one of the uniformed services, were structured like military divisions. There was a hierarchical chain of command trickling down from the omnipotent laboratory chiefs and their lieutenants, the section heads, to the lowly foot soldiers who did the real work of the lab, the postdocs and lab technicians. Tenured scientists even held Navy ranks, like admiral, captain, and commander, reflecting the NIH's origins as a maritime hospital laboratory.

Much as had been done in World War II with the Manhattan Project, which was overseen by the Army Corps of Engineers, the autocratic discipline of the military was imposed upon the scientific research process, which is essentially unruly and defies regimentation. So while this system provided focus and spurred productivity, it was a fundamentally incompatible combination, stifling the flashes of inspiration that spark the truly astonishing breakthroughs which drive science forward.

The NIH's eventual emergence as a peerless research empire was propelled indirectly by its worst disaster, which occurred during the successful campaign to vanquish one of the great scourges of the twentieth century: polio. In 1954, Jonas Salk formulated a polio vaccine from polio-causing viruses that were inactivated by formaldehyde; the deadened virus would stimulate a protective immune response but cause no damage. One batch of vaccine, however, was defective—apparently, some virus particles had survived the inactivating treatment. At least 80 youngsters were inoculated with faulty vaccine, which they passed on to another 120 people. Within weeks, three-quarters of the victims were crippled and eleven died. Vaccine production was abruptly halted, and the Secretary of Health, Education, and Welfare (HEW), the director of the NIH, and several other officials resigned.

In the wake of this scandal, James Shannon, a physiologist who had pioneered in the development of antimalaria drugs, assumed the directorship, with a congressional mandate to clean house. Shannon proved to be an adept politician in his thirteen years at the helm of the NIH, navigating through congressional appropriation hearings with the aplomb of a seasoned diplomat. He used his power to convert what he viewed as a second-rate agency into the world's premier biomedical research facility. By the 1960s, a research network had been erected "with components in every substantial university and medical school in the country, with the NIH at its center," notes Susan Wright in *Molecular Politics.*[22] "Work sponsored by the NIH was pursued with the general goal of understanding and controlling disease, and a major assumption underlying this support was that progress in basic research was a necessary condition for progress in medicine." And the covenant forged between government and academic investigators in the heady postwar years—that government-subsidized scientists would make key discoveries that accelerated industrial innovation—paved the way for American supremacy in medicine and in pharmaceuticals, just as Vannevar Bush promised. It was an agreement that survived pretty much intact until Ronald Reagan swept into office in 1980.

CHAPTER 2

A FREAK FIND

Vannevar Bush's sweeping vision of a new scientific order failed to include molecular biology, a discipline that would come to dominate medical research and create intellectual traditions that persist to this day. In 1945, it was in its chaotic infancy, a backwoods intersection of biology, chemistry, genetics, and physics, pursued by an insular fraternity of brilliant theoreticians, eccentrics, and lunatics who were arrogant enough to believe they could unlock life's deepest secrets. "DNA, you know, is Midas' gold," proclaimed Maurice Wilkins, who shared the Nobel Prize with Francis Crick and James Watson. "Everybody who touches it goes mad."[1]

The field of molecular biology was so small its disciples could all gather at a bar called Neptune's for a beer in the village near Long Island's Cold Spring Harbor Laboratory, where summer biology conferences were convened. It would take the elucidation of the structure of DNA, the master molecule of heredity, in 1953 to launch the long ascent of molecular biology to the virtual hegemony it enjoys today. By the late 1960s, the field would split into two distinct but overlapping camps: the geneticists, who grappled with unraveling the biological laws of heredity, and the virologists, who employed the tools of molecular biology to study cancer-causing viruses. And later still, the invention of gene splicing in 1973 would merge the once separate paths of biology, medicine, and drug development under the rubric of biotechnology—and pave the way toward making genetics and virology fabulously profitable.

In the early days, however, molecular biology meant Warren Weaver and Oswald Avery of New York City's Rockefeller Institute. The two scientists were the architects of an obscure research backwater that Weaver had christened molecular biology, where the rigorous scientific methods of physics and chemistry were applied to biology, in hopes of understanding the molecular mechanisms that determine heredity and govern reproduction. Except that no one had any idea what those mechanisms were.

In the beginning of the twentieth century, organic chemists probed deep inside the cells, focusing on the chemicals contained in the cell's nucleus, the aptly named nucleic acids. But the technology was primitive, and their methods rudimentary, so investigators often unwittingly destroyed the very chemicals they were attempting to analyze. By the late 1930s, however, chemists refined their techniques, thanks to the development of more precise instruments like ultracentrifuges, which enabled them to pick apart the constituent components of the cells. As Warren Weaver noted in the Rockefeller Foundation's 1938 annual report: "Among the studies to which the Foundation is giving support is a series in a relatively new field, which may be called molecular biology, in which delicate modern techniques are being used to study even more minute details of certain life processes."[2]

In 1944, Weaver's patronage of this embryonic discipline paid off. After nearly a decade of false starts and frustration, Oswald Avery, along with two colleagues, Colin MacLeod and Maclyn McCarty, performed an experiment that yielded what Nobel laureate Joshua Lederberg later hailed as "the pivotal discovery of 20th century biology."[3] They found what they called the transforming principle—that is, a specific molecule inside the cell of pneumonia bacilli responsible for passing on hereditary information. That molecule was deoxyribonucleic acid or DNA, then considered a highly unlikely candidate to carry such precious cargo.

In his landmark paper, Avery described the outcome of the experiment, but, in what became a legendary model of understatement, he stopped tantalizingly short of making the conceptual leap about the significance of this discovery—that DNA, in fact, contains the genetic code, then the holy grail of molecular biology. It was as if someone were describing the parts of an elephant but refused to declare that yes, indeed, that large gray animal with the long trunk and massive ears is an elephant. Privately, though, Avery confessed his suspicion to his brother, Roy, a scientist at Vanderbilt University. At "last *perhaps* we have it . . . something that has long been the dream of geneticists,"

Avery wrote, a known chemical substance that induces *"predictable* and *hereditary* changes in cells."[4]

Oswald Avery's public discretion was the restraint of maturity; Avery, who had spent most of his career in the collegial embrace of the Rocke-feller Institute, which he joined in 1913, was sixty-seven. With his round wire-framed glasses and owlish features, Oswald Avery looked more like a small-town pharmacist straight out of a Norman Rockwell print than a scientist who forever changed the direction of medical research. His achievement was, a colleague later noted, "the ever rarer instance of an old man making a great scientific discovery."[5] But Avery had witnessed the downfall of more than one eminent scientist whose extravagant claims later proved erroneous. He had no intention of sab-otaging his own distinguished career by hatching outlandish theories.

Avery's reticence, which probably cost him the Nobel Prize he so richly deserved, starkly contrasted with the heady brashness of the "Phage" group, the young stallions of this infant discipline. The Phages were led by a handful of maverick physicists. In the 1940s, some quantum physicists, who were intellectually restless by nature, were then hungry for new worlds to conquer. They became intrigued by the notion that the laws of physics, which had been deployed to harness the forces of nature and build the ultimate weapon, could also be applied to living organisms. By studying the gene, and learning how hereditary information was transmitted from one generation to the next, they thought they might uncover "other laws of physics."

To glean insights into the mechanisms of heredity, the Phages ana-lyzed the life cycle of bacteria and their natural enemies, a set of viruses called bacteriophages that prey upon bacteria. The leaders of the Phage group, noted Nobel laureate James Watson, a junior mem-ber of the Phage group, "changed the face of genetics by making bac-teria the obvious organisms for research on the nature of the gene [rather than plants or other organisms]. Experiments could be done in a day, instead of weeks, and billions of cells could be examined in searching for mutants and determining mutation rates."[6] They believed that determining whether bacteria were altered when they came into contact with the phages would illuminate how the genetic code operated. Did bacteria mutate to outwit these wily predators? And if so, was this phage-resistant information passed on to succeed-ing generations of bacteria?

The Phage group was also intrigued by the bacteriophage viruses. The study of viruses dated back to legendary microbe hunters like Edward Jenner and Louis Pasteur in the eighteenth and nineteenth centuries, who accidentally stumbled upon viruses in their search for infectious pathogens. But it wasn't until 1892 that an actual virus was first isolated. Dmitri Iwanowski, a Russian botanist, extracted fluid from tobacco plants stricken with the mosaic disease. He strained the liquid through a filter so fine that no bacteria could possibly escape. Yet when he poured the liquid into new plants, they sickened and died. Clearly, a microbe smaller than a bacterium was the infectious agent. The common analogy is that if a bacterium is equivalent to the size of a man, then a virus would be as large as an arm. Viruses hover in a mysterious limbo between life and death, tiny capsules of protein that are smaller even than bacteria, and are incapable of reproducing themselves. Viruses replicate by penetrating the cell wall of the bacteria and commandeering the genetic machinery of the host's cells to churn out identical copies of themselves. Members of the Phage group were convinced that determining exactly how the bacteriophage did this might shed light on how all living organisms reproduced and transmitted hereditary information.

The lords of the phage realm were Max Delbrück and Salvador Luria, two European émigrés steeped in the Continent's rigorous scientific traditions. The totalitarianism sweeping across Europe transformed both men into itinerant scholars. Delbrück, a German theoretical physicist who migrated to biology, arrived in the United States in 1937 on a Rockefeller fellowship. He encamped initially at the California Institute of Technology, located on a sun-washed strip of land dotted with palm trees and adobe-style buildings near downtown Pasadena, a deceptively casual place of unpretentious old California money, and quietly driven scientists like Linus Pauling who win Nobel Prizes with a metronomic consistency. Delbrück, whose parents were esteemed intellectuals in his homeland, refused to return to Nazi Germany once his fellowship was over, and taught physics at Vanderbilt University for the war's duration. Afterward, he secured a permanent appointment at Caltech.

Luria, a voluble northern Italian Jew with strong leftist leanings, was trained in medicine in his native Turin. He was a radiology specialist in Rome, and a protégé of Enrico Fermi, Italy's leading physicist, before rising anti-Semitism forced Luria to flee to Paris in 1938. After the Nazi conquest of France in 1940, Luria fled once again, this time to the United States. He worked briefly at New York's Columbia University before he landed at Indiana University, which is nestled in the rolling hills surrounding Bloomington.

The Phage group itself originated in a genetics symposium held at Cold Spring Harbor Laboratory in the summer of 1941. There, Luria and Delbrück joined forces with Alfred Hershey, who would later take up permanent residence at the Carnegie lab at Cold Spring Harbor, and embarked on joint studies of these tiny predators in order to understand inheritance and reproduction (Delbrück, Luria, and Hershey shared a 1969 Nobel for their phage research). Each summer, they'd return to Cold Spring Harbor, which was an unlikely haven during World War II for many European scientists seeking refuge from tyrannical regimes.

Initially, however, Delbrück and Luria didn't find many converts to their cause. "But in 1945, Delbrück took a step that was to set off a rapid and autocatalytic growth of the Phage Group," recalled Gunther Stent, who was Delbrück's first postdoctoral fellow at Caltech. "He organized the annual summer phage course at Cold Spring Harbor. The purpose of this course was frankly missionary: to spread the new gospel among physicists and chemists."[7] The group that gradually formed around Delbrück and Luria imitated the freewheeling intellectual ferment of quantum physics in the 1920s, of which Delbrück had been a young disciple, when that field was in its giddy ascendancy. The Phage group grew into "a republic of the mind . . . a commonwealth of intellect held together by the subtlest bonds, by the excitement of understanding, the promise of the subject, the authentic freedom of the style."[8]

Cold Spring Harbor's matchless setting, situated on lushly wooded grounds near a bird sanctuary on the edge of Long Island Sound, enhanced the communal ambience, encouraging and nurturing the free exchange of ideas that was the lifeblood of academic science. A famous photograph of Delbrück and Luria taken in 1953 captured the convivial atmosphere at Cold Spring Harbor, as well as the personalities of the two men. Both men, jauntily attired in shorts, are sitting cross-legged on two wooden chairs outside one of the lab's residential cottages. The relaxed and expansive Luria, then forty-one, is bare-chested and wears black sneakers without socks. He grins like a mischievous schoolboy, just oozing his fabled Mediterranean charm. In contrast, Delbrück, in sandals and a short-sleeved shirt, sits stiffly, with Teutonic reserve, and smiles shyly at the camera, almost embarrassed to be caught in such a casual pose.

The annual summer meetings inevitably ended with impromptu strategy sessions, distinguished by a remarkably egalitarian division of labor and spirit of cooperation that embodied Delbrück and Luria's social democratic ideals. During those halcyon days after the war, the question they were grappling with was: If DNA does, in fact, carry our genetic code, then how does this chemical transmit this information?

The answer would come nine years after Oswald Avery's veiled confession to his brother. One of Luria's acolytes was a socially awkward twenty-two-year-old named James Watson, whose personality even then was a curious combination of diffidence and prickly bluntness. Born into a family of ardent New Dealers on Chicago's South Side, the precocious young Watson, a former radio "quiz kid" who earned a zoology degree from the University of Chicago at age nineteen, considered himself a "leftist." So it was only natural that he gravitated to the similarly inclined Luria. And within the Luria-Delbrück circle, with their almost nostalgic references to their early years, Watson got "the unmistakable feeling that Europe's slower-paced traditions were more conducive to the production of first-rate ideas."[9]

After Watson completed his Ph.D. at Indiana University in 1950, Luria helped him secure a Merck fellowship to study in Europe and later arranged for Watson to work in Cambridge's Cavendish Laboratory. Before Watson set sail for Europe to do his postdoctoral research— "when he was on the road to Damascus," wryly recalls Gunther Stent— he made one last appearance at the meeting of the Phage group, which had grown to more than thirty members, in late August at Cold Spring Harbor. No one suspected then, though, that what Watson would do in Europe would alter all of their lives.

It was in England a year later, in the Cavendish Laboratory, the experimental physics laboratory at the University of Cambridge, that Watson met the man with whom his name would forever be linked, Francis Crick, a loquacious thirty-five-year-old physicist who had yet to find a suitable project for his doctoral dissertation. The urbane British-born Crick, who had spent World War II devising torpedoes for the

Royal Navy, was, in the words of the great British philosopher-scientist Sir Peter Medawar, "a man of very great intellectual powers."[10] But the chance collaboration between Watson and Crick turned out to be Kismet. "Jim and I hit it off immediately," Crick noted in his autobiography, *What Mad Pursuit,* "partly because our interests were astonishingly similar and partly, I suspect, because a certain youthful arrogance, a ruthlessness, and an impatience with sloppy thinking came naturally to both of us."[11] One afternoon in March 1953—after more than a year of interminable discussions that often lasted well into the night, fiddling with cumbersome models that resembled Tinkertoys, and poring over crude X-ray crystallography pictures of DNA taken by Rosalind Franklin and Maurice Wilkins—this improbable duo, later nicknamed the "bad boys of science," figured it out. They unraveled the structure of DNA: it was a double helix, and looked like a long, circular staircase composed of two parallel winding structures joined by "steps" of chemical bonds, or base pairs, dotted like diamond-encrusted jewelry with genes.

That night, they went to the Eagle, a pub near Cambridge, to celebrate. "We have discovered the secret of life," Crick crowed to anyone who would listen. "We knew that a new world had been opened and that an old world which seemed rather mystical was gone," recalled Watson, who immediately wrote to Delbrück about their discovery.[12] The news sparked a sensation as it spread through the scientific grapevine. Gunther Stent, who was teaching at UC Berkeley, heard about their breakthrough when he picked up a colleague at the bus depot in San Francisco. "As he got off the bus he was excitedly waving a paper, which turned out to be a photocopy of Watson's letter, shouting, 'The structure of DNA has been found.' By the time we had gotten across the Bay Bridge, which is about a twenty-five-minute drive, he had told me everything, about the double helix and about the base pairs. But the greater the discovery, the less time it takes to tell it."

This was just the way scientists like it: a simple but elegant solution to the mystery that had confounded scientists for nearly a century. Several weeks later, Watson and Crick announced their discovery to the world in a brief—and surprisingly restrained—900-word article in the science journal *Nature.* Watson, in a rare display of reticence, was afraid that they'd overstate the case. "The less said, the better," he told Crick. "Well, we've got to say *something,*" Crick testily responded.

"Otherwise, people will think those two unknown chaps are so dumb that they don't even realize the implications of their own work."[13] Crick gave in to Watson, and avoided making any grand claims, though they both knew their discovery assured their place in history. Consequently, one of the paper's closing paragraphs rivals Oswald Avery for understatement: "It has not escaped our notice that the specific pairing we have postulated immediately suggests a possible copying mechanism for the genetic material."

The paper was published on April 25, 1953, just a few weeks after Watson celebrated his twenty-fifth birthday. "Watson was a highly privileged young man. . . . Almost at once (and before he had done anything to deserve it), he entered the privileged inner circle of scientists among whom information is passed by a certain beating of tom-toms, while others wait the publication of a formal paper in a learned journal," Sir Peter Medawar noted. And in the partnership between Watson and Crick "each provided the right kind of intellectual environment for the other. In no other form of serious creative activity is there anything equivalent to a collaboration between scientists, which is a subtle and complex business, and a triumph when it comes off, because the skill and performance of a team of equals can be more than the sum of individual capabilities."[14]

Their finding was hailed as comparable in importance to Einstein's papers on the theory of relativity. Simply stated, DNA is composed of two microscopically thin strands that are tightly coiled inside each of the cell's twenty-three pairs of chromosomes. Each strand is made up of four smaller chemicals, known as nucleotides, that are arranged in a variety of combinations and line up next to each other like two sides of a zipper. These complementary base pairs of the nucleotides, adenine (A) and thymine (T), and guanine (G) and cytosine (C), are always bonded together in those specific pairings by hydrogen. When DNA replicates itself, the two strands separate and act as a template for the formation of a mirror image, matching each A with a new T, and each G with a new C. Consequently, when a cell divides, each new cell receives a complete copy of the original cell's genetic information. At the same time, each gene codes for the synthesis of a specific protein, the next critical step in the complex chemical cycle that we know as life.

What's equally significant is that the two sides of the zipper—the opposing strands of the double helix—can fit together in only one way. Thus, if the sequence of nucleotides on one strand is known, then that of its partner is also known. In practical terms this means that even tiny fragments of DNA will bind or attach only with segments of DNA that have the same complementary structure. This seemingly simple concept opened the doors to whole new worlds of research and is the foundation upon which scientists constructed the science of the mechanics of genetics. "In many ways, the double helix was a freak find," Crick later recalled. "It was so revealing of deep biological secrets that it gave the game away. More importantly, people and money were available to exploit the discovery, leading to new techniques to create new breakthroughs."[15]

Suddenly, Watson and Crick were household names, a duo as familiar to the American public as Lucy and Ricky. Their discovery transformed molecular biology from an arcane pursuit on the fringes of science into a respectable mainstream discipline. "A period of explosive development now set in, made possible not only by [Crick and Watson's] intellectual breakthrough but also by the sudden increase in government support for biological research," notes Gunther Stent.[16] Or, as British geneticist Sydney Brenner succinctly put it: "Watson and Crick may have invented [molecular biology], but Uncle Sam certainly fueled it."[17]

After World War II, in fact, government funding of medical research grew exponentially, leading to the emergence of so-called Big Science, where "the normal type of research ceased to be the private research of individual scholars at the great universities and came to be a highly organized mass undertaking," noted MIT mathematician Norbert Weiner in 1958. It marked the dawn of "a new era in which the research of the individual scholar has become a marginal and somewhat exceptional phenomenon, and in which highly organized mass research prevails."[18] The independent, small-scale projects that had typified scientific inquiry before the war were gradually replaced by complex enterprises undertaken by large teams requiring sophisticated technology and heavy infusions of money. And the role of scientists shifted from the rigorous problem solvers to managers who could formulate projects that attracted funding. "A professor's life nowadays is a rat-race of busyness and activity," one leading scientist ruefully noted, "managing contracts and projects, guiding teams of assistants, bossing crews of technicians, making numerous trips, sitting on committees for government agencies, and engaging in other distractions necessary to keep the whole frenetic business from collapse."[19]

Throughout this period of expansion in the 1950s and early 1960s, the progeny of molecular biology's first generation fanned out across the country to other institutions, like UC Berkeley, the University of Wisconsin, Stanford, and MIT (where Luria landed in 1959). Watson himself—"Lucky Jim" as Sir Peter Medawar dubbed him—was hired as an assistant professor at Harvard in 1955. There, he built Harvard's Biological Laboratory from the ground up, exhibiting an unexpected genius for administration that would consume his later years. While Francis Crick moved on to grapple with equally formidable scientific questions—How does the brain function? What are the biological underpinnings of consciousness?—Watson's scientific output slowed and stopped altogether by the mid-1960s.

At Harvard, Watson had a reputation as a terrible lecturer—he swallowed his words and his thoughts often tumbled out in a disjointed jumble. But he excelled at turning out corps of young scientists with whom he was rigorous, demanding, and intellectually provocative. When he was awarded the Nobel Prize in October 1962, he chose to savor his triumph at a seminar for his graduate students rather than celebrating with his peers. "We were all sitting waiting for Watson to come in," one of them recalls of that fateful morning, "which was most unusual because he was usually there right on time. So somebody went down to the departmental office on the first floor to ask where he was, whether he was sick, whether we should go home, or what the problem was. This guy came back into the room and had this very funny look on his face. Without saying a word, he walked up to the front blackboard and wrote on it, 'Dr. Watson has just won the Nobel Prize.'"[20] When Watson showed up about fifteen minutes later, the class gave him a standing ovation. Then he proceeded to spend the next two hours telling his captivated protégés the story of the extraordinary collaboration with Crick, Rosalind Franklin, and Maurice Wilkins.

It was fitting that Watson and Crick received their Nobel in 1962, right on the cusp of a breathtaking cascade of discoveries in the field they helped establish. By 1957, scientists had determined that DNA employs some type of code to order up the synthesis of proteins, which was the next crucial step in the mysterious process of life. However, elucidating this process proved daunting, even to heavyweights like Francis Crick and fellow geneticist Sydney Brenner. But in 1961 a young scientist who wasn't a member of the profession's elite inner circle known as "the club" did just that. At a conference in Moscow, Marshall Nirenberg, a somewhat disheveled thirty-four-year-old biochemist and junior NIH researcher, gave a short report to a small audience in a classroom on the conference grounds. But in less than fifteen minutes, Nirenberg told his incredulous listeners that he and Heinrich Matthaei, a German postdoc at the NIH on a NATO training fellowship, had unraveled the intricate biochemistry that enables the nucleotides that form the base pairs of DNA to orchestrate the production of RNA (ribonucleic acid) and then proteins. These two young unknowns had, in short, cracked the genetic code.

Francis Crick, who was in Moscow, heard about the discovery and arranged for Nirenberg to be added to the main conference program. The audience, Crick later wrote, was "electrified" when Nirenberg delivered his paper. Geneticist Severo Ochoa, fresh from winning the 1959 Nobel Prize in medicine and obviously gunning for another, immediately ordered all his underlings in his vast lab at New York University to do the next series of experiments to decipher the genetic code. When Nirenberg got wind of Ochoa's plans, he was heartsick. Ochoa had acres of lab space and battalions of graduate students and postdocs, whereas Nirenberg's domain was a little hole in the wall at the NIH—a few feet of bench space in the corner of an NIH laboratory. "The competition between Nirenberg and Ochoa became as intense as any in the history of science," noted science historian Horace Freeland Judson.[21]

The two scientists' bitter rivalry proved to be Ochoa's undoing. "Depriving this junior guy of the opportunity of harvesting the implications of his discovery was considered a very serious violation of scientific etiquette," recalls Gunther Stent. "When Nirenberg got back to the NIH [from Moscow], his fellow postdocs were so enraged that they gave up their own projects to help him. Suddenly Nirenberg had a crew of five or six postdocs, including Phil Leder and Maxine Singer, who later became superstars in their own right. By 1966, Leder and Nirenberg, along with Har Gobind Khorana at the University of Wisconsin, had elucidated the entire code. Ochoa was no place and he never regained his standing in the scientific community. It was the end of Ochoa—God punished him."

By 1970, scientists had formulated a general idea of how organisms reproduce: exactly what a gene was, how genes replicated themselves, how they directed and controlled the synthesis of proteins, how proteins performed and interacted, and how organisms constructed themselves. It took the development of gene-splicing technology, however, known as recombinant DNA (for recombining DNA), to blast molecular biology into the stratosphere, and the mushrooming field divided up faster than amoebas into specialties like sequencing, cloning, and virology. But the intellectual legacy of the pioneering molecular biologists endures. Each lab represents different lineages or bloodlines, part of an intertwined network of connections and overlapping alliances as inbred as European royalty—and just as contentious. Where young scientists train is like a pedigree, and their thinking is indelibly stamped by those early influences. And the spiritual heirs of the group who convened each summer at Cold Spring Harbor still believe science should be an aristocracy of excellence.

James Watson remained a driving force at the forefront of molecular biology for four decades. As the man who helped launch a new age of biology, the blunt-spoken Watson, with his nimbus of gray hair, glacier-blue eyes, and perpetual air of impatient distraction, enjoys a special place in the galaxy of science superstars. While Francis Crick sequestered himself at the Salk Institute in La Jolla studying the brain, Watson took over the reins of Cold Spring Harbor Laboratory, and spearheaded the U.S. Human Genome Project, part of the international effort to map the human genome.

When he arrived in 1968, Cold Spring Harbor had fallen on hard times and had deteriorated into little more than a run-down summer camp for biologists. Despite the luminous presence of Nobel laureates like Barbara McClintock on the rustic campus, the lab was drifting, with no clear scientific direction. The epoch of the legendary Phage group, which had made Cold Spring Harbor the epicenter of the genetics revolution, was supplanted by newer trends in molecular biology. And the laboratory itself was in such precarious financial straits that the trustees debated about shutting it down. Under Watson's uncompromising leadership, however, Cold Spring Harbor was modernized into a peerless research facility and mecca for the world's most distinguished scientists. Staff mushroomed tenfold, from 50 in

1968 to nearly 500 today, the operating budget ballooned from a paltry $600,000 to $28 million backed by an enviable $45 million endowment, while the laboratory's annual conferences are considered among the biggest events in science, with invitations as highly prized as private audiences with the Pope.

This rebirth was sparked by two key decisions Watson made when he took over the floundering laboratory. First, he recruited intensely competitive young investigators, rather than trying to lure established stars. They were at or near their peak of scientific productivity, and they were willing to toil long hours for low pay. "At 40, you realize you have other obligations," Watson has said. "At 30 you can work all the time."[22] And the handpicked postdocs who labored in Watson's labs were like the farm team for the invincible 1927 Yankees. Many of them now head high-profile labs of their own, and a few have even won the Nobel. "Jim's presence infuses everything, the way science is done, the people who are in the labs," says one former postdoc who is now a top AIDS researcher. "It's an extraordinarily exciting place because you're working on the frontiers."

It was, in fact, cutting-edge research that restored Cold Spring Harbor's preeminence in molecular biology. "We rescued it by doing good science," Watson flatly stated. Watson galvanized the laboratory by astutely selecting a scientific problem that challenged his restless Young Turks yet was important enough to attract desperately needed capital. The problem he picked was tumor viruses, in order to elucidate the biological roots of cancer. It was, by all accounts, another of Lucky Jim's inspired choices, and helped push tumor viruses to the forefront of molecular biology in the early 1970s.

Like the lowly bacteriophages, upon which Cold Spring Harbor had originally built its reputation as the epicenter of the genetic revolution, tumor viruses provided an excellent model system, giving scientists tantalizing glimpses into the inner life of the cell. "The tumor viruses . . . offered a kind of experimental probe that would be analogous to the use of phages in the bacterial system," explained Paul Berg, a pioneering molecular biologist at Stanford University.[23] Scientists believed that studying tumor viruses could not only shed light on how genes were expressed in life forms higher than bacteria on the evolutionary ladder but also illuminate how a normal cell turns cancerous.

*   *   *

The study of tumor viruses had a long and distinguished pedigree. In 1911, Peyton Rous, a virologist at the Rockefeller Institute, discovered that viruses extracted from a chicken with a large tumor could produce similar cancers in healthy chickens within a few weeks or months. Rous's experiment could not be reproduced in other animals, however, so biologists dismissed the tumor-causing virus—dubbed the Rous sarcoma virus (RSV)—as a peculiarity of chickens. The notion that viruses may cause cancer was revived in the early 1950s when Ludwig Gross, of the Bronx Veterans Administration Hospital in New York, discovered viruses that were the culprits behind leukemia in mice. Subsequent experiments by other researchers uncovered other cancer-causing viruses in mice, cats, cattle, monkeys, and fowl. Cancer in humans is not contagious, however, and viruses normally kill the cells they infect rather than prompt them to grow wildly out of control, which is the hallmark of cancer. Consequently, scientists were dubious that viruses played any role in human cancers.

But Wendell Stanley, who won the Nobel Prize in 1946 for crystallizing the tobacco mosaic virus, used his bully pulpit to push the virus-cancer hypothesis. The war on polio was winding down, leaving many virologists with little to do. So Stanley, a poliovirus veteran, shrewdly lobbied for funds for a cancer virus program. In a speech at the Third National Cancer Conference in Detroit in 1956, Stanley proclaimed, "I believe the time has come when we should assume that viruses are responsible for most, if not all, kinds of cancer, including cancer in man, and design and execute our experiments accordingly."[24]

Harry Rubin also suspected studying these tiny predators would yield important clues as to why ordinary cells suddenly go haywire and spread through the body like a prairie fire. Tall and gaunt, with the mournful visage of a rabbinical scholar and the confident gait of a former college football star, Rubin had worked as a veterinarian throughout the United States and Mexico before becoming an academic. He was intrigued by the RSV because he sensed it might provide insights into how viruses could cause cancer in humans. Now considered the father of retrovirology, Rubin, with his postdoc at Caltech, Howard Temin, devised an innovative method for growing the finicky RSV in cell cultures, so they could have quantities of pure virus to study and to analyze its chemical structure. Viruses fall into two broad categories: some viruses' genetic content is comprised of DNA while others are composed of RNA. The Rous virus was an RNA virus, but Rubin and Temin noticed that RSV was quite peculiar. Unlike other viruses, which go on commando raids, destroying cells and then moving on, the RSV seemed to embed itself into the DNA of the cell. Rubin gradually lost interest in RSV, however, lured by other, more beguiling pursuits, such as the genetic underpinnings of cancer.

But Temin was fixated, fanatical in his obsession to understand how this enigmatic virus operated. In 1964, Temin theorized that RSV somehow converted its genetic information from RNA to DNA, and then inserted this piece of DNA into the infected cell's genetic code after it invaded the host's cells. Temin's hypothesis was met with disbelief, even ridicule in some quarters, because it contradicted the central dogma of molecular biology, as postulated by the redoubtable Francis Crick—namely, that genetic information flowed from DNA, where it is stored, to RNA, which serves as a signaling system to the proteins, not the other way around.

Harry Rubin, already an immensely powerful figure, thought the whole notion was hogwash. "RNA doesn't go to DNA," he would impatiently fume. And when Peter Duesberg, a junior researcher in his department at UC Berkeley, proposed an experiment to clarify how this transference might possibly occur, Rubin reputedly told participants at a faculty meeting, in no uncertain terms, that "the plan to do this experiment was a *career-endangering* experiment." Duesberg, a young German émigré whom Wendell Stanley had recruited in 1964 from Germany's prestigious Max Planck Institute, got the message and backed off. "Harry was furious," Duesberg recalls. "'Oh, you think like Temin,' he said. I almost lost my job. Harry was the absolute kind of retrovirology—he could make you or break you."

Temin stood his ground, though it took seven long years for him to be vindicated. But in 1970, Temin, now head of his own lab at the University of Wisconsin, isolated an enzyme that produced a DNA copy of the Rous sarcoma virus's RNA. When he announced his findings to a group of virologists at the International Cancer Conference in Houston, Texas, in May 1970, it triggered a wave of excitement that eventually carried retrovirologists to the top of the medical research establishment.

Since the Rous virus copied genetic information from RNA to DNA, so that information flowed in reverse, it earned the appellation of "retrovirus," while the enzyme that catalyzed this transformation was designated "reverse transcriptase." David Baltimore, a young foot soldier in the polio wars at MIT, quickly confirmed Temin's discovery (the two men shared the 1975 Nobel Prize in medicine for this astonishing advance). "When this proof was finally presented, the effect was remarkable," noted Peter Vogt, another eminent virologist. "Seldom has there been such an instantaneous and complete conversion of a field as that triggered in retrovirology by the discovery of reverse transcriptase. . . . Howard Temin turned the central dogma of molecular biology on its head . . . changing our view of biology."

Once scientists knew how the Rous retrovirus hijacked the genetic machinery of the cell, the next logical question was: How did it cause cancer? That same year, Peter Vogt, another of Rubin's former postdocs who was then at the University of Washington, collaborating with Peter Duesberg, uncovered the answer. In a tricky bit of biochemistry, the two scientists diagrammed the genetic structure of the RSV, an accomplishment in those days that was the equivalent of charting a microbe without the aid of a microscope. They did it all by touch, mincing tiny fragments of genetic material with a scalpel and what one colleague called "two of the best pairs of hands in the business." What they discovered was that the RSV gene had an extra, mutant gene— later known as the *src* oncogene—that provoked the wild cell growth that is the hallmark of cancer. Vogt and Duesberg had stumbled upon an oncogene, one of the renegade genes which were believed to be the chief culprits behind cancers. "We thought then 'now we have it,' that we were closing in on the causes of human cancer," Duesberg recalls rather wistfully. "We finally had a molecular target."

The two experiments catapulted the field of virology into its commanding ascendancy. In this heady atmosphere, scientists hunkered down for what they thought would be the final stretch in the lengthy marathon to reveal the root causes of cancer and reach deep inside the cell to unlock its secrets. If these malevolent retroviruses somehow prompted healthy animal cells to grow unchecked, perhaps identifying retroviruses that infected humans would shed light on what caused human cancers. The excitement that swept the field that year was palpable, and kindled the scientific impetus behind the funding the following year, in 1971, for President Nixon's War on Cancer.

Richard Nixon, the poor boy who never forgot the bitter hardships of his early years, was an improbable benefactor of medical research. He harbored an innate distrust of scientists, whom he viewed as a pack of snobbish troublemakers, especially since so many left-leaning scientists had participated in the upheavals on the nation's campuses. During Nixon's administration, the position of presidential science adviser had been eliminated and budgets for basic research were slashed.*

But Richard Nixon had been on the receiving end of some masterful arm twisting by members of the powerful cancer lobby, most notably the formidable Mary Lasker, a politically well-connected New York socialite and philanthropist who had tirelessly promoted federal funding for medical research in the decades after World War II. In December 1969, a full-page advertisement, bought by the Citizens Committee for the Conquest of Cancer, a group that not coincidentally had the same address as the Lasker Foundation, appeared in *The New York Times.* The ad implored Nixon to devote the same collective national will and resources "that went into putting a man on the moon" to combating this deadly foe. Compounding this was the fact that Nixon wasn't happy with the prospect of facing Senator Ted Kennedy, a high-profile champion of health care, in the 1972 election. A war on cancer, Nixon and his aides believed, would deprive Kennedy of his signature issue.

In his 1971 State of the Union message, Nixon called for "an extra $100 million to launch an intensive campaign to find a cure for cancer." Echoing the stance of the Lasker lobby, he asserted, "The time has come in America when the same kind of concentrated effort that split the atom and took a man to the moon should be turned toward conquering this dread disease. Let us make a total national commitment."[25]

But Nixon's cancer legislation languished in a Senate subcommittee

---

*In fairness, this was part of a trend that began in the 1960s under Lyndon Johnson, when the Vietnam War began draining the economy and siphoning away resources from domestic programs. Politicians suddenly wanted to see some return from the government's heavy investment in basic research. In June 1966, Johnson asked his top public health officials—including the NIH director, the Surgeon General, and the HEW Secretary—whether "too much energy was being spent on basic research and not enough on translating laboratory findings into tangible benefits for the American people." Scientists were horrified by this suggestion, and in the uproar that followed, Johnson felt compelled to helicopter to the NIH's campus in Bethesda to placate scientists and lavish grandiose praise on the agency for its "billion dollar success story."[26] Nevertheless, the long honeymoon was over and federal support for basic research, which had grown exponentially in the two preceding decades, fell by 10 percent between 1968 and 1971.

until an incident occurred that has since assumed mythic proportions on Capitol Hill. Three months after his State of the Union speech, Ann Landers devoted a column to cancer. This deadly scourge, she wrote, claims the lives of more Americans each year than perished on the battlefields in World War II. A comprehensive program to vanquish this killer was stalled in the Senate, she noted, so write your senators.

Americans did.

Senate offices were so swamped by the flood of more than 100,000 letters that arrived within the next few weeks that beleaguered Senate typists posted signs which read IMPEACH ANN LANDERS. The bill was swiftly resurrected, and on December 23, 1971, in a White House ceremony attended by more than a hundred guests, including many prominent cancer research advocates, Nixon signed the National Cancer Act of 1971.

The War on Cancer offered scientists the opportunity to restore their public esteem, which had eroded in the decades after World War II. By conquering the scourge that claimed a half million lives every year, they could prove their worth and justify the nation's generous support of science. And veteran virus hunters like Harry Rubin and David Baltimore, who still enjoyed considerable cachet from the defeat of polio, were recruited to be the elite shock troops on the front lines of this war.

No laboratory was better positioned to cash in on Uncle Sam's renewed largess than Cold Spring Harbor—thanks to James Watson's almost omniscient selection of the tumor virus as its chief research target. "It's part of [Watson's] genius—and it is genius—to be able to put together a laboratory to successfully carry out advanced biological research," David Baltimore once said, "to put together the right people and the physical facilities, and to see the direction things would go, to understand the dynamics of intense, extremely bright people working together."[27]

CHAPTER 3

CROSSING THE RUBICON

James Watson's "first among equals" status in the scientific community was amply demonstrated by an inconsequential incident at a symposium held in San Francisco in September 1992 to commemorate the fortieth anniversary of the discovery of the structure of DNA. At the opening session, Watson was flanked by a veritable rogues' gallery of molecular biology—Nobel laureate Harold Varmus, soon to be head of the NIH, looking like the casual California academic in sport jacket and tortoiseshell glasses; Paul Berg, a 1980 Nobelist, stiff and graying, with alert terrier eyes; and the two fathers of biotechnology, Stanley Cohen and Herbert Boyer.

Watson's rambling discourse on the race to discover the double helix was met with rapt attention from the standing-room-only crowd gathered in the auditorium of the Palace of Fine Arts, an opulent building on a bluff overlooking San Francisco Bay. Once he finished, he moved his chair back and proceeded to take a nap. With his head thrown back, and mouth agape, the apparently jet-lagged Watson's snoring was audible through the others' speeches. But no one on the venerable panel dared awaken him.

Ironically, Herbert Boyer, the scientist who arguably exerted the most influence on biomedical research in the past two decades, seemed somehow out of place, like a ghostly relic from a bygone era. When he stepped up to the podium to give his talk, Boyer, his once dark curly hair and mustache now silver, seemed tentative and uncertain, his normally expansive personality muted around this gallery of Nobel laureates. The buzz that steadily rose from the increasingly disinterested audience seemed to confirm that he was indeed an impostor who had somehow bluffed his way onto the stage. Even his former collaborator, Stanley Cohen, sober and bearded, in a sport jacket with patches on the sleeves, sat on the opposite end of the dais, a fitting symbol of the light-years of distance that now separated the two men who once made scientific history together.

Boyer was the hippie scientist turned entrepreneur who founded Genentech, one of the first and still the foremost of the biotechs. But as the unwitting catalyst behind the creation of the golden biolab, Boyer became a touchstone for all the criticism that swirled around the commercialization of molecular biology. Money has smoothed the rough edges off Boyer, a burly former high school football player who always seemed uncomfortable around the cultured Ivy Leaguers who dominate the upper strata of science. Boyer, a cheerful workaholic who thrived on the tedium of laboratory bench work, retired from the University of California at San Francisco (UCSF) at an age when many of his peers were hitting their professional peaks because he could no longer serve two masters.

"Herb really loved science but the main thing that's happened since Genentech hit it big is that in a sense he's dropped out of the scientific community," a colleague observed. "You just don't hear about him anymore. He lost his ability to go to people, talk about results, see what's going on. See, when you get tied up with a company, you have secrets. You can't give your competitor the edge. It's not science anymore. You're in business."[1]

Of course, commercial ties between academics and industry were commonplace in fields like physics, chemistry, and electronics, where research could often be spun off into marketable products. But medical research was different. Medical investigators felt it was unseemly to profit from people's ills. When Jonas Salk, for example, who was funded by grants from the March of Dimes, developed the polio vaccine, legendary newscaster Edward R. Murrow asked him why he never patented his invention. "How can you patent the sun?" Salk replied. For Salk and his contemporaries, commercialism cast a shadow, tainting the integrity of pure research.

And the virtuous biologists, whom one observer called the "Trappist monks of science," were downright contemptuous of industry, and looked down upon scientists who patented research and started companies with the haughty disdain of old money glaring at gaudy parvenus. They preferred doing basic research, like unraveling the genetics of fruit flies or delving into the sex lives of bacteria, that they hoped would yield secrets that would ultimately benefit humankind. Biologists were guided by what Sir Peter Medawar called the "dire equation" of basic research: *Useless=Good.*

"Biologists in the old days took a high moral stand, that this has to be pure science, unsullied by commercialism," Gunther Stent recalls. "Besides, those of us in the first generation thought it was fantasies, Buck Rogers in the twenty-third-century stuff, that we could intervene genetically, that molecular biology would be of any practical use. We didn't have the slightest idea the field would so explode and become big bucks."

The development of gene-splicing technology inverted Sir Peter Medawar's cherished equation, sharply narrowing what had once been a vast gulf between basic and applied biological research. What's more, Herbert Boyer's decision to "go commercial" was an almost inevitable consequence of the social and political forces that subtly shaped and set the agenda for medical research during that era. While the high-profile virologists grew fat from Nixon's War on Cancer, molecular biology's poor country cousins, bacteriologists like Boyer, scrambled for an ever-dwindling slice of federal research dollars. The loss of government funding, coupled with the increasing demand that research be useful, put financially squeezed academic scientists in a bind. Many felt their only alternative was to abandon basic research and hunt for practical applications for their research and corporate partners to underwrite it.

Ironically, industry was slow to recognize the enormous commercial potential inherent in the ability to splice genes from one organism into another. But once it did, the way biomedical research was conducted in the United States was changed forever. And Genentech wasn't even the first biotech company—though it certainly was the splashiest. Of course, in those unimaginably heady days in the early 1970s, when the UCSF biochemistry department was the center of the genetic engineering universe, no one expected things would turn so sour. Herb Boyer presided over one of the hottest labs in the country, a benevolent paterfamilias who inspired his dedicated crew—the technicians, graduate students, and postdoctoral fellows who perform the experiments, grinding out massive volumes of data and grant proposals that keep the laboratory engines lubricated with money—to do groundbreaking work. "Herb would get so jazzed on an apparently trivial result, he'd get people going harder and harder and harder," one recalled. "It was one of those times when everything seemed possible."[2]

Over the years, his cramped laboratory stretched out to encompass a healthy chunk of the fourth floor of the UCSF Medical School. Housed in a cluster of aging buildings and two gleaming white high-rises that jut out of the fog bank that perpetually blankets San Francisco, the medical school is in a working-class neighborhood near Golden Gate Park. Throughout the 1970s, Boyer displayed a real flair for running a modern lab: he was brilliant at conceiving and designing experiments, he kept petty rivalries among his prodigiously talented staff to a minimum, and he seemed to handle the mind-numbing chores of a lab chief with equanimity.

It was a time when people got to work early in the morning and toiled late into the night, baby-sitting experiments, or simply congregated in the hallways swapping gossip, loath to leave in fear they might miss something. Amid the controlled chaos of the cluttered lab—crammed with sinks, refrigerators, cabinets, and long Formica-topped tables covered with batches of chemicals, glass beakers, wires, and equipment—the excitement was palpable. Everyone knew they were making scientific history. "After all these new techniques started coming out, it was like discovering the Rosetta Stone—everyone was just going nuts," recalls Stanley Falkow, a longtime colleague of Boyer's. "It was an incredibly exciting time and you felt you really had your fingers on the pulse of biology—you just couldn't wait to get into the lab."

Herbert Boyer was an unlikely candidate to expand the frontiers of science. Born in the depths of the Depression, he grew up in Derry, Pennsylvania, a rural hamlet of about 3,000 in the Appalachian foothills, the son of a former coal miner and railroad man who never finished grade school and refused to own a car. Boyer attended such a small high school that the football coach doubled as the science and math teacher, which was the first in a series of fortuitous accidents. The teacher awakened a love for science in his star player that might have remained dormant otherwise. The only career advice Boyer received from his parents was his mother's suggestion that he learn to type; there would always be jobs for typists, she felt, even in another Depression. But the intrinsic logic of science appealed to Boyer's orderly, practical mind. With vague notions of becoming a doctor, he majored in biology and chemistry at St. Vincent College, a rigorous Benedictine school in nearby Latrobe that served as the summer training camp for Boyer's beloved Pittsburgh Steelers. But two summers slaving in the clinical labs of a mental hospital near his home extinguished his interest in medicine. "To hell with medicine," he thought at the time. "Who needs all these sick people to take care of; I want to do something interesting."[3]

What now gripped Boyer's imagination was a relatively new discipline that was just starting to filter down to college textbooks: genetics. He even named his two Siamese cats Watson and Crick, though he clearly had no intimations then how integral a role the scientists' discovery would play in his career. He did his graduate work at the nearby University of Pittsburgh, the place where Jonas Salk had staged his successful assault on polio only a handful of years before, because, he once said, "a small-town boy doesn't stray too far from home."

By Boyer's own estimation, his "awakening" as a scientist came while he was studying bacteriology at the University of Pittsburgh. But it was as a postdoctoral fellow at Yale, where he added enzymology, biochemistry, and protein chemistry to his repertoire, that Boyer was inducted into the scientific priesthood, embraced and encouraged by Yale's collegial scientific community, who recognized his innate gifts. He also was politicized in the progressive intellectual incubator of New Haven, where he participated in the civil rights movement, and began to espouse liberal views that his conservative family found heretical.

In 1966, he headed West just as the Vietnam War was escalating, and joined UCSF's biochemistry department, situated only a few blocks from the Haight-Ashbury, which was about to explode into the nation's counterculture capital during 1967's LSD-fueled "Summer of Love." The intellectually inquisitive Boyer couldn't help but be swept up in the currents of that incendiary era, reading Krishnamurti, Fritz Perls, and Hermann Hesse as much as scientific journals, and attending nearly every antiwar demonstration in the Bay Area.

But while the big bucks were in virology and tumor viruses as part of the well-financed federal quest to cure cancer, Boyer seemed content toiling in a research backwater, studying bacteria that secreted a class of enzymes that had the uncanny ability to snip out portions of DNA. This work was a natural evolution of the experiments he had conducted at Pittsburgh and continued at Yale. When attacked by viruses, these bacteria produced what are called restriction enzymes to thwart the viral invasion. The enzymes were somehow programmed to recognize the viral DNA, which they'd dice up and disarm, thus preventing the virus from penetrating the bacteria's cell and reproducing itself. In another bit of the providence that's punctuated Boyer's career, these lowly enzymes ultimately were the prized drones of the genetic engineering revolution because of their adroitness in cutting, shaping, and manipulating DNA.

In the early 1950s, Salvador Luria, one of the Phage group patriarchs, had noticed that not all bacteria were helpless in the face of a viral onslaught. Some were able to repel the foreign invaders. He theorized that these bacteria produce a substance, probably an enzyme, that prevented viral replication. It wasn't until 1968, though, that two MIT researchers, Matthew Meselson and Robert Yuan, actually discovered the restriction enzymes that pulverized viral DNA, reducing them to useless fragments of nucleic acid, the chemical building blocks of DNA. This key finding opened the door to a flood of tantalizing discoveries. A year later, a group at Johns Hopkins uncovered restriction enzymes that home in on specific sites in the DNA and form unique rather than random breaks. This breakthrough armed scientists with unprecedented control in snipping DNA, and in isolating specific genes embedded along the long strands of the double helix. In the next few years, dozens of even more precise restriction enzymes would be found.

In the spring of 1972, one of Herb Boyer's postdocs unearthed a restriction enzyme produced by the *E. coli* bacteria, dubbed *EcoR1*. But what was so exceptional about this particular enzyme was that when it cut DNA, it left what came to be known as "sticky ends." These were complementary sequences of DNA on the two projecting ends, genetic mirror images that attracted each other like magnets. This meant that any two pieces of DNA, even from different species, could be fused together by first cutting them with *EcoR1* to generate the sticky ends.

On Sunday evening, November 12, 1972, Herbert Boyer and Stanley Falkow, who was then a bacteriologist at the University of Washington in Seattle, were sitting in the bar of the Miyako Hotel in Honolulu, sucking down Blue Hawaiians. "Unlike a great number of basic scientists, who tend to be social misfits, Herb had a great sense of humor," recalls Falkow. "We liked to smoke and drink and have fun." The night was clear and balmy, heavy with the humidity that lulls vacationers into a somnolent torpor in this lush tropical paradise. But they weren't on holiday. The two men had just arrived for a three-day conference sponsored by the National Science Foundation on a U.S.-Japanese cooperative program on plasmids, which are tiny ringlets of DNA with a few genes that drift languidly inside bacteria cells.

Contrary to the popular image of isolated researchers driven by their private muses, science is a collective venture, with laboratories throughout the world tackling different aspects of the same problem. Ideally, each successive experiment builds upon the last, as research teams slowly converge on a solution, like an armada of battleships bearing down on the enemy. Of course, the competition to be first can be ferocious, with the Nobels going to the winners. But it's also supposed to be a civilized contest among scholars who are expected to behave in accordance with a genteel Marquis of Queensberry set of rules. Unlike the Darwinian tradition of business, once scientists publish their work, they're expected to actually *help* their competitors by sharing their data and their reagents—the special chemicals or microbes they used in their experiments. Those who breach this etiquette quickly get shut out of the mainstream.

Falkow and Boyer were soon joined by Boyer's former colleague from the University of Pittsburgh, Charles Brinton, his wife, Ginger, and Stanley Cohen, a Stanford University geneticist. Brinton suggested going somewhere for a late-night snack. No one was in the mood for Japanese food, which would doubtless be the staple at the conference, so the group meandered down the beach until they discovered a Jewish delicatessen improbably situated at the end of Waikiki Beach. "When we walked in, the waiter said 'Shalom,'" recalls Stanley Falkow. "I thought I had died and gone to heaven."

As the scientists wolfed down corned beef sandwiches on the patio, conversation inevitably turned to the esoteric arcana of their work, specifically about how bacteria pass on antibiotic resistance genes through the exchange of plasmids, which could reproduce themselves and often jumped from one bacterium to another. If they could decipher how nature transferred genes from one organism to another, perhaps it would suggest an efficient pathway to do this artificially, in the laboratory.

Antibiotic resistance was a convenient genetic trait to transplant—a good model system, scientists like to say—because it was easy to verify whether the experiment worked. If bacteria with the modified plasmids died after being doused with antibiotics, then the experiment failed. But if the bugs lived, they had succeeded. Boyer sketched out what he had recently uncovered in his lab, that his enzymes, *EcoR1* and *EcoR2*, made staggered cuts in DNA, leaving cohesive ends which permitted the ends to be rejoined. The normally low-key Cohen, one of the world's experts on plasmids, enthusiastically raced ahead, speculating about a cascade of dizzying possibilities.

Already abuzz with the notion of gene splicing, the molecular biology community was dreaming about somehow manipulating genes and about putting bacteria to work as factories to produce mammalian proteins. Everyone knew that was where the field was headed. In 1971, a series of experiments conducted by Paul Berg, chair of Stanford's biochemistry department and chief of a high-profile and well-funded lab, had taken a giant leap forward in that direction. In one experiment, his team had created a hybrid DNA molecule by inserting genes into the chromosome of the SV40, a simian virus first isolated in 1960 from the kidney cells of the rhesus monkeys used to culture the polio vaccine. Berg's strategy was to exploit the virus's ability to penetrate cell walls like a hot knife slicing through butter, and to employ the virus as a "vector," from the Latin "to carry," a tiny cargo ship to shuttle the gene inside bacteria cells and animal cells.

But Berg's method was intricate and laborious, requiring expensive equipment and technical sophistication beyond the scope of most labs. Thus, no one had yet hit upon an efficient technique of combining DNA. Nor had anyone devised how to fashion copies, or clones, of these genetically altered molecules to give scientists enough material to study them. But a critical mass of information was accumulating, and key technologies had emerged that accelerated the pace of research, so it was only a matter of time before someone took that quantum leap forward.

Perhaps the tiny plasmids, which promiscuously jump from one cell to another, could be pressed into service as more convenient vectors. Stanley Cohen had figured out how to remove the plasmids with genes for resistance to the antibiotic tetracycline from the bacteria's single chromosome, and then coax the plasmids back inside the cell. Boyer's enzymes sheared DNA with such precision and left those marvelous sticky ends, a scissors and paste kit all in one, like microscopic snap couplers. They might very well be the key to splicing together disparate genes easily. Intriguingly, when Boyer was still a postdoc at Yale in 1965, he predicted, in a bit of prescience, that these enzymes would be quite useful. As he wrote in a grant proposal: "The applications of this area of research to the possible future of 'genetic surgery' are obvious."[4] Cohen wondered if it was possible to use Boyer's enzymes to pluck out these resistance genes from a plasmid. Could this bit of genetic material then be grafted onto a plasmid cut with *EcoR1* so they had matching sticky ends? If so, could the modified plasmid ferry these antibiotic resistance genes into a bacterium? And finally, would the newly altered bacteria be resistant to antibiotics? Or, in scientific parlance, would the foreign genes be expressed?

"Potentially, we could take any gene we want and put it in there," said Cohen. "Yes, in theory," responded Boyer, "if it works." A current of excitement swept through the group as they strolled down the beach on their way back to the hotel. Everyone knew exactly what it would mean if the implanted genes did their jobs. It was a big if, but if the genes functioned correctly, they would have devised a simple way of cloning just about any gene, whether it was from a fruit fly, a toad, a horse, or a human. As the altered bacteria reproduce themselves, they replicate the foreign gene too, converting the tiny microbes into molecular photocopying machines.

In the spirit of scientific cooperation, Boyer offered to give Cohen a sample of his enzymes. But Cohen insisted on a full collaboration. "It suddenly became very clear from their conversation that you could link together diverse pieces of DNA," Falkow remembers. "I went back to my hotel room and lay awake in bed that night thinking if these experiments worked, things would never be the same again."

Stanley Falkow was right.

That meeting in Hawaii kicked off several months of intense collaboration between Cohen and Boyer, as well as Annie Chang, Cohen's research assistant, and Robert Helling, a microbiologist from the University of Michigan and an old friend of Boyer's from the University of Pittsburgh, who was on sabbatical in Boyer's lab. Conveniently, Annie Chang lived in San Francisco, so she shuttled reagents back and forth between the two labs. In the evening, Chang would drop off the pSC101 plasmids, which had a gene for resistance to the antibiotic tetracycline. Boyer's team would then cleave them with *EcoR1*. Chang would then pick them up in the morning on her way back down to Stanford in Palo Alto, which was about twenty miles south of San Francisco.

Normally, laboratory research moves at a snail's pace, in frustrating fits and starts, with experiments constantly mired in unforeseen glitches. Nothing ever works the first time. But in this instance, it did. Research proceeded at warp speed, almost as if destiny were pulling them along. Within four exhilarating months, the experiments were done. By March, the team had cut open the plasmid, spliced in genes for resistance to a second antibiotic, kanamycin, and then smuggled the hybrid plasmid into the *E. coli* bacteria, which obligingly churned out copies of the implanted gene. They had boldly gone where no scientist had gone before. "It was very fast," Boyer said later. "All of these things just dropped in our laps, practically . . . the technologies just emerged at the right time."

That spring, Herbert Boyer was invited to the Gordon Conference on Nucleic Acids scheduled for June. The Gordon Research Conferences are exclusive retreats for different scientific disciplines convened at private academies in New England every summer, a scientific Bohemian Grove sans the sophomoric male-bonding rituals. Organized by the big guns in each field, these cloistered, by-invitation-only gatherings afford the elite intellects a chance to commune with each other and learn about the cutting-edge work of the scientific vanguard.

This Gordon Conference on Nucleic Acids, the chemical building blocks of DNA, took place at the New Hampton School in New Hampshire, in the verdant foothills of New Hampshire's White Mountains. The subject of Boyer's panel, held on the conference's fourth day, was "Bacterial Restriction Enzymes in the Analysis of DNA." Techniques for using restriction enzymes to chop up the lengthy strands of DNA into more manageable segments were a hot topic in molecular biology circles. But so insular is the world of science that no one expected not to have heard already of something new concocted in someone's lab. Consequently, no one anticipated anything particularly earthshaking from the half dozen scientists sharing the dais that Thursday morning with Boyer.

If Stanley Cohen, who tended to be secretive and circumspect, had participated rather than Boyer, perhaps it would have turned out differently. But Boyer, says one associate, "can't keep *anything* to himself." Cohen had extracted a promise from his gregarious collaborator that he would stifle his natural impulses and not reveal the results of their recent—and as yet unpublished—experiments. Boyer, they had agreed, should confine his remarks to research he had already written up in the scientific literature.

But Boyer was so excited by their work—and perhaps a little awed by the company—that he couldn't restrain himself. He spilled the beans and told them what he and Cohen had done. His unexpected revelation sparked a sensation among the audience, who understood immediately the implications of the discovery of this new technique. This method was far easier than Berg's cumbersome, technically daunting way of fusing DNA molecules, akin to the difference between making automobiles by hand and making them on an assembly line. Now any lab—not just the well-funded ones with state-of-the-art equipment—could fuse disparate genes with the *EcoR1* enzyme.

Several scientists were disturbed by this turn of events, however, and voiced grave worries about the unregulated application of this new technology. As key discoveries were made throughout the late 1960s and early 1970s, research into gene-manipulation techniques had gained an almost uncontrollable momentum, which in turn provoked a growing alarm within the ranks about biohazards. There were dark mutterings about the threat of spawning mutant bugs that could escape from the lab, true Andromeda strains that could plague humankind. A handful of scientists, many of whom had been anti-Vietnam War activists, saw themselves in the same position as nuclear physicists in the late 1930s. Like the physicists, they halted at the threshold of the genetic engineering age.

But Boyer and Cohen's astonishing advance wasn't speculation or the stuff of science fiction. It was real. There was no turning back now. The genie had been let out of the bottle. The conference co-chairs, the NIH's Maxine Singer, who had helped Marshall Nirenberg elucidate the genetic code, and Yale biochemist Dieter Soll, agreed to a brief impromptu meeting on Friday morning, the last day of the conference, to allow everyone to air their anxieties.

There was no time left, though, for a thoughtful debate. Many participants had already left, and those who remained were eager to head home. So the group hastily voted to draft a letter, later published in the esteemed journal *Science*. The missive expressed their "deep concern" about the ability to fashion "new kinds of hybrid plasmids and viruses, with biological activity of unpredictable nature" that "may prove hazardous to laboratory workers and to the public." They also requested that the National Academy of Sciences form a subcommittee to examine the controversies raised by recombinant DNA technology. Over the next year, this committee, which was chaired by Paul Berg, would become the locus of the first major attempt at self-regulation within the international scientific community since the early 1940s, when physicists agreed to deny their German colleagues access to nuclear data. "The Gordon Conference," noted science historian Susan Wright, "was the first in a long chain of events, surrounded by public controversy and debate, that eventually resulted in the formation of national controls for genetic engineering."[5]

On that last day, a group portrait of about ninety of the Gordon Conference participants was taken by the conference's official photographer to immortalize this historic occasion. The jeans-clad Boyer, with long sideburns and mustache, his thick mop of curly hair brushed haphazardly to the side, stood awkwardly on one end of the back row. A few weeks shy of his thirty-seventh birthday, the unassuming small-town boy—who didn't attend the Bronx High School of Science or MIT, enter the Westinghouse Science Talent Search, or go through any of the other early rites of passage that anoint those who are destined for scientific greatness—had shaken the lofty Brahmins of biology to the core. So perhaps Boyer's dazed look in the photograph wasn't surprising—he looked as if he had just realized that *he* was ground zero of this gathering storm.

What the Cohen and Boyer team had achieved, however, though certainly an estimable accomplishment, was merely a preliminary to the main event. Bacteria are among the simplest of living organisms, with a single chromosome and a cluster of genes. But could they synthesize proteins made by higher organisms using *E. coli* bacteria? Crossing the species barrier, the great evolutionary divide in biology, would be the real proof of the utility of this technology. Then, *any* gene could be replicated every time the bacteria cells divided, which occurs a few times an hour. Within a relatively short time, large quantities of this implanted DNA could then be harvested from the bacteria.

By August 1973, Boyer, Cohen, Helling, and Chang, along with John Morrow, a graduate student in Paul Berg's laboratory, and Howard Goodman, a UCSF colleague of Boyer's, had crossed this scientific Rubicon. Using the uncannily precise cuts of the restriction enzymes, they snipped out a gene from the chromosome of the African clawed toad (*Xenopus laevis*), then used the sticky ends to splice it into the DNA of the *E. coli*. When the team determined the genetic code of succeeding generations of the bacteria that carried the toad DNA, they realized they had concocted an entirely new life form. They had, in essence, synthesized life.

An obviously delighted Boyer called Stanley Falkow to tell him about their startling breakthrough. Falkow was naturally curious as to how Boyer's team had determined which bacterial colonies—one out of perhaps a million—actually had the toad DNA. "Herb said he kissed every colony on the plate until one turned into a prince," Falkow recalls. "Then he hung up on me. I had to call him back to get the real answer."

Boyer's and Cohen's discovery electrified molecular biologists when they published their findings in the November 1973 issue of the *Proceedings of the National Academy of Sciences* (*PNAS*). Soon after, articles began appearing in the popular press, in *The New York Times*, in the *San Francisco Chronicle*, and in *Fortune*, optimistically predicting these new techniques would "revolutionize" the pharmaceutical industry. This method of transferring genetic material offered the first new drugmaking approach in decades. Traditionally, big drug companies screened thousands of chemicals to find one that would cure disease. It was a costly, time-consuming, hit-or-miss process that one observer aptly characterized as "molecular roulette"; it often produced drugs with undesirable side effects. By the mid-1970s, the pharmaceutical industry's after-tax return on R&D, which required battalions of scientists, was only 3.3 percent, a drop from 12 percent in the 1960s.[6]

Gene splicing gave scientists the tools to mine the world's best pharmacopoeia for combating disease, the human immune system. By coaxing foreign genes to function in bacteria, they could devise drugs derived from the body's storehouse of proteins that have specific missions, like human growth hormone or insulin. Other potential applications were in agriculture, in the formulation of, say, genetically engineered crops resistant to insect infestations, and in industry, to devise solvents, plastics, fertilizers, and natural sweeteners.

But all this media attention, coupled with the mad dash to do recombinant DNA experiments in labs around the world, was nerve-racking to the high priests of science. "Telephone calls were coming into our laboratory daily," recalled Paul Berg. "Send us pSC101 [plasmids]. 'What do you want to do?' we'd ask. And we'd get a description of some kind of horror experiment and you'd ask the person whether in fact he'd thought about it and you found that he hadn't thought about it at all."[7] Little wonder the biohazard debate ratcheted up several notches. "The future will curse us," one top biochemist darkly warned, with the gravity of a biblical prophet, "if we continue to engage in a destructive colonial warfare against nature."[8]

Others were stricken more by fears of unwanted public intrusions than by any real pangs of social conscience. They worried that if the scientific community didn't police itself and rein in this emerging technology, the government would—and impose draconian controls that would make it impossible to conduct further research. So in July 1974, three visibly nervous scientists faced the Washington press corps and told them they had written a letter, which was published simultaneously in the three top scientific journals, *Nature, Science,* and *The Lancet,* calling for a global moratorium on certain recombinant DNA experiments. The letter was signed by eleven leaders in the field, including James Watson, David Baltimore, Paul Berg, Herbert Boyer, and Stanley Cohen.

The letter sent shock waves through the international molecular biology community, which had been excitedly poised to proceed with experiments that many had dreamed of doing for their entire professional lives. But the work halted in virtual mid-step. Everyone pretty much observed the moratorium, though there was an undercurrent of grumbling about an "intellectual lockout" and about pulling up the drawbridges, since the letter was signed by the pioneers in the field, who presumably had already finished the research that would put *them* in Nobel contention.

"Stan Cohen admitted to me [earlier in the year] . . . that something was brewing among some of the virologists . . . and they were thinking about recommending that all research on drug-resistant bacteria cease and desist," recalled Roy Curtiss III, another early molecular biologist. "I said, 'You've got to be kidding!' [When the letter appeared in *Science*] I was very annoyed at Stan and Herb because I knew what the hell they were doing . . . because there were aspects that to me looked like 'Blow the whistle on experiments that you've already done; don't preclude your ability to do those experiments that you're now doing or you want to do.'"[9]

Curtiss's attitude was fairly typical. Ironically, the anger directed toward Boyer and Cohen was a bit unfair because their inclusion in the letter was an afterthought. Pressure for a moratorium *had* emanated from the enormously influential virology contingent. They were biology's elite corps of virus hunters and cancer researchers, people like David Baltimore, who, in the intricate pecking order of molecular biology, were far more powerful than the lowly bacteriologists. Apparently, one of the titans on the august National Academy of Sciences committee that drafted the moratorium letter descended from Olympus long enough to solicit Boyer's and Cohen's participation. After all, it was their research that had developed the first real tools of genetic engineering—and mired science in this mess in the first place—endowing scientists with the ability to manipulate the stuff of life itself.

Despite the moratorium, the commercial potential of this method of transferring genetic material was not lost on officials at Stanford University, the birthplace of the semiconductor industry, which, in turn, spawned Silicon Valley. Stanford had gained millions by leasing its unused acreage to semiconductor start-ups, and from endowments from grateful alumni, like Hewlett-Packard founders William Hewlett and David Packard, who became fabulously wealthy by commercially exploiting discoveries they made while they were on the Stanford faculty. Which explained why Niels Reimers, Stanford's patent administrator, was stunned when a colleague sent him a newspaper article that quoted Stanley Cohen rhapsodizing about the immense potential for bacteria "factories" churning out antibiotics or insulin.

"I called up Stan and said, 'This looks like it's important,'" Reimers recalled. Cohen, however, who trained to be a physician, demurred. Reimers was aware of the possible payoffs in this technology, so he persisted, and implored Cohen to put aside his natural antipathy toward commercialism. Reimers invoked the story of penicillin. When Sir Alexander Fleming discovered penicillin he refused to patent it, preferring "to make a gift to mankind." But no company would manufacture penicillin without patent protection, according to Reimers. It wasn't until the government intervened during World War II that the antibiotic was developed. In the meantime, said Reimers, "Fleming's decision not to patent cost the world eleven years."[10]

This wasn't quite accurate—though Reimers didn't intend to mislead Cohen. British drugmakers hadn't developed penicillin chiefly because it was so difficult to work with and their resources were devoted to defeating the Nazis. But the clock was ticking on gene splicing—patent law required that the patent application had to be filed within twelve months of the publication of their original 1973 paper—and time was slipping away. Cohen finally relented. He and Boyer applied for a patent, though they initially ceded their share of any royalties from the rights to their universities. Stanford, which handled the administrative chores, filed the paperwork barely a week before the deadline.

The fallout was immediate. Fellow scientists were outraged. Hundreds of taxpayer-supported researchers toiling at dozens of institutions over three decades, in an ascending arc of discovery that began with Oswald Avery, had contributed to the body of knowledge that led to this breakthrough. For two men and one institution to claim all the credit, not to mention millions in royalties, was unconscionable.

Stanford's patent application intensified the antagonisms within the molecular biology fraternity about the global moratorium. "That's just the Stanford people wanting to tie it up and halt the competition," scoffed British geneticist Sydney Brenner[11] when he got wind of the patent application. The simmering hostilities came to a boil a few months later at the now famous Asilomar Conference, held in February 1975 at the Asilomar Conference Center, a rustic seaside retreat nestled in a secluded wood on California's Monterey Peninsula. About 150 scientific leaders from around the world congregated in the center's redwood cottages, meeting rooms, and barnlike cafeteria for four days to hammer out safety guidelines for recombinant DNA.

But what was billed as a scientific Woodstock, set against the incomparable backdrop of the rugged northern California coast, with its Monterey pines, towering redwoods, and vast expanse of sparkling

white beaches, quickly degenerated into esoteric schoolyard squab-
bles among a bunch of men who were accustomed to being the
smartest kids in the class. The freewheeling discussions were reminiscent of the anarchic student movement of a few years before, with
their emphasis on an open, democratic exchange of ideas at the
expense of any semblance of order. As one reporter sarcastically noted:
"The proceedings rapidly develop[ed] the appearance of some
obscure primitive tribe eons ago, accidentally stumbling by trial and
error onto the secret of parliamentary procedure."[12]

In the aftermath of Vietnam and the Watergate scandal, scientists
convened at Asilomar to show the world they could behave responsi-
bly. But the net effect was quite the opposite. Meetings turned into
petty turf wars, where scientists seemed more interested in protecting
their area of research from restrictions than in honestly talking about
the consequences of concocting mutant pathogens in the lab. The
undercurrent of all these discussions seemed to be to agree on some
perfunctory guidelines that would placate the public so they could
continue their work. This was especially true of the younger scientists,
who were champing at the bit to get the moratorium lifted with as few
restrictions as possible. "But no one will come out and say it," said one
of the conference's organizers. "They're all chicken."[13]

Not surprisingly, the overall impression that emerged was that scientists were incapable of regulating themselves. Nevertheless, there
was a great deal of pressure to emerge from this meeting, which had
been paid for by the taxpayers, with some kind of consensus. Otherwise, there was a very real threat the government would impose stringent controls on their research. "We can't say that 150 scientists spent
four days at Asilomar and all of them agreed that there was a hazard—
and they still couldn't come up with a single suggestion," Paul Berg
ominously warned attendees. "That's telling the government to do it
for us."[14] And so it was that on the morning of the last day, after intense
debates that lasted well into the night, a provisional document was
adopted by the bleary-eyed participants.

In the midst of the fractious atmosphere at Asilomar, Herbert Boyer
and Stanley Cohen tried to maintain a low profile, though both men
were churning inside. The last thing Stanley Cohen grabbed before
leaving for Asilomar was a box of antacids. And Boyer later said that
the whole experience was so emotional, he didn't sleep the entire

week, mulling over every session in his mind all night long. But Stanley Cohen, to his immense chagrin, was forced to face his colleagues. At one point during a particularly heated discussion about the propriety of patenting, Cohen, who was standing in the back of the auditorium, was asked to come to the stage and explain the rationale behind Stanford's patent application. Cohen later said it was the longest walk he'd taken in his life.

But it was Boyer who was the convenient scapegoat, a flash point for the controversies that would dog him for the rest of his career. Stacks of hate mail from environmentalists, consumer groups, and the usual assortment of kooks, condemning him for tampering with nature and playing God, regularly arrived at his lab. The real low point for Boyer, however, was reached in the fall following Asilomar: the *Berkeley Barb*'s special Halloween edition named him as one of the Bay Area's top ten bogeymen.

In hindsight, however, scientists' weighty concerns about Frankenstein monsters crawling out of the lab were greatly exaggerated, and their crisis of conscience unnecessarily inflamed public fears, rather than allaying them. The chances of laboratory strains of *E. coli,* dulled by decades of pampering in the lab, mutating into lethal bugs that could survive long enough in the real world to wreak havoc were about as likely as a Park Avenue preppie destroying the Cali cartel.

Just how misguided their well-meaning attempts to curb this new technology were was crystallized by an incident that occurred the day after the Asilomar Conference ended. In a small conference room in a swank hotel in downtown San Francisco, sixty miles—and light-years—away from the rugged natural wonders of Asilomar, a select group of NIH scientists and officials were seated around a sleek wooden table. There, the assembled gathering spent an intense day plowing through the densely written Asilomar manifesto, with all its murky caveats and foggy addenda, to hash out formal guidelines for recombinant DNA research, along with methods of enforcing these rules. Late in the afternoon, some levity intruded upon their earnest deliberations on how to police experiments with recombinant DNA. Suddenly, one female participant started to laugh. The other members of the group looked up, startled.

"Do you realize," she said, smiling wryly and staring intently at the paper in front of her, "what this *means?*"

Her question was met with silence, as all eyes regarded her expectantly.

"This means," she continued, "that we have just made human sex a moderate-risk experiment."

"But that's only," someone else interjected, "in the *laboratory*."[15]

CHAPTER 4

THE BEST
AND THE BRIGHTEST

While molecular biologists flocked to California, the scientific hinterlands, to debate the propriety of patenting their research, it was not even remotely an issue within the National Institutes of Health, the hub of the nation's vast medical research enterprise. There, the virology troops were mobilizing to battle cancer, and the NIH itself, one HHS Secretary would later say, was still "an island of objective and pristine scientific research excellence untainted by commercialization influences."[1] But that era would soon end. The incipient commercialization of research, and its consequences, was like a slow-growing cancer that would eventually infect the entire system, even the mighty NIH.

With its low-slung brick buildings surrounded by expanses of lush greenery, the NIH looks more like a bucolic Ivy League college campus than a globe-girdling research empire. Located on a former country estate, the NIH—jokingly called the "Reservation" by staffers—now occupies sixty-four buildings scattered over three hundred acres in Bethesda, Maryland, a prosperous Washington, D.C., suburb. Up until the 1960s, however, staff scientists at the NIH were considered government hacks by their colleagues at the top research universities, also-rans who couldn't cut it in the competitive environs of academia. But the presence on the NIH campus of people like Marshall Nirenberg, who cracked the genetic code and who in 1968 became the first NIH scientist—in fact, the first federal employee—to win the Nobel Prize, elevated the stature of the NIH in the eyes of the snooty scientific elite.

By the late 1960s and early 1970s, the NIH was a magnet for the best and the brightest emerging from the nation's medical and graduate schools—the "Yellow Berets" who joined the Public Health Service to fulfill their military obligations and to avoid Vietnam—inaugurating an era of blazing discovery unparalleled in the agency's history. "There was an entirely different atmosphere in research then," one recalls. "There was an incredible excitement and enthusiasm for what could be done." And many of them were enlisted in another epic struggle: President Nixon's much vaunted—and highly politicized—cancer blitzkrieg.

The National Cancer Institute, flush with War on Cancer funds, was a mecca for the most ambitious of the rising young stars. And few stars shined brighter than that of Robert Gallo, who would come to personify the changes wrought in research by the opportunity to amass great affluence and influence. Gallo was a young physician when he reported to the NIH in 1965 after completing his internship and residency at the University of Chicago. An abrasive man with sharp features, a mercurial temperament, and the rough edges of a street tough, Gallo was a second-generation Italian who grew up in Waterbury, Connecticut, a decaying mill town at the edge of New England's rust belt. His father, Francis, a dour workaholic, owned a metallurgy foundry and the family was relatively well off.

But his idyllic world was shattered by an event that would alter the course of his life. When he was eleven, his only sibling, Judy, was stricken with leukemia. "The jolly, plump, pretty sister I remembered was now emaciated, jaundiced, and covered with bruises," he observed, recalling his visit to her in the hospital, in what must have been a horrifying experience for a sheltered young boy. "When she smiled I saw only the caked blood covering her teeth. This was the last time I would ever see Judy, and it remains the most powerful and frightening demon of my life."[2]

After her death, a pall settled over the family, and Gallo's adolescence was spent in a gloomy household where holiday festivities— even music—were taboo. He resolved then that he would pursue medical research and study the biology of blood cells. He graduated summa cum laude from Providence College in Rhode Island, and received his medical degree from the Thomas Jefferson University School of Medicine, a respected but lesser-known institution in Philadelphia. The lack of impressive academic credentials was a perceived handicap he seemed to feel keenly, and it fed the apparent deep sense of inferiority that permeated every facet of his life and drove his career.

Gallo found a home at the NIH, which was full of brash streetwise kids like himself who didn't have fancy Ivy League educations yet were determined to succeed. Like all new M.D.s who are required to go through an apprenticeship doing hands-on medicine in the NIH's hospital, Gallo started his tenure at the NIH in the cancer wards in Building 10, the ten-story building which houses the hospital where patients are treated. Initially, Gallo was ecstatic to be at the NIH, where he could commence his research career in earnest. But his enthusiasm quickly eroded under the daily grind of dealing with very sick people. Especially wrenching were his last six months when he was assigned to the pediatric leukemia wards, an experience that chillingly echoed his own childhood and his sister's untimely death. And some of his contemporaries fell apart under the strain. "One colleague began literally running away from the wards whenever a crisis with one of his patients seemed imminent. . . . Another went to a nearby hotel and killed himself with morphine," Gallo grimly noted. "It was my last direct involvement with clinical medicine."[3]

During this time, however, Gallo was befriended by two men who would exert a tremendous influence on the course of his career. One was Robert Ting, a top NCI virologist from a prominent family in Hong Kong, who had studied under Salvador Luria at MIT, and who had encouraged Gallo to study viruses. The other, Vincent DeVita, was a fellow Italian-American and an established star in the NCI firmament for his pioneering work devising potent chemotherapies to combat Hodgkin's disease, a lymphatic cancer. DeVita was a powerful mentor—he won a 1972 Albert Lasker Award, the nation's highest biomedical award, and was appointed NCI director in 1979. He also had a reputation for being tenacious and difficult, an abrasive taskmaster; intriguingly, these echoed complaints that would later be made of his young protégé.

But DeVita quietly bore his own secret sorrow that few beyond his immediate circle knew about. In 1972, his son, Ted, then nine, was diagnosed with aplastic anemia, an often fatal bone marrow disorder that severely compromises the immune system, leaving victims defenseless against even minor infections. The young boy was treated with massive blood transfusions, and confined to a sterile, germ-free

71

chamber in the NIH clinical center. DeVita would do his daily patient rounds, then visit with Ted in the evenings. The boy survived for another eight years until May 1980, when he died at age seventeen, just a few months after his father was appointed head of the NCI.

By 1972, Gallo was head of his own lab, which he named the Laboratory of Tumor Cell Biology (LTCB). "Gallo was in the right place at the right time and he was embraced by the NCI's Italian Mafia," says a colleague of his meteoric rise. He was quite adept at attracting gifted investigators who did much of the groundbreaking work that has since made him famous, and shrewdly surrounded himself with talented foreign nationals, from places like China, the Philippines, India, Japan, and Czechoslovakia. Over the years, some of Gallo's most trusted lieutenants were highly trained foreigners who willingly logged long hours. They tolerated conditions one called "involuntary servitude" because they were given the rare chance to do cutting-edge work. "The pay is low, and the hours are long, sometimes fourteen hours a day, seven days a week," recalls one former NCI scientist. "But they love it because they can't do this kind of science anywhere else—they couldn't get the position or the grants. Gallo always said, 'If you have to hire, hire a foreigner because they work hard, and they don't expect much. And if they don't do what you want, you can deport them.'"

Working for Gallo often took on the tenor of the emotional whipsaws of an abusive marriage, observes another. Temper tantrums and corrosive black moods alternated with disarming displays of a winning charm and genuine contrition for previous bad behavior. "I get my stimulation out of trouble," he confessed to one reporter. "The ferment gets me somewhere. But deep down I know I'm soft. I have no real enemies except myself."[4] Even in the view of his detractors, says one, "Bob Gallo is an extremely charismatic and dynamic person."

This duality in his nature was reflected in the prevailing atmosphere of his lab, which was sharply divided between those who were only passing through, getting their tickets punched on their way to better things, and those whose blind allegiance to Gallo bordered on fealty. "This is a guy who always has to be dominant," says one fellow scientist, echoing the sentiments of other colleagues who describe him as having the persona of a combative schoolyard bully. "Anytime you meet, even if you've met him a thousand times before, the first thing he has to establish, his number one goal, is that he is in charge."

Gallo's laboratory was engaged in a search for human tumor viruses—specifically, retroviruses, which are a special class of viruses—that may be linked to common cancers. His staff combed through tumor cell cultures for evidence of these microscopic invaders, in a tedious process not unlike panning for gold. The rationale was that if a virus was responsible for cancer, then it might be possible to prevent the disease with the magic bullet of a vaccine in the same way other viral diseases, like smallpox and polio, had been eradicated.

But the first step was to find a human retrovirus, which is what Robert Gallo, among numerous others, set out to do. Not long after Temin's and Baltimore's discovery of the reverse transcriptase (RT) enzyme, the Pasteur Institute convened a tumor virus conference in Paris in November 1970. There, several top virologists announced they had found traces of reverse transcriptase in tissue samples from leukemic patients. Subsequently, a researcher in Gallo's lab, J. Bhattacharya, identified RT floating around in human leukemia cells, a finding that Gallo thought vindicated "our beliefs that a human retrovirus was indeed present in human leukemic cells."[5] But when the results were published in the esteemed journal *Nature*, there was little response from the scientific community. The paper sank like an anvil in quicksand. Gradually, Gallo, baffled by this indifferent reaction to what he believed was a great discovery, realized that detecting "a putative footprint (in the form of an RT enzyme) of a human leukemia virus would never be a substitute for isolating and growing the virus itself."[6]

An intense hunt commenced. Gallo was determined to silence skeptics who questioned the significance of his results. After all, recalls Robert Gallagher, a virologist who was one of Gallo's lab chiefs, "if this sign of the virus is there, why can't we find the virus?" Starting in 1971, Gallagher, collaborating with Zaki Salahuddin, another researcher in Gallo's lab who had recently arrived from Pakistan, initiated a series of experiments in which they attempted to induce human leukemia cells freshly harvested from bone marrow to grow. The theory was that the more they grew, the more chance there was that the cells would shed virus particles. They weren't having much luck until Robert Ting, who had left the NCI to head up Litton Bionetics, a research outfit that did contracting work for Gallo's lab, furnished the two researchers with some frozen mixed cells derived from human embryo tissue. Suddenly, the cell cultures from one of these embryos had prompted the leukemic blood cells to grow like a prairie fire. Gallagher detected consistent RT activity, indicating the presence of a retrovirus. An electron microscopy confirmed his suspicions, revealing a type C retrovirus, the same kind of retrovirus that causes leukemia in many animals.

Gallo was elated when he heard the news, certain *this* discovery would catapult him into the same rarefied ranks as Temin and Baltimore, who were then front-runners for the Nobel. In January 1975, Gallo announced that he and Robert Gallagher had isolated the first human cancer retrovirus, which he named HL-23. Normally, scientists first publish results of their experiments in peer-reviewed professional journals so that the research would be vetted by experts in the field. It also provided colleagues with the chance to confirm the experiment's accuracy before the results were disseminated to the general public. But news of Gallo's discovery was leaked to the media before it appeared in the scientific literature. "I got up one morning and read the headlines of *The Washington Post*," Robert Gallagher told the *Chicago Tribune*. "I was shocked to find that he'd been talking to the press."

Gallo then invited Robin Weiss and Natalie Teich, two renowned British virologists, to conduct experiments with the new retrovirus in his laboratory. By now, Gallo's lab had swelled to nearly fifty researchers and support staffers. It was housed off the crowded NIH campus in a commercial building in downtown Bethesda that had once been a bowling alley and was conveniently located a block from a McDonald's, which staffers frequented for late-night snacks. "Gallo thought by bringing in other prominent scientists, this discovery would be more accepted," Gallagher remembers. "But somewhere in there, a contamination occurred and what finally came out was a whole garbage pail of different viruses."

Gallo and Gallagher had no idea this had happened, however, when they confidently headed for the annual meeting of the Virus Cancer Program in Hershey, Pennsylvania, in the spring of 1976. Prior to the meeting, they had sent samples to other scientists for independent confirmation of their results, which is a common practice. After Gallo delivered his presentation, the other researchers reported that the cell cultures were contaminated with a mixture of ape, monkey, and baboon viruses. Members of the audience pounced on him like a pack of jackals. The ultracompetitive cancer research establishment, particularly the heavyweights at the NCI, had been quite chagrined that an upstart lab that didn't even rate on-campus housing had possibly uncovered the first cancer-causing virus. They were almost gleeful in their attacks now that it appeared Gallo had failed.

Gallo was blindsided by this unexpected finding. Contaminations were a common laboratory hazard. But the unspoken accusation here was that in Gallo's haste to stake his claim to this discovery and earn a spot on the Nobel podium in Sweden with Temin and Baltimore he had failed to do the most basic confirmatory tests, a colossal blunder even a first-year graduate student wouldn't make. Gallo was utterly humiliated in front of his peers, who unabashedly ridiculed his work. "Human tumor viruses," they joked. "Or human *rumor* viruses."

After the meeting, Ludwig Gross, whose own research had once been derided, comforted the disconsolate Gallo. "Science is a tough game," Gross told him, and if he was truly on the right track, then he would ultimately be vindicated. Gallo retreated to his lab, and a pervasive atmosphere of gloom settled over the LTCB in the wake of the HL-23 fiasco. "The damage had been not just to myself, but to every one of us working in LTCB and to researchers elsewhere who had invested time and effort working with human retroviruses," Gallo noted.[7] Gallagher and Salahuddin spent two frustrating years afterward trying to replicate the original experiment, though neither one quite understood how the contamination occurred, or if what they had uncovered was an artifact, an anomaly in that particular patient. "There has never been for me an adequate explanation to this day as to how you can have all this positive data and then all of a sudden there's no evidence and it is totally discredited," Gallagher says, shaking his head in retrospect. "The most likely explanation is that someone just got sloppy." But the notion that retroviruses could cause a serious illness was now contemptuously repudiated. Ambitious scientists, eager for the next big score, jumped on the oncogene bandwagon, now the hot cancer research arena.

And the virus cancer program itself was in a shambles. A 1974 investigation of the NCI's Special Virus Cancer Program (SVCP), which consumed nearly 100 million taxpayer dollars annually— roughly 12 percent of the NCI's budget—was particularly damning. The panel of university scientists appointed to probe the program were horrified by what they uncovered: most of these funds were siphoned off into subcontracts to industrial firms, none of which were subjected to the gauntlet of rigorous peer review that grant applicants from universities faced. "Practically every NIH lab has contact rela-tionships with private industry, which often allow a lab to use special technology without making enormous investments in equipment or personnel they will not use on a regular basis," Robert Gallo blandly noted in his autobiography, *Virus Hunting*.[8] "Such contractual relation-ships have long been part of government biomedical research."

The academic investigators viewed these arrangements with a more jaundiced eye, however. Two scientists who observed one meeting where contracts to outside companies were awarded were shocked at how cavalierly taxpayer money was dispensed. Discussions were "per-functory," and "no hard questions were asked about the scientific con-tents of the proposal, the past productivity of the contractor or the program relevance." Another participant dismissed these meetings as "a farce."

The report concluded that there were flagrant conflicts of interest in the SVCP, money was dispersed to a tight clique of cronies, rather than on the basis of real merit, and the program itself was "unproductive" and "intellectually shoddy." Those who run the program, the report con-cluded, "are also often the recipients of large amounts of the money they dispense . . . [and when] the Segment Chairmen decide that a particu-lar scientific problem should be studied, usually this study is dele-gated to a friendly colleague." The inquiry instigated a dismantling of the SVCP, sharply reduced the use of outside companies, and shifted the focus to research by university and NCI scientists.[9]

Gallo's lab was singled out as one of the chief offenders in doling out NCI money to subcontractors like Litton Bionetics, but Gallo emerged from this major housecleaning unscathed. One former NCI scientist sourly observes, "Gallo managed to land on his feet on a consistent basis, even though things happened in his career that would fell a lesser scientist."

By this time too the War on Cancer was a dismal disappointment. The gargantuan research juggernaut had failed to yield fresh insights into cancer causes or more humane therapies than surgery, radiation, and the ghastly chemotherapy—cut, burn, and poison—that had been standard since the 1950s. And survival rates for most cancers remained stubbornly unchanged. As Charles Edwards, an eminent physician and research administrator, noted, the cancer program was based "on the politically attractive but scientifically dubious premise that a dread and enigmatic disease can, like the surface of the moon, be conquered if we will simply spend enough money." Former FDA Commissioner Donald Kennedy, who would soon have troubles of his own as president of Stanford University, put it more succinctly: the cancer program was "a medical Vietnam."[10]

Throughout the 1970s, however, important discoveries did emanate from Gallo's lab, most notably Interleukin-2 (IL-2), a crucial growth factor produced by the immune system that later became a tool in cancer treatment, and the HL-60 cell line, an exceptionally fertile human cell line that is still widely used for biological studies around the world. These two discoveries could have generated hefty licensing fees but Gallo never attempted to cash in. Government scientists weren't allowed to patent inventions arising out of their research. Besides, for Gallo, it was about glory, not money, and profiting from your work simply just wasn't done.

He made his feelings on this issue quite clear when he tangled with David Golde, a UCLA Medical School hematologist, over the commercial rights to KG-1, a rare cell line that was used to clone interferon, once touted as a miracle cancer cure. Gallo had received samples of KG-1 from Golde, which he forwarded to researchers at Hoffmann-La Roche, the multinational drugmaker, for testing for interferon. Golde allegedly claimed the cell line was "stolen" and "hijacked" by Hoffmann-La Roche employees, whom he described as "crooks" and "thieves." (Golde later denied making these allegations.) Gallo, who saw nothing wrong with sharing cell lines "with any qualified investigator," felt personally defamed by Golde's accusations and reputedly offered to punch him out.

On the strength of these genuine advances, the LTCB, one of the first of the large laboratories, cut a wide swath through the research establishment, like a enormous supertanker plowing through the open seas and swamping smaller vessels in its wake. By 1978, the LTCB took up most of the top floors of Building 37, a gleaming new six-story concrete-and-glass structure perched on a hill at the edge of the sylvan NIH campus. But the price tag for these breakthroughs was exorbitant. The LTCB's annual budget had climbed to $8 million, and fees to subcontractors like Litton Bionetics ate up another $3 to $4 million each year. A comparable academic lab might receive $250,000 in yearly NIH grants, which spurred fellow scientists to question Gallo's lab's actual productivity in light of its vast resources.

That same year, however, a postdoc in the LTCB named Bernard Poiesz produced a seminal discovery that would elevate Gallo into the rarefied ranks and rekindle the search for retroviruses. Poiesz had joined the lab in July 1978, after completing his medical training at the University of Pennsylvania. He had spent a year as a clinical oncology fellow in the cancer wards in Building 10 before settling in at Gallo's lab for the second year of his postdoctoral fellowship at the NIH. Poiesz piggybacked on research that was already underway in the laboratory, where researchers were attempting to elucidate the mechanisms that provoked cancer cells to grow wildly out of control. He wanted to examine whether there was something awry in the growth regulator of these malignant cells. Before Gallo left for a sabbatical in Europe that fall, he approved Poiesz's proposal. Gallo thought this was a reasonable approach, but he cautioned Poiesz that he would have to abandon this line of inquiry if he didn't find anything by the time Gallo returned several months hence. "As an aside, since I knew how to look for retroviruses," Poiesz recalls, "I decided I would also screen [the cancer cells] for the presence of retroviruses by doing RT assays." Poiesz didn't suspect this afterthought would revitalize retrovirology.

Almost immediately, Poiesz detected reverse transcriptase in human cancer cells extracted from a man named Charlie Robinson, who was coincidentally one of Poiesz's former patients from Building 10. An African-American from Alabama, Robinson was stricken with mycosis fungeoides, a rare type of cancer that affects the T cells, the immune system's front line of defense against disease. Poiesz could hardly believe what he was seeing the first time he peered through the microscope and saw the telltale signs of reverse transcriptase floating around inside the cells. "I stayed up all night because I was afraid I'd lose it," Poiesz recalls. "My first thoughts were: Was this a novel retrovirus? Or was this just a contaminate?"

Clearly, memories of the HL-23 debacle were still fresh. Consequently, Poiesz, working under the supervision of cell biologist Frank Ruscetti, spent the next four months confirming his findings, often laboring through the night and taking every precaution to ensure that no contamination had occurred. "The philosophy in the lab was that you had to be very careful because contamination had misled folks before," Poiesz recalls. "We grew tons of this virus and we characterized it with all the reagents. And everything we did said this was different than anything we had ever found before. By Christmas, we had nailed this down pretty well."

When Gallo returned from Europe, he was dubious about their research's significance. And it didn't help their case that Gallo first heard about this discovery in *his* lab at a party given by a neighbor and colleague, who was bursting with the news about "Bernie's new virus." "Gallo was pretty upset we hadn't told him and he had every right to be," Poiesz readily admits. "But Frank feared a reenactment of HL-23, so we explained that we waited because we wanted to be 100 percent sure before we said anything. Gallo remained extremely skeptical. I guess he thought that a young person in a few short months couldn't have found the first human retroviruses, that the deities wouldn't smile on us." Gallo insisted they go back to the lab and do more research. To his credit, he allowed the two Young Turks to use the resources of the LTCB, and assemble a first-rate research team culled from the lab to prove beyond a doubt that Poiesz had, indeed, detected a new human retrovirus.

By May 1980, Poiesz and Ruscetti were ready to present their results at the prestigious Cold Spring Harbor Conference. Gallo was supposed to come as well, but at the last minute he bowed out, because, some said, he was incapable of sharing the limelight with his underlings. But once their results were confirmed, says another scientist, "Gallo got very excited and tried to take it over." While Ruscetti and Poiesz were writing up a paper to report their results to the scientific community, Gallo summoned Ruscetti to his office for a confidential meeting. "You know, Frank, the person in the lab who did the work doesn't always have to be first author," said Gallo.[11] But Ruscetti insisted that Poiesz receive the proper credit. Scientific etiquette dictates that the person who does the creative work in the lab receives first authorship, the equivalent of top billing. Poiesz was even more incensed when he heard of Gallo's intentions. "Of all the people on the project, I did the most work and I was the one who made the original observation and it *had* to go down that way," Poiesz recalls. "Gallo may have provided the environment but I made this discovery—no one else was in the room that night when I saw this virus. I knew what my legal position was and what my ability was to press a complaint within the NIH system. I communicated to Gallo that I expected to be treated fairly and appropriately."

Gallo backed off. Poiesz was first author on the paper that appeared in December 1980 in the *Proceedings of the National Academy of Sciences* announcing the isolation of a new human retrovirus, as well as on a series of more than a dozen other publications regarding the retrovirus Gallo named human T-cell lymphoma virus, or HTLV. Soon after, Poiesz moved on to a faculty position at the State University of New York Medical Center in Syracuse. Ruscetti, however, was summarily fired with virtually no explanation. Despite having conducted distinguished research—he played a key role in the discovery of IL-2, as well as in HTLV—he was unemployed for a period because, some say, Gallo gave him poor ratings to prospective employers. Gallo even circulated a copy of the unflattering letter he had written about Ruscetti to members of his lab, in a potent reminder to all of them of just how powerful he was. "It was very clear [after that incident] that Bernie wouldn't be able to stay in the lab," recalls a former colleague. "And Frank made the major mistake of backing Bernie. . . . That's how Frank lost his job." However, Gallo told *Spy*, "I never intervened to harm Frank Ruscetti. I've never, ever been asked about Frank Ruscetti. Maybe his first boss asked me—I'm not sure."

The discovery of HTLV, the first known human retrovirus to be implicated in cancer, electrified fellow scientists. Though it didn't seem to afflict much of a disease population, it was a noble start, and revived the sagging fortunes of the virus hunters. And on the strength of this discovery, which Gallo characterized as "one of the most exciting stories of 20th Century biology," his reputation was rehabilitated. The Nobel Prize that had eluded him for so long was now within reach.

Once the furor died down, however, the discovery didn't seem quite so extraordinary in the harsh light of serious scrutiny. Poiesz and Ruscetti hadn't demonstrated that HTLV actually caused mycosis fungeoides, or any other disease, for that matter. So HTLV was in danger of turning into a forgotten laboratory curiosity. In 1978, a group of Dutch researchers found themselves in a similar predicament. They had detected levels of reverse transcriptase and identified what looked like a retrovirus in cells culled from patients stricken with mycosis fungeoides. But very few people in the Netherlands suffered from mycosis fungeoides, so they couldn't test a large enough pool of patients to prove the retrovirus was responsible for the cancer.

Halfway around the world, however, a team of Japanese medical scientists were investigating an outbreak of a rare form of leukemia that afflicted residents on Kyushu, an island in southern Japan. *Their* research would ultimately rescue human retroviruses from medical irrelevance. In the fall of 1977, they identified a new type of cancer that afflicted the T cells, which they called adult T-cell leukemia, or ATL for short. A few months later, another Japanese scientist noticed that some type of infectious agent was being transmitted in the cells taken from a patient who died of ATL. Since there was evidence of RT activity, he surmised that the most likely culprit was a retrovirus. This was later confirmed by Yorio Hinuma, a prominent Japanese virologist, who detected retrovirus particles in the cells by using an electron microscope.

When another scientist in Kyoto heard about Poiesz's paper, he wondered if there was a connection between HTLV and ATL, so he sent blood samples to Gallo's lab. By 1983, in an elegant and carefully crafted document, a hallmark of the Japanese style of science, several Japanese researchers confirmed that ATL was caused by a retrovirus, and that it was, indeed, the same retrovirus that Bernard Poiesz had retrieved in the fall of 1978.

As time went on, though, Gallo alone would be associated with HTLV, whose name metamorphosed from human T-cell lymphoma virus to human T-cell leukemia virus, to reflect its link to ATL. In November 1982, when Gallo was awarded his first Albert Lasker Award for the discovery of HTLV, he was hailed for his "revolutionary discovery of the first retrovirus known to be associated with a human malignancy." Bernard Poiesz, Frank Ruscetti, and the considerable contributions of the Japanese and Dutch scientists were scarcely acknowledged. "He absolutely has to be the one to get sole credit," says one former colleague. "How it happens is that he is the one who is invited to international meetings or to write reviews and his name becomes ever more prominent. After a while, his name is the only one that becomes associated with the discovery."

Gallo's insistence on hogging *all* of the credit was excessive even given what one called "the plantation mentality" of science, where lab chiefs who haven't done experiments in years are credited with discoveries made in their labs; this is comparable to portraying Bill Gates as the sole inventor of Windows. "The big guys don't do any lab work," observes one scientist. "They spend 99 percent of their time traveling, or talking to people consolidating the old boys' network." Gallo's drive for recognition went beyond what was acceptable even among the insatiable egos at the pinnacle of the scientific establishment. And like the protagonist in a Shakespearean tragedy, it was the fatal flaw that would lead to his undoing.

CHAPTER 5

AFTER THE GOLD RUSH

Herbert Boyer didn't share Stanley Cohen's misgivings about commercializing gene splicing. Shortly after Asilomar, he pondered the possibility of inserting human genes into bacteria, even genes for human hormones, and then inducing the bacteria to yield functional proteins. "We're in the process of having a look at the expression of this material in bacteria," he said in a May 1975 interview. "I think this has a lot of implications for utilizing the technology in a commercial sense—that is, one could get bacteria to make hormones."[1]

This research would take money, though, money for the new equipment and the reagents this sophisticated technology required, and money for the postdocs who perform the laborious bench work, more money than Boyer was able to squeeze out of the NIH or other public funding sources. The big federal bucks—billions of them—were pouring into the War on Cancer. Genetic engineering may have been the subject of morbid public fascination, with its dazzling possibilities and sinister Brave New World undertones, but government bureaucrats were more interested in pumping increasingly scarce federal dollars into science that had the prospect of an immediate payoff—both medically and politically.

Despite having done pioneering research, Boyer's laboratory remained underfunded and overcrowded. He could only accommodate a few of the gifted postdocs who were clamoring to work in his lab, eager to be in on the ground floor of this exciting new technology. The ones he did accept usually had to provide their own funding, and even for them money was drying up. It was incredibly frustrating to make a discovery that had opened up a new field of research and be unable to get grants to continue those experiments. Boyer, however, compelled by a 1960s-style idealism, refused to be downbeat. He believed recombinant DNA technology could be harnessed to save lives. If he couldn't get cash from traditional sources, he'd try a more unorthodox route. Throughout 1975, he sounded out several companies about translating gene-splicing technology into marketable products. None were encouraging.

Someone else, though, was thinking along parallel lines, so it was inevitable their paths would converge. Robert Swanson was a junior partner at Kleiner & Perkins, a thriving venture capital firm that specialized in seeding the risky high-tech enterprises that had transformed the orchards and farmlands surrounding Highway 101 between the Stanford campus in Palo Alto and San Jose, about thirty miles to the south, into one sprawling industrial park. Short and stocky, with thinning hair and jowly cheeks that made him look like a preternaturally old chipmunk, Swanson exuded the edgy cheeriness of a natural-born salesman. Like Boyer, Swanson was convinced genetic engineering had enormous commercial potential. It could possibly even eclipse the profitable semiconductor industry.

Swanson was uniquely qualified to midwife the birth of the biotechnology industry. He had raced through his undergraduate work in chemical engineering at MIT in three years, then switched to graduate work in business at MIT's Sloan School of Management. At MIT, Boston's monument to Yankee ingenuity, with its magisterial granite buildings arrayed like Sphinxes on the banks of the Charles River in Cambridge, Swanson learned a valuable lesson in managing people, especially headstrong young scientists, that later characterized his managerial style.

During a demonstration in the late 1960s, a group of undergraduates barricaded themselves inside MIT's student union, protecting an Army deserter, who had somehow stumbled onto campus, from arrest. Their protest interfered with a spring dance scheduled at the center, however. In their infinite wisdom, MIT's tweedy dons simply asked the students to move their barricades, along with their ward, to another protected building. "They worked to manage it, rather than bring in the storm troopers, the way others would," Swanson recalled. "MIT was a good place, where people were encouraged to go their own way."[2]

From MIT, Swanson finessed his way into a job at Citibank in 1970, and was soon dispatched to open Citicorp Venture Capital Ltd.'s San

Francisco office. Four years later, at the ripe old age of twenty-six, Swanson, now a venture capital veteran, joined Kleiner & Perkins, which had offices on Sand Hill Road, in a wooded knoll in Menlo Park conveniently situated at the northern mouth of Silicon Valley. Identifying promising start-ups and shepherding them through their initial development phase wasn't satisfying Swanson, however. Instead of kibitzing from the sidelines and riding roughshod over Silicon Valley's unruly and flamboyant entrepreneurs, Swanson realized he wanted his own shop, one that related to science. So he holed up in local university libraries, devoured technical papers on the new recombinant DNA technology, then methodically compiled lists of the articles' authors, whom he methodically called, one by one.

Each phone conversation was pretty much the same. Scientists didn't mind spending a few minutes talking about their research, especially with someone like Swanson, who was conversant in the complicated lexicon of genetics. Commercializing this technology, though, was another story—that was decades away, twenty-first-century stuff. Besides, the very notion of commercialism was crass, anathema in the sheltered world of molecular biology. In January 1976, Swanson finally hit pay dirt when he called Herb Boyer, though at the time Swanson had no inkling he was talking to one of the two men most responsible for the invention of the technology he was so eager to exploit. On his end, about the only thing Boyer heard was that there might be some money. He was willing to give ten minutes to anyone who might subsidize his perpetually cash-starved lab.

Late one Friday afternoon, Swanson wended his way through UCSF's mazelike medical school complex to Boyer's lab. Conservatively attired in a dark suit and tie, Swanson looked conspicuously out of place among the casually clad graduate students and postdocs. Boyer, in faded jeans and vest, didn't look much older or more authoritative than his underlings, though he was nearly forty. He and Swanson made an incongruous pair but they seemed to hit it off immediately. The ten minutes lengthened to several hours, as the two repaired to Churchill's, a local saloon frequented by UCSF's legion of lab rats. Over several beers, they agreed to put up $500 apiece—Boyer had to borrow his share—to form a partnership. Boyer had even thought about a name for the company, a shortening of "genetic engineering technology," Genentech, with the accent on the second syllable.

Fortuitously, Boyer's and Swanson's strengths melded together like two complementary strands of DNA. They both were certainly ambitious, but not in a self-aggrandizing way. Swanson possessed considerable entrepreneurial skills, but he had the soul of an accountant, organized and disciplined, colorless even, in a world populated by reckless visionaries. Boyer had the same practical, down-to-earth quality about him. He wasn't driven by a reservoir of toxic insecurities to win at any cost. Nor did he have the stomach for the corrosive power games of high-stakes science, which can seem more like Roller Derby than a civilized competition among highly educated professionals. Science for him meant doing productive research, earning the respect of his peers, and, with a little luck, landing in the history books on the strength of a great discovery. He had already gone farther than he ever expected, and swelling his paltry bank account would be icing on the cake.

Swanson was determined to hammer out a virtually airtight marketing strategy that would be adhered to every step of the way. He had seen too many promising high-tech start-ups founder, burning through millions of dollars in expenditures on plants and equipment and hiring personnel, because they dabbled in too many areas and didn't stick to a clear-cut plan. Following the advice of his mentor, Tom Perkins, Swanson contracted out their work to university labs like Boyer's at UCSF, thus saving unnecessary overhead expenses. And instead of developing a product right away—and risk being sucked into a quagmire of costly and unforeseen delays—they'd engineer a simple prototype to demonstrate the use of the technology. Once the novel technology was proven, they reasoned, then they could generate plenty of capital to finance a full-scale operation. Boyer, for his part, brainstormed to come up with products that were technically feasible and genuinely useful. Together, they crafted an innovative business plan that later was a much imitated model for the as yet unborn industry. "You take two naive people and put them in a room," Boyer once said, "they just boost each other over the bar."[3]

Swanson rented a small office on Sansome Street in San Francisco, near the financial district. He put up out-of-town business associates, who were accustomed to more deluxe accommodations, on the couch of his modest apartment. Instead of being wined and dined at fashionable restaurants, Swanson would amuse his guests with Ping-Pong matches on the table he'd set up in his dining room. But if the external trappings of Boyer's and Swanson's fledging enterprise seemed humble, their ambitions were grandiose. Though they had no employees or facilities, Swanson's intent was to institute the first major new full-scale pharmaceutical company since Syntex was founded to take advantage of the discovery of the birth control pill in the early 1960s. And Boyer planned, quite simply, to alter nature.

In Boyer's original experiments with Stanley Cohen, they had inserted a foreign gene into a bacterium, which the bacterium then replicated, or cloned. Now he wanted not only to implant a foreign gene but to then induce the bacterium to *express* the gene and produce a functional *human* hormone inside a petri dish. It was a scientific accomplishment most researchers believed was decades away from being accomplished, a daring feat of technical legerdemain comparable to embarking on a mission to Mars after the Wright brothers first, uncertain flight at Kitty Hawk.

But which protein? Selection of the company's first drug was essential to establish their credibility. Swanson came up with a long laundry list of requirements that had to be met in order to convince the investment community that this was a viable company with a practical new technology. The product had to have an existing market, because they didn't have the resources to do what Swanson called "missionary marketing" to stimulate a demand for their product. Plus, the product would then have a proven track record with the FDA, expediting the agency's often glacial approval process that can drag on for years, leaving companies in a costly purgatory of uncertainty. It would also make more economic sense if the genetically engineered version of the product was cheaper and easier to manufacture. All these conditions narrowed the field considerably, and for Swanson, given the marketplace's intricate calculus, the natural choice, indeed the only choice, was genetically engineered synthetic insulin.

Recruiting gifted young scientists to carry out this task was daunting, however, since biologists who worked in industry were considered second-raters by their academic counterparts. And Swanson didn't want just anyone. He wanted the best. Part of Swanson's genius is that he "recognized that the entrepreneur and the postdoc had much in common, and he worked to cement that bond."[4] The postdocs are science's workhorses, the dedicated lab rats who have no responsibilities other than the hands-on bench work of pure science. Like entrepreneurs, postdocs have to be aggressive risk takers because they're under enormous pressure to perform revolutionary research, to execute the elegant experiments that result in a key discovery— which, of course, is credited to the lab chief even if he hasn't touched a test tube in years—or, at the very least, to do work with enough cachet to assure them a faculty position.

Consequently, they're intrigued by the seemingly insurmountable—and potentially career-making—problems that established scientists shun because they fear frittering away scanty resources on ventures that are almost certainly doomed to failure. Creating a gene from scratch using materials pulled off the laboratory shelf certainly fell into this category. Hardly anyone in the scientific community believed it was possible to synthesize a protein as large as insulin. Swanson, in his recruitment pitches, slyly appealed to his quarry's infatuation with pushing the envelope. "Clone insulin, and *we got it made!*" Swanson would exhort.[5] And a few exceptional young scientists heeded his siren's call.

It was fortuitous Swanson enlisted such talent because he soon discovered they faced some very stiff competition. In April 1976, Boyer and Swanson incorporated their company with $100,000 in seed money from Kleiner & Perkins. A month later, Eli Lilly & Co., the pharmaceutical giant, sponsored a symposium on insulin. The hundred-year-old drug company was one of the world's leading producers of insulin. Their domestic insulin revenues amounted to $160 million annually, comprising about 80 percent of the U.S. insulin market. Lilly officials had summoned scientists to talk about using the new techniques of recombinant DNA to engineer insulin genetically.

The conference had been prompted by an FDA statistician who had noticed a sobering trend. Pancreases from slaughtered pigs and cows were used to manufacture therapeutic insulin, but in the past several years, consumer meat consumption had leveled off considerably, while the diabetic population rose steadily, inexorably, at a rate of about 5 percent a year. If these two trends continued the implications were ominous: sometime soon, whether it was in 1980 or 1990, a shortage would develop that could be catastrophic for the nation's 1.5 million insulin-dependent diabetics.

Some of the nation's top insulin researchers, along with major players in the embryonic genetic engineering revolution, met on May 24 near Lilly's corporate headquarters in Indianapolis to ponder possible solutions to this impending crisis. Among those present were Harvard's Walter Gilbert, another physicist turned molecular biologist, and William J. Rutter and Howard M. Goodman, UCSF colleagues of Herbert Boyer. By the time the conference ended two days later, they realized it was feasible. The technology had matured to the point where they could isolate the insulin gene, churn out copies of it using their trusty *E. coli* bacteria, and then prod the bacteria to secrete human insulin. When they returned to their labs, an informal consensus was reached that they would, in scientific parlance, "go for the gene."

Boyer and Swanson weren't thrilled that developing genetically engineered insulin was suddenly a race. They were already committed to first synthesizing somatostatin, a powerful hormone secreted by the hypothalamus, a small gland at the base of the brain. Somatostatin has a simple chemical structure, comprised of only fourteen amino acids, which Boyer thought would be relatively easy to synthesize. Those experiments would convince dubious investors that the technology worked, Swanson maintained, *and* arm them with insights into how to synthesize the infinitely more complex insulin molecule.

But what if they just lost precious time? The fate of their fledgling company hinged upon the successful synthesis of insulin—and they didn't intend to come in second in what was now a three-way race.

What's more, Howard Goodman was an old friend of Boyer's, family almost, and one of his chief collaborators during his most productive period in the late 1960s and early 1970s. And William Rutter, the department chair, had revitalized the once moribund UCSF biochemistry department after his arrival in 1969 and transformed it into an academic hotbed. Boyer didn't want bruising scientific rivalries to sour those relationships. Unfortunately, as one writer noted, "the UCSF biochemistry department became, unwittingly and rather traumatically, a social laboratory for all the growing pains associated with fame and achievement in genetic engineering"—not to mention the prospect of amassing vast riches.[6]

Almost immediately, Genentech's contractual arrangement with Herbert Boyer's UCSF lab ruptured these established alliances. It spawned a raging controversy about the propriety of these industrial ties, which was hotly debated in the hallways of the medical school and in the academic senate, and caused ugly fissures that ran like a fault line through the lab. Suddenly, a chosen few were expected to protect proprietary information and keep secrets, which was in direct conflict with the canon of open communication that traditionally propelled science forward. "I remember that first day," recalled one postdoc. "There were only twelve or so of us in Boyer's lab, and one guy was singled out to have a confidential meeting with Herb and Bob Swanson. We all wondered what was going on, and he came back out and couldn't tell us. Right then, that very moment, things changed in the lab, and it sort of all fell apart from that point."[7]

The first research team under the Genentech banner was assembled, composed of members of Boyer's lab working in collaboration with scientists at Caltech and at the City of Hope National Medical Center in Duarte, California, which is located on a patch of flat, sun-parched land on the outskirts of Los Angeles. What they ultimately accomplished was later hailed by Philip Handler, president of the National Academy of Sciences, as "a scientific triumph of the first order,"[8] but not before the group experienced a heart-stopping crisis that almost scuttled Genentech. In the spring of 1977, two of Boyer's postdocs, Herb Heyneker and Paco Bolivar, finally synthesized and cloned the somatostatin gene, using DNA fragments that had been laboriously concocted in labs at the City of Hope after several setbacks over the previous year.

Were the altered bugs actually secreting somatostatin? The way to find out was to clone lots of colonies of the bacteria to get enough of a sample, and then test for the presence of the hormone using specially outfitted radioactive antibodies that home in on somatostatin like heat-seeking missiles. On the morning of June 16, researchers at the City of Hope hooked up a gamma counter to perform the radioimmunoassay. But nothing happened. There was no trace of hormone.

Robert Swanson, who had flown down to Duarte for the demonstration, was devastated. "I saw my whole career and everything else pass before my eyes," Swanson recalled. Swanson was unaccustomed to the pace of scientific research, which tends to lurch forward in sporadic bursts after seemingly interminable delays. He had quit his job at Kleiner & Perkins, staking everything on the success of these experiments, and the unpredictable nature of scientific progress was anxiety-provoking. He could feel the hot breath of Harvard's Walter Gilbert and UCSF's William Rutter and Howard Goodman—not to mention that of an increasingly impatient Thomas Perkins, who was underwriting the endeavor. Another setback could shatter Perkins's already shaky confidence and demoralize Boyer's overworked troops. Swanson was fast running out of money, and he really thought they couldn't recover from this failure.

Surprisingly, they did. The scientists figured out what went wrong. Apparently, another protein in the *E. coli* recognized the somatostatin as foreign and was gobbling it up. They devised an ingenious subterfuge to slip the hormone past the bacteria's defenses. They hid the somatostatin gene inside a much larger gene, which camouflaged the hormone enough so that it wasn't emulsified. When they repeated the assay in mid-August, it worked. On December 1, 1977, at a press conference held at the Biltmore Hotel in Los Angeles, the UCSF–City of Hope research team told the world about what *The New York Times* called a "biomedical research coup"—that they had cloned and expressed somatostatin. It didn't matter that somatostatin would never be produced commercially. Their scientific tour de force demonstrated the practical use of this technology. As Herbert Boyer told reporters: "The man on the street can now finally get a return on his investment in science."[9]

Robert Swanson suddenly had no trouble raising $1 million to bankroll their insulin project. Swanson even took the bold step of actually renting out space for the infant company's laboratory in January 1978. He leased 8,000 square feet of a warehouse in a South San Francisco industrial park situated on a strip of land perched on San Francisco Bay called Point San Bruno, where the locals congregated to fish. And he hired Genentech's first full-time scientists, Dennis Kleid and David Goeddel, two gifted postdocs who were intoxicated by the prospect of working on the edge of the scientific frontiers without being handicapped by lack of funding or equipment.

Despite the Genentech–City of Hope group's stunning achievement, trying to synthesize the insulin gene was a long shot, an audacious, dark-horse strategy in a race against molecular biology's dependable Man o' War, Walter Gilbert. A scientist of intimidating brilliance who cast a long shadow over every facet of molecular biology, Gilbert was an odds-on favorite to win a Nobel Prize for any one of a number of key discoveries he had unearthed in a distinguished career. Unlike Boyer, who came up the hard way, Gilbert had the right pedigree. He headed a large research team at the Harvard Biological Laboratories and his illustrious work had earned him an appointment as the American Cancer Society Professor at Harvard. He even *looked* like a scientist, with his black horn-rim glasses, nondescript features, and short, dark curly hair.

Biology, for all its politicking, backbiting, and intellectual snobbery, is, at bottom, an unforgiving meritocracy. Old school ties are irrelevant in the crucible of the laboratory, where all that matters is whether the experiment works or not. In this instance, Boyer's singular background at the intersection of bacteriology and biochemistry provided him with a decisive edge. "The chemical synthesis of DNA was waiting for the cloning techniques to make its usefulness known," he later said. He recognized it was possible to mimic artificially the sequence of DNA for any human gene with common laboratory chemicals, and he also knew the few scientists who possessed the cunning to execute this tricky piece of technical wizardry.

Here again, providence played a crucial role. Boyer sensed correctly that growing political opposition to recombinant DNA experimentation would prompt the government to impose severe restrictions on research. As expected, in June 1976, the NIH mandated that recombinant DNA research requiring human genetic material must be done in P4 laboratories, those forbidding, hermetically sealed maximum-security facilities where space-suited military researchers conduct the most hazardous germ warfare experiments. Since no such labs were open to civilians in the United States, William Rutter and Howard Goodman's UCSF group and Gilbert's team at Harvard struggled to find a suitable venue in Europe. After some intense negotiations, Gilbert's group bivouacked at a P4 military facility in Porton, England, where their research was bedeviled by a series of distressing snafus. Members of the UCSF team hit similar snags in Strasbourg, France.

The Boyer-led Genentech group was employing synthetic genetic material, so they weren't fettered by the NIH's constraints. Their competitors were stymied by the logistical difficulties inherent in performing intricate experiments in unfamiliar surroundings. Kleid and Goeddel had to journey no farther than a few miles up Highway 101 from their homes in Menlo Park to their lab at Point San Bruno, where they'd sneak out to catch a few fish while waiting for experiments to cook. After a heated two-year race, during which the fortunes of each team rose and fell faster than a soprano's bosom, an exhausted Genentech team staggered across the finish line first. However, Gilbert's group stoutly maintained they would have won handily if they hadn't been forced to go abroad.

Robert Swanson moved swiftly to capitalize on their breakthrough. Throughout 1978, he had been in informal negotiations with Eli Lilly to license this technology. Lilly officials were willing to talk to Genentech but they balked at signing any agreements. They even hedged their bets by investing money in the rival UCSF insulin initiative. Lilly could afford to be choosy. After all, they held all the cards. Genentech wouldn't have a prayer marketing their product in a head-to-head competition with the entrenched pharmaceutical giant. Nor did the tiny biotech have the capability to scale up production, shepherd the drug through the FDA's regulatory hurdles, and market it.

All Genentech had going for it was superb science, and a brazen CEO in Robert Swanson. It turned out to be enough.

On August 24, 1978, Dave Goeddel finished the experiment that confirmed that their genetically altered bugs were secreting human insulin. The next day, Swanson closed the deal with Lilly. Two weeks later, on a hot, smoggy September day, the Genentech team gathered in a sweltering conference room at the City of Hope Medical Center in Duarte to announce to a packed house of television and print journalists that they had made human insulin using the techniques of genetic engineering.

The story was front-page news across the country, and featured on all three networks' nightly news broadcasts. The press conference was, said one, "a monster" and put the tiny biotech on the map. There were a handful of skeptical reporters in the mostly adulatory crowd, however, who had the bad manners to interrupt this lovefest by asking some pointed questions. Did the genetically engineered insulin actually work? Was it biologically active—that is, did it reduce high blood sugar in test animals? Had they even tested the metabolic effects of this insulin? The answers, of course, were no. In their mad dash to claim victory, clinch the deal with Lilly, and beat out Walter Gilbert, who, rumor had it, was planning a major announcement at a scientific meeting in Munich on September 7, Genentech hadn't bothered to perform these critical studies. "It was just a big media hype," Judy Ismach of *Medical World News* later said. "It was done because Genentech was going public and they wanted the coverage."[10]

Genentech, despite the squeaky-clean image that Bob Swanson so carefully cultivated among the generally adoring members of the press, was not above playing very hard ball when it came to protecting its corporate interests. In the company's haste to bring genetically engineered human insulin to the marketplace, Genentech evaded the NIH's stringent guidelines on the use of genetic material. In the fall of 1978, Genentech was ready to scale up production of insulin, but NIH rules limited them to only ten liters of the substance in their laboratory. Ten liters was hardly enough to proceed. In October, Robert Swanson wrote to the NIH director that they were starting a pilot project to produce insulin in a P1 laboratory, a lower-level containment facility than the NIH required.

Genentech's act of defiance put the NIH in an untenable position. If NIH officials reprimanded the company publicly, it would reveal the agency as a toothless tiger with no legal power to enforce these controls. But if the NIH did nothing, the vast gulf regarding compliance that already existed between academia and industry would only widen. Several months later, NIH officials informed Swanson that P2 conditions "are appropriate for the clones mentioned in your letter." Genentech disregarded the NIH directive and forged ahead with its original plan. The company justified its flagrant violation of the NIH rules with confusing doublespeak. If they complied with the NIH rules, Robert Swanson told *The New York Times* in June 1979, they might be forced to divulge trade secrets to their rivals. Besides, he dismissively added, "the risks involved in this are minuscule."[11]

It was the NIH that blinked, and embarrassed agency officials concocted all sorts of transparent excuses to indicate "the company had been in compliance all along." The correspondence between the NIH and Genentech proves otherwise. It reveals "a company threatening to make policy decisions by itself and a government agency taking no action to prevent it from doing so," notes science historian Susan Wright. "To avoid congressional intervention, the NIH left such backstage arm-twisting unpublicized, and companies like Genentech took the opportunity to press their agendas with impunity."[12]

These high-pressure tactics were a portent of what was to come, an early glimpse into the more ruthless underside of a company that liked to portray itself as the Tiffany of the biotechs, with its emphasis on revolutionary science and the laid-back working environment that *Esquire* magazine dubbed "postindustrial management." And the doubts voiced by the handful of skeptics at Genentech's press conference were drowned out by the deafening euphoria about the shimmering promise of biotechnology. "This was the watershed," says Susan Wright. "After this, corporations began to invest in academic labs."[13]

And events were moving swiftly a continent away—in Washington and on Wall Street—that turned this trickle of industrial interest in academic bioscience into a torrent. In 1980, two seemingly unrelated events would set in motion a revolution that altered the ethos of science and the way therapeutics are devised in the United States. It is only now, some seventeen years later, that the disastrous consequences of these actions are stunningly clear.

"It is scarcely an exaggeration to say that right now American business is facing its most severe public disfavor since the 1930s," David Rockefeller, the chair of Chase Manhattan Bank, said in a speech to the Advertising Council in December 1971, at the height of the protests that divided the nation into warring camps. "We are assailed for demeaning the worker, deceiving the consumer, destroying the environment, and disillusioning the younger generation."[14]

Rockefeller, scion of one of the world's most powerful families, echoed concerns being voiced privately by members of the nation's corporate elite. The U.S. economy, drained by the Vietnam War, deteriorated throughout the late 1960s and early 1970s. Industry felt economic growth was shackled by the onerous restrictions prompted by the consumer safety, environmental, and occupational health and safety movements. Corporate leaders like Rockefeller were at the forefront of a crusade to derail the regulatory juggernaut of the early 1970s. They advocated rapid technological development, which could nurture productivity and improve America's perceived declining presence on the international market.

Forming closer ties between industry and science, and academic scientists, in particular, who were at the forefront of innovation, was integral to this process. Corporate leaders warmed to the notion of tapping into academia's vast research enterprise, rather than spending money to expand their own in-house research and development capabilities. With the Vietnam War winding down, college campuses were no longer antagonistic to the presence of corporations on campus. And universities, many of which had severed their industrial ties during the upheavals of the 1960s, were now caught in a serious cash crunch due to stringent government funding cutbacks. So they too welcomed the revival of relationships with industry.

In 1974, Frank Cary, chair of IBM, championed a new alliance between academia and industry at a dinner for the heads of the nation's largest high-tech companies, thirteen Nobel laureates, and several academic leaders. Behind the scenes, David Rockefeller's brother Nelson, who served as Vice President during Gerald Ford's brief administration, was the architect of a coalition between government-sponsored science and the corporate sector. This resulted in the reestablishment of the Office of Science and Technology Policy in 1976, an agency that had been dissolved during the Nixon era. (Nixon distrusted academic scientists; a handful even appeared on Nixon's infamous "enemies list.")

"In response to all the movements going on in the early seventies that called for regulation of science and technology," observes Susan Wright, "the corporations started a major counteroffensive to figure out what to do with the increasingly regulatory climate. They then launched a campaign aimed at deregulation but also aimed at forging much closer ties between science and industry." The patent law was standing in the way of the consummation of these unions, however. At the time, if a researcher took one dime of government money, then the rights to his or her discovery were in the public domain. Corporations wanted exclusive licensing agreements on all breakthroughs achieved under a company's sponsorship. Otherwise, they had no real incentive for investing in university research. Industry and academic officials began to call for changes in the patent law that would hasten the transfer of technology from the public to the private sector and so speed the development of promising technologies.

Republicans rallied around technology transfer as a way of sharing the cost burdens of academic research with industry. Democrats were reluctant, though, to sanction this corporate intrusion on campus, but technology transfer advocates found an unexpected ally in President Jimmy Carter. Carter liked to portray himself as the quintessential Washington outsider, the simple, God-fearing peanut farmer from rural Georgia. In reality, though, he was a far more complicated man. An engineer by training and an Annapolis graduate, Carter had been a disciple in his youth of the venerable Admiral Hyman G. Rickover, the crusty father of the United States' fearsome nuclear submarine fleet. Carter, generally considered one of our brightest Presidents, was infatuated with technology and embraced the notion that harnessing its power could transform society. In May 1978, he initiated a domestic policy review of industrial innovation.

Suddenly, technology transfer was bandied about on Capitol Hill as a vehicle that could spearhead a broad-based industrialization. The fruits of biotechnology, then the product of academic laboratories, would generate new world markets for American industry and ensure America's continued global supremacy in pharmaceuticals—one of the few bright spots in an otherwise dreary economic landscape. And at a time when federal resources were dwindling, university officials could compensate for the shortfall by attracting corporate dollars in exchange for exclusive licensing agreements on discoveries made under a company's sponsorship.

Bipartisan support grew when Democrats were convinced that technology transfer could help jump-start the stalled economy and rescue Jimmy Carter's foundering presidency—or at least limit the damage to Democrats in the 1980 election. Birch Bayh, one of the Senate's most distinguished liberals, teamed up with Bob Dole, a conservative Republican whose star had ascended when he was Gerald Ford's 1976 running mate, to sponsor a bill that would give companies exclusive licensing rights to discoveries arising from federally funded research and encourage scientists to seek commercial applications for their work.

The debates that raged at the congressional hearings held in September 1980 to discuss the proposed Bayh-Dole Act still resonate strongly today. Secretary of Commerce Philip Klutznick candidly conceded that "some have likened our proposed policy to using tax money to pay a contractor to build a road and then allowing the contractor to charge an additional toll to those who would travel the road. Let me offer a different analogy," he told the congressional panel. Then he proceeded to articulate the Carter White House's position. "Imagine ourselves back in the early nineteenth century," he continued. "The government hires a contractor to explore new territory. The contractor goes out and returns to tell us he crossed swampy, bandit-infested territory, crossed deserts and mountains, and, before turning back, saw from a distance a promising land. It would be in the public interest to give the contractor an exclusive right to try—to invest his own money to build a road across the swamp, desert, and mountains with the further right to collect a toll for a limited period of time should he succeed and be able to entice anyone to make the journey."[15]

It was a intriguing conceit, but Admiral Hyman G. Rickover, who testified after Klutznick, dismissed his fanciful arguments with an impatient wave of his hand. The iconoclastic Navy man had an unblemished reputation. He believed Bayh-Dole was one of the greatest giveaways in American history—much to the chagrin of his former protégé, President Jimmy Carter. "This whole thing is an exercise in semantics by the patent lobby. . . . They are always figuring out things to keep them in business," he said, fixing his interlocutors with the icy stare that had devastated adversaries for more than four decades. Rickover, who had spent much of his career policing profligate defense contractors, had a keen insight into the proposed law's ultimate consequences. "Based on 40 years' experience in technology and in dealing with various segments of American industry," he gravely intoned, "I believe the bill would achieve exactly *the opposite* of what it purports." It would throttle technological development, hurt small business, stifle competition, and cost the taxpayer plenty while promoting "greater concentration of economic power in the hands of large corporations."[16]

Despite the high esteem in which Rickover was held, his dire predictions were ignored, and Bayh-Dole was enacted in October. But few politicians in Washington truly fathomed the ramifications of this legislation, so no one thought to implement provisions to safeguard the public's interests. That Rickover would later be a vindicated prophet gave him no satisfaction. Although the bill's passage came too late to rescue Jimmy Carter's presidency, the timing couldn't have been more fortuitous for the incoming resident of the White House, Ronald Reagan.

Unlike Carter, a thoughtful humanist who had darkly warned of a national malaise, Reagan was an amiable optimist who had stumped throughout the country with the message that it was "morning in America." Or morning at least for his clique of corporate cronies who got him elected. He was delighted to shift the burden for federal programs from the public to the private sector, and give away the rights to billions of dollars' worth of taxpayer-supported research. With the enactment of Bayh-Dole, science historian David Nobel caustically observes, "people were now able to trade in public goods with impunity and total immunity from public scrutiny. They just hid behind the refuges of scoundrels: academic freedom and proprietary interests."[17]

At the same time, a key court case, known as *Diamond* v. *Chakrabarty*, was wending its way through the judicial system on its way to the U.S. Supreme Court. Legal scholars believed the outcome of this lawsuit would remove the last remaining obstacle to patenting gene-splicing technology. In 1972, Ananda Chakrabarty, a microbiologist with General Electric, had devised a superstrain of the *Pseudomonas* bacterium by crossbreeding several existing strains of that bacterium. The new bacterium could gobble up four different components of crude oil, rendering it extraordinarily useful in mopping up destructive oil spills. His initial patent application was turned down by the Patent Office because microorganisms are a "product of nature" and therefore not novel, so they are not patentable. GE, on behalf of Chakrabarty, appealed, contending that his hybridization techniques had synthesized an entirely new life form.

On the third Monday of June 1980, the Supreme Court agreed, in a 5–4 decision that modified patent law in the same way that *Roe* v. *Wade* forever altered the abortion debate. The high court ruled that scientific discoveries were, indeed, inventions and that new life forms can be patented. Writing for the majority, Chief Justice Warren Burger said Dr. Chakrabarty's discovery "is not nature's handiwork, but his own; accordingly it is patentable subject matter."[18]

It is ironic that only one vote shifted the course of history, though a coalition of biotech firms stood ready to lobby lawmakers to amend the patent law if the decision had gone the other way (Genentech had filed a friend-of-the-court brief). This landmark ruling paved the way for patent protection for genetic engineering and allowed the burgeoning biotech industry to exploit the staggering commercial potential in the development of new life forms.

But the decision touched off a firestorm of controversy, reigniting the biohazard debate about "the gruesome parade of horribles" that could emanate from the laboratory, and fanning scientists' fears that patentability of microorganisms would encourage secrecy and inhibit the free flow of information and materials that is so essential to scientific research. A handful of critics detected an even darker, more sinister undertone to this ruling, which they believed opened the door to a frightening *Blade Runner* future where a monolithic corporation owns everything, right down to each base pair on the human genome. "The Supreme Court usurped the responsibility of Congress—they had absolutely no judicial right to make law, which is essentially what they did," charged Jeremy Rifkin, who was then director of the People's Business Commission, which opposed the ruling. "Now, in the eyes of the law, a living creature is no different than a toaster oven or a computer. This decision will open up the floodgates for the commercialization of the gene pool which inevitably leads to the patenting of life itself."[19] Rifkin, an implacable foe of genetic engineering, sounded like a raging fanatic, but subsequent events over the next decade would prove him right.

Genentech continued to garner headlines, first with the successful synthesis of human growth hormone, then with interferon, a scarce natural protein touted as a potent cancer cure. By the time the company was ready to go public, expectations about biotechnology, and particularly about Genentech, had been roused to a fever pitch. No one could have predicted, however, the blowout that occurred when the first publicly traded shares of Genentech went on sale on the morning of October 14, 1980. Within twenty minutes of the opening bell on the New York Stock Exchange, one million shares had been eagerly snapped up, and the stock jumped in price from $35 to $89 a share. Throughout the day, fortunes were earned and lost as the price skyrocketed and then precipitously dropped, only to climb upward again, driven by an unprecedented speculative frenzy, before it settled down to $71 1/4 by the end of the day. In a few frantic hours, Genentech, a company which posted barely $80,000 in earnings and didn't have a single product to offer, raised $38.5 million. Herb Boyer and Robert Swanson's original $500 investment in the company had been magically transformed into a paper $60 million.

In the stampede to scramble onto the biotech bandwagon, the financial fundamentals—profit and loss, price-to-earnings ratios, the complicated calculus which analysts use to determine value—were left in the dust. The Genentech offering signaled the start of an unprecedented bull market for biologists and generated profound changes in academic research. Biology was suddenly big business, with projected sales from bioengineered products topping $500 billion by the year 2000. In the ensuing months, similar scenarios were played out as dozens of other biotech companies debuted on Wall Street, ultimately raking in more than 500 million in investment dollars. The financial press even gave this speculative hysteria a name: biomania.

The Gold Rush was on.

In a bit of curious synchronicity, on the exact same day Genentech stormed Wall Street, the Nobel Prizes for 1980 were announced. As had long been predicted, Walter Gilbert, along with Frederick Sanger of Great Britain, was awarded the chemistry prize for developing a method of rapidly sequencing DNA. Sharing this award was Stanford's Paul Berg, for his pioneering research in recombinant DNA—though some cattily said it was for "integrity" for convening Asilomar. Yet none of the press releases emanating from the Royal Swedish Academy mentioned Boyer and Cohen.

That same year, Stanley Cohen and Herbert Boyer shared the Albert Lasker Award, the nation's most prestigious medical honor and generally considered a forerunner to the Nobel. By any yardstick, Herbert Boyer had performed seminal science, first in gene splicing and then in godfathering the effort to synthesize the somatostatin and insulin genes. Boyer's considerable achievements were undercut in the eyes of his peers by his decision to be among the first to go commercial, though Boyer always insisted the money was incidental. "When the first patient gets treated with something my company makes," he muttered, "that's going to be a big day for me."[20]

Many of his detractors were simply jealous—"there was much gnashing of teeth when Boyer formed Genentech," one UCSF staffer waggishly recalls. Others, though, liked to counter with the story of two of Boyer's contemporaries, Cesar Milstein and his postdoc, Georges Koehler, of the British Medical Research Council Lab. In 1975, Milstein and Koehler discovered a technique to produce monoclonal antibodies in the laboratory, a discovery that earned the two scientists a Nobel Prize in 1984. Monoclonal antibodies are the cruise missiles of the immune system, specifically targeted disease fighters that home in on foreign invaders with unerring accuracy. Like gene-splicing technology, their breakthrough served as the basis for a whole new class of therapeutics. They were aware of their invention's financial potential, Milstein has said, "but I do not think we ever guessed at the number of zeros involved in the estimate." They took the moral high ground, however, and declined to patent their invention based on principle. "The practical achievements of science," insisted Milstein, clearly a scientist of the old school, "are part of science itself. They are advances in public knowledge and therefore don't belong to anybody, but to society."[21]

Ironically, many of the scientists who ostracized Boyer soon went down the same trail he blazed. They started their own biotech outfits, got rich off discoveries made at the taxpayers' expense, and privately chortled that Cesar Milstein "was a sucker." Drugmakers and venture capitalists were soon swarming over campuses dangling money and stock options, like baseball scouts cruising the minors for talent. The twenty-mile corridor along Highway 101 between UCSF and Stanford University, as well as the industrial areas near UC Berkeley, Harvard, and MIT, was dotted with start-ups. Genentech set the pattern for what followed: assemble a consortium of five or six scientists, split the company between the scientists and the people who put in the money, and those scientists will do the work in their university labs. In the mad dash to clone money, however, the spirit of cooperation, a bedrock of the scientific ethos, was shattered. "People were loath to ask questions and give suggestions in seminars or across the bench," according to one report, "for there was a feeling that someone might make money from someone else."[22]

For many top scientists, it was like winning the lottery. Investors were so eager to be on the ground floor of Silicon Valley II that financing for biotech companies was often obtained without products, prototypes, or even patents. Merely a biology superstar or two on the board of directors or in a key position was virtually all that was needed to solicit millions in venture capital. Between 1979 and 1981, more than 150 small biotechs were founded by university scientists eager to exploit their research, while dozens of other academics entered into lucrative cooperative alliances with industry.[23] Prominent researchers and Nobel laureates like Paul Berg, Walter Gilbert, and David Baltimore, who followed Boyer into the corporate boardrooms, now possessed unprecedented power. Their presence on a faculty could catapult a second-tier institution to the front rank, enabling the university to lure corporate sponsors. So they were courted and cosseted as assiduously as Heisman Trophy winners.

But for Herbert Boyer, who continued to run a research lab at UCSF, there would be no redemption, and his career never quite recovered from the stigma of his being the first to make a big score. He stopped granting interviews, and gradually withdrew from the academic science community. He siphoned off his considerable energies into consulting and cheerleading for Genentech. He used his wealth to seed his favorite charities—he donated $10 million to Yale and set up a philanthropic foundation that bears his name—and indulge his hobbies. The man who grew up in a home without a car traded in his aging Porsche for a top-of-the-line Targa and collected classic cars. He took up flying, and headed a little theater group in Marin County, the hip, affluent enclave north of San Francisco, where he and his family lived like landed gentry among the other newly minted biomillionaires. "Herb got more than any scientist can ever ask for," said a former member of his lab team. "He made an important contribution, he got recognized, and he became a millionaire. It was hard for him to handle. Science not only requires your mental concentration, it requires your physical presence. He just got distracted."[24]

CHAPTER 6

Margaret Heckler
Had a Cold

Despite Robert Gallo's strenuous efforts to resurrect retrovirology, the study of these tiny predators had fallen out of favor, regarded by mainstream scientists as a dreary backwater that would shed little light on the mechanisms of cancer or any of the other common ills that afflict most Americans. Nevertheless, Gallo, along with a small band of his acolytes at labs around the country, soldiered on in an almost quixotic quest to gain scientific respectability for retrovirology. Once Robert Gallo's lab discovered HTLV, his loyal lieutenants commenced the painstaking work of dissecting the virus, and mapping out its genetic structure, in order to analyze how it actually works.

One of them was biochemist William Haseltine, who hunkered down for the arduous job of deciphering the virus's genetic makeup in 1981 in his laboratory at Harvard's Dana-Farber Cancer Institute. To do this intricate piece of chemical wizardry, and plunge deep inside the lilliputian universe of viruses, required costly equipment, however, a more expensive arsenal than Haseltine could afford on his paltry grants. Though government scientists at the NIH were still prohibited from profiting from their discoveries, the traditional taboo against commercializing research in the ivy-covered halls of academe had been shattered. Gene splicers were routinely grabbing headlines for their Wall Street scores. Why shouldn't members of the once lofty virology contingent join the gold rush? The thirty-six-year-old Haseltine, who possessed the relentless drive of an entrepreneur, launched a biotech, Cambridge BioScience, to subsidize his retroviral research and to capitalize on any discoveries made in his lab.

Although Haseltine had a relatively easy time rounding up financial backers for his company, he knew it was risky to bet against the prevailing wisdom on retroviruses. In what later seemed like an uncanny bit of prescience, Haseltine believed these fragments of genetic material played a far more crucial role in the onset of disease than anyone imagined. He speculated they were the culprits behind perhaps one-quarter of all cancers, and they also might be causing a mysterious new malady that struck pockets of young homosexuals in New York, Los Angeles, and San Francisco. "Bill has a smell for what's important in molecular biology," Robert Gallo would later observe.

Haseltine invited two of the leaders in the field of retrovirology—Robert Gallo himself and Harvard's Max Essex—to join his venture. Initially, Gallo accepted 10,000 shares of stock in the company, along with options to buy an additional 40,000 shares of stock at $1.00 per share. As a federal employee, though, Robert Gallo was forbidden from joining an outside company because of the potential for conflicts of interest. So he was forced to return the stocks and options, though he was permitted to act as a paid consultant for the firm, receiving a stipend of $2,000 a day. Essex, however, had no problems with accepting an equity position in exchange for heading up the company's scientific advisory board. Haseltine owned 414,000 shares, Essex 208,000 shares, which would eventually make them multimillionaires.[1] And Harvard University, much to its dismay, was forced to enter into what one called "a shotgun marriage" with Cambridge BioScience.

The university had been looking for a corporate sponsor to help underwrite Essex's research at the Harvard School of Public Health. The big pharmaceuticals were interested in work on common ills like heart disease and ulcers, however, that could lead to new therapies that had blockbuster potential—not esoteric studies on obscure viruses. Cambridge BioScience was the only firm willing to support Essex's work, which meant that Essex and Haseltine would directly benefit financially from research conducted in Essex's laboratories at Harvard. Harvard would hold the patents on any discoveries arising out of Essex's work, but Cambridge BioScience would be awarded the exclusive licensing rights, which would generate far bigger bucks. Understandably, Harvard officials had considerable misgivings about this arrangement. In those early days, everyone, particularly at Harvard, was tiptoeing around, exercising scrupulous restraint about mixing academia with industry. After some hesitation, the university "became, in essence, a de facto partner in the biotech company, by providing lab space, labor (in the form of graduate students) and a good name."[2] "If there'd been *anyone* else" willing to back Essex's research, one Harvard administrator said, they never would have bothered with Cambridge BioScience.

And because of Cambridge BioScience's strategic position at the cutting edge of retroviral research, Haseltine and Essex would cash in on any breakthroughs the company made in treating and controlling diseases induced by retroviruses. None of this really mattered much then, however, since the only known human retrovirus, HTLV, and its more recently discovered first cousin, dubbed HTLV-2, sparked isolated outbreaks of a rare form of leukemia on islands in the Caribbean and in tiny fishing villages in Japan. Hardly enough of a patient population to make Essex and Haseltine rich.

No one knew then that Haseltine's vague hypothesis would prove correct and that a retrovirus would be implicated in the bizarre illness that was killing young gay men, or that the disease would evolve into a frightening global pandemic that came to be known by its acronym, AIDS. When the disease first emerged, scientists hashed out dozens of theories as to what could possibly be causing this deadly malady. Some thought it was the result of venereal diseases gone haywire, or the prolonged ingestion of amyl nitrites—known as poppers on the gay party circuit—in combination with other drugs, or simply the cumulative effects of the fast-line gay lifestyle wearing out the immune system. And there were, of course, persistent paranoid whispers in the gay community about lethal bugs concocted in military germ warfare labs that were being unleashed to wipe out homosexuals.

Nor could anyone have predicted that William Haseltine would one day be a powerful gatekeeper over the direction of AIDS research, by serving on three scientific committees that dispensed money for AIDS, and a member of the editorial boards of five scientific journals, the forums through which scientists communicate with each other, two of which were concerned with AIDS. By that time, Haseltine was such an influential national presence, testifying before Congress, advising the staffs of presidential campaigns, crafting NIH policy, and constantly quoted by the sound-bite-hungry media, that few dared question whether his decisions were influenced by personal interests rather than being motivated solely by a professional dedication to conquer this plague. AIDS research would come to be dominated by what one top AIDS researcher bitterly called "the Haseltine-Essex-Gallo Axis which boycotted ideas that were incompatible with their own." Ironically, the fortunes of Cambridge BioScience throughout the 1980s would eerily parallel that of the research establishment's war against AIDS.

Cambridge BioScience was an apt name for a company founded by a man who had spent most of his career ensconced in the cozy intellectual environs of Cambridge, across the Charles River from Boston. The son of a Navy physicist, Haseltine was trained by a trio of Nobel laureates, first as a graduate student at Harvard, where he studied under James Watson and Walter Gilbert, then as a postdoc in David Baltimore's laboratory at MIT. The bespectacled Haseltine, with his slicked-back hair and bland features, looked like a colorless science nerd.

He had a penchant for the outrageous, however, that grated on his buttoned-down Bostonian colleagues—he once roared up to Gallo's NCI lab behind the wheel of a fire-engine-red Mustang convertible, which he drove around the courtyard in front of the building several times in case anyone had missed his arrival, and he loved to swagger into meetings decked out in an Indiana Jones–style hat. There was more to Haseltine than just attention-seeking flamboyance, though. When he was reputedly having marital problems in the late 1970s, he was occasionally seen sitting alone in the bar of a seedy old hotel in downtown Cambridge, where the postdocs from Harvard's biology lab congregated, pensively nursing a beer into the wee hours of the morning. And colleagues grudgingly conceded he did good work.

Haseltine's linking of a retrovirus with the deadly ailment afflicting gay men wasn't quite the stunning intuitive leap that it seemed. His friend and fellow virologist Max Essex had made the intellectual connection first, soon after reports about this new disease blipped across the radar screens at the Centers for Disease Control (CDC) in Atlanta. In June 1981, Essex received a telephone call from Don Francis, a CDC epidemiologist who had worked in Essex's lab in the late 1970s.

In reading over the agency's *Morbidity and Mortality Weekly Report*, a bulletin distributed to health-care professionals that tallies illnesses and deaths in the United States, Francis was struck by a report from a UCLA physician. It concerned five young homosexuals who were at an age when they should have been in perfect health, yet their immune systems were so severely damaged they couldn't ward off even the most benign germs. Their T-cell counts, the white blood cells the body mobilizes to repel foreign invaders, were dangerously low. Their bodies were ravaged by normally innocuous infections— yeast infections and *Pneumocystis* pneumonia, a rare pneumonia that strikes cancer patients on chemotherapy, which destroys the immune system and leaves patients vulnerable to assault by microbes.

The infectious agent, if this was, in fact, an infectious disease, prob- ably attacked the T cells, hence the low T-cell counts. And the disease, whatever it was, seemed to have a long incubation period, since it appeared out of nowhere simultaneously in three cities on both coasts. If the new pathogen had been a more recent arrival, the pattern of infection would follow a more traditional route, starting in one city, which would be its point of entry into the population, and then spread to another, nearby locale, along an easily delineated path—not emerg- ing full-blown in three geographically diverse areas. And if it did have a lengthy latency period, then there was no telling how many people were infected, how many time bombs there were out there that could explode anytime. The public health implications, if Francis's instincts were right, were staggering.

Don Francis had a notoriously short fuse and was legendary for jumping up in the middle of otherwise sedate meetings and pounding on tabletops to drive points home. But he was a veteran epidemiolo- gist—a medical detective who was part of the CDC's elite corps of physicians known as the "medical CIA"—who had been dispatched all over the developing world to contain mysterious disease outbreaks. He was accustomed to sifting swiftly through mountains of conflicting and confusing data to pinpoint the source of trouble, quickly deter- mining from often sketchy clues whether an illness was infectious and spread by insects, animals, or humans, or whether it was caused by poor sanitation or the myriad of other social ills endemic to impover- ished nations. In this instance, from Francis's perspective, the avail- able evidence pointed to only one thing. "This is feline leukemia in people," he flatly told Max Essex.

Max Essex was one of the world's leading authorities on feline leukemia, and he agreed with Francis that the two illnesses appeared to have some striking similarities. Essex's subsequent conversation with Don Francis would shape thinking about AIDS for many years to come. Essex, who had a Kewpie doll face and an unruly thatch of graying hair, was a veterinarian by training, with the kindly nature of someone who originally intended to devote his life to caring for animals. Recruited to Nixon's War on Cancer in the 1970s, the avuncular Essex had chosen to study feline leukemia in ordinary house cats, an illness which is transmitted by a virus. Essex observed that cats spread the leukemia virus through sexual contact and saliva. So if cats can infect each other with cancer through intimate contact, Essex had wondered, why not people? Essex also noticed that most infected cats weren't dying of the leukemia, but that their immune systems had collapsed, giving way to an onslaught of "opportunistic" disease.

Now Don Francis was raising the possibility that something similar was happening in humans. Perhaps a cancer virus was decimating the white blood cells, rendering victims susceptible to other infections that normally don't kill. Essex took Francis's theory one step further. Perhaps this new pathogen was a member of the same retroviral family as HTLV-1, the human leukemia virus discovered in Robert Gallo's NCI lab some months earlier, which Gallo believed triggered adult T-cell leukemia after a long incubation. Perhaps it was even HTLV-1 itself that was crippling these patients' immune systems. Throughout 1982, Essex tested blood samples from young homosexuals stricken with this mysterious ailment for the presence of antibodies to HTLV. If it was HTLV-1, or a variant of it, then the virus should be immortalizing T cells—prompting them to grow wildly out of control, the hallmark of cancer—not killing them. Essex chose to ignore this apparent contradiction. It was a seemingly inconsequential oversight that would have disastrous consequences later on.

Initially, however, Essex couldn't interest his colleague and friend Robert Gallo in this new disease. In fact, the discovery of HTLV-1 in Robert Gallo's lab made him the most likely candidate to discover the culprit behind AIDS. In late 1981, the CDC's James Curran made the trip up to Bethesda from the CDC's headquarters in Atlanta to enlist Gallo's help in identifying what triggered this malady. Again, he demurred. But when several other scientists raised the possibility that this new disease might be induced by HTLV-1, Gallo reluctantly assigned one team in his giant lab to look for the presence of HTLV in AIDS patients. By late 1982, Gallo and Essex reported many AIDS or immune-suppressed patients were infected with HTLV-1.

By the spring of 1983, Gallo convinced his superiors at the NCI to seize the initiative by creating a task force on AIDS, with him as head. Normally, finding the cause of a new infectious disease should have been the domain of the National Institute of Allergy and Infectious Diseases (NIAID), while battling the disease and safeguarding public health would be the responsibility of the CDC. In the early stages of the epidemic, however, when the Reagan White House cut federal funding for medical research to the bare bones, these niceties were ignored as cash-starved agencies engaged in unseemly back-room brawls to muscle in on the action. NCI director Vincent DeVita, who had a reputation as a tough street fighter, was determined to claim a hefty slice of the federal funds earmarked to battle this deadly new pathogen for the leviathan NCI, by far the largest institute on the NIH campus.

Robert Gallo was the NCI's standard bearer, a position he took quite seriously. Throughout 1982 and early 1983, Gallo's lab worked overtime trying to identify the microbe responsible for AIDS. But they were operating under an unforeseen handicap. Gallo and his troops were searching for a variant of HTLV-1, a blind spot that contributed to their failure to get cell cultures extracted from the blood of AIDS patients to grow. For some inexplicable reason, the cells kept dying off.

This strange new malady was also making its presence felt on the other side of the Atlantic. In late 1982, Luc Montagnier, chief of viral oncology at Paris's Pasteur Institute, met with a group of Parisian physicians who were treating young homosexuals afflicted with this mysterious wasting disease. The doctors wondered if this lethal ailment could possibly be sparked by a retrovirus, and begged Montagnier to investigate the possibility. Two of his assistants, Jean-Claude Chermann and Françoise Barré-Sinoussi, had experience working with retroviruses, so he asked them to check it out. Within a few weeks, Barré-Sinoussi uncovered something startling in cells from a young French fashion designer named Frédéric Brugière, who had swollen lymph nodes but wasn't as yet stricken with this new disease.

In February 1983, one of Gallo's assistants, Zaki Salahuddin, received a phone call from Françoise Barré-Sinoussi, who had recently completed a sabbatical in Gallo's lab. The young French scientist had spent several months in the LTCB working with Salahuddin, the man with a fabled "green thumb" who could grow anything in a petri dish. Peering through the microscope at her workbench in Montagnier's cramped lab, Barré-Sinoussi had seen something quite extraordinary in the cells from the young Parisian. It was definitely a novel organism, she excitedly told Zaki. "And there are rods sticking out of the top," she added, almost cooing into the phone in her heavily accented English. They both knew what the presence of rods meant— she had found a virus, possibly a retrovirus.

Montagnier began calling Gallo every Wednesday afternoon, ostensibly to ask him for reagents to test whether the virus discovered at the Pasteur was related to HTLV-1. Mostly, though, Montagnier, a bookkeeper's son from the Loire Valley, seemed to hope he could ingratiate himself with the powerful American scientist with whom he had enjoyed a collegial relationship over the years. The mild-mannered French virologist, with the soft, doughy features and guileless gaze of a provincial peasant, shrewdly realized he'd need a strong ally to ensure that the Pasteur discovery was considered seriously.

By April, Montagnier informed Gallo there was no way this new virus could be related to HTLV-1. The antibodies for HTLV-1 Gallo had sent to the Pasteur in February hadn't reacted with the French virus. Even more important, this new virus was killing T cells, so they were constantly adding cells to keep the virus growing; HTLV-1 didn't kill T cells, it made them multiply. He also told Gallo that he was writing up a paper reporting his findings. At that point, Gallo told him that he and Max Essex were also preparing papers which demonstrated a link between AIDS and HTLV-1. If Montagnier finished his soon, Gallo said, perhaps all three papers could appear simultaneously.

Essex's paper revealed that the blood of perhaps 40 percent of the AIDS patients he had tested had antibodies to an as yet unidentified protein on the surface of the leukemic helper T cells. Essex acknowledged his blood test wasn't accurate enough, and it needed to be refined. If it ultimately proved to be an effective test for the pathogen causing this deadly disease, it could be quite lucrative. Before his paper was published, Harvard quietly filed for a patent on the Essex test. Cambridge BioScience, however, which would automatically own the licensing rights if the test was approved, would be the big beneficiary.

Montagnier truly believed he had found the cause of AIDS, but in his paper he cautiously named his virus lymphadenopathy-associated virus (LAV); in other words, a virus associated with lymph inflammation. He observed that LAV appeared to be a lentivirus, a slow-acting virus that spawns anemia in horses and was not a member of the HTLV family. What this meant was that Don Francis's original instincts had been chillingly accurate. If this virus was a lentivirus, then it had a long incubation period, so there was no telling how many people were already infected and were now unwittingly passing the virus on to countless others. The paper also pointed out that Gallo's leukemia virus and this new virus were "not immunologically related."

The Pasteur paper, which was co-authored by Barré-Sinoussi, Chermann, and Montagnier, was hand-delivered in April 1983 to Gallo's lab in Bethesda. However, the manuscript didn't have an abstract, which is the paragraph preceding a scientific paper that summarizes its contents. This wasn't a minor oversight. Abstracts are essential, and they're often the only thing busy scientists have time to read to ascertain a paper's contents. Gallo called Montagnier. Since time was of the essence, he told the Frenchman, he would write an abstract.

Gallo sent the Pasteur paper to the editors of *Science,* along with a strong letter of recommendation that said, "This paper is of obvious immediate great importance and relevance. . . . It should be published as rapidly as possible." Appended to the Pasteur manuscript was Gallo's abstract. He wrote that the French virus was a C-type virus, the same class of viruses as HTLV-1, that the core protein was similar to that of the leukemia virus, and that antibodies to HTLV-1 had reacted with the French virus. Gallo also added a sentence to the text itself: "The virus appears to be a member of the human T-cell leukemia virus (HTLV) family."

None of this was true, however. The Montagnier team's paper said exactly the opposite; their virus was most emphatically *not* a leukemia virus. Dr. Gallo's backstage maneuvers with the Pasteur paper were designed to bolster the case for HTLV-1 as the cause of AIDS. His actions were later characterized by the NIH Office of Scientific Integrity as "gratuitous, self-serving, and improper," reflecting "Dr. Gallo's propensity to misrepresent and mislead in favor of his own research findings or hypotheses." Montagnier was extremely "distressed" by Gallo's inaccurate additions when the paper appeared in *Science.* The subtle but critical distinctions between the French virus and the ones isolated by Essex and Gallo were lost on the press, which never bothered to read past the abstracts. Newspapers across the country dutifully reported that researchers at Harvard, the National Cancer Institute, and the Pasteur Institute had found evidence of HTLV-1 in patients with AIDS, which *The Boston Globe* called "the leading suspect for causing the illness."

Over the summer, Gallo's lab requested samples of the virus the French discovered. Françoise Barré-Sinoussi asked someone in Gallo's lab if she should send them on. "Are you crazy?" the researcher responded. "He'll rob you blind." Nevertheless, the Pasteur, in keeping with accepted scientific practice, continued to share their virus with the LTCB. Subsequent tests revealed what Montagnier had been saying all along—the French virus was not HTLV. However, the competitive undercurrent that had been roiling beneath the surface between the Pasteur laboratory and Gallo's LTCB finally flared up into open hostilities at a special meeting devoted to HTLV and retroviruses that was held at Cold Spring Harbor on September 14, 1983, in honor of Mary Lasker, the longtime benefactor of cancer research.

First Robert Gallo, then Max Essex presented the latest findings from their labs. They, along with other researchers, had found evidence of reverse transcriptase (RT) activity in cells extracted from AIDS patients. They had uncovered some indications there was a link between HTLV and AIDS. But they couldn't seem to grow the virus in cell cultures.

Luc Montagnier was given only twenty minutes to make his presentation. He was scheduled to speak next to last, on the second day of the conference in the early evening when most people were tired and many had already left. Once he stepped up to the podium, though, it was evident the Pasteur group was way ahead in the race to identify the infectious agent. The team had isolated a new retrovirus in eight AIDS patients, including one from each of the key risk groups—gay men, hemophiliacs, and Haitians. They had devised a blood test that already had about a 60 percent accuracy in identifying the virus, but what really shocked the audience was that electron microscope photographs and biochemical analysis indicated this new pathogen bore no relation to HTLV-1.

Montagnier's talk illuminated exactly why Gallo and Essex were having so much trouble keeping samples of their virus alive. This putative retrovirus wasn't a transforming virus like HTLV-1, which prompted cells to grow wildly out of control. It was a cytotoxic virus, which destroyed cells. This was why the scientists who were looking for a variant of HTLV couldn't grow their virus; HTLV would have grown in any nutritive media, but this virus didn't because it killed the cells off. The French didn't have those biases, though, so they continued to add fresh cells to the growth medium, which is why their viruses stayed alive.

Even more startling was the implicit message of Montagnier's discoveries—namely, that the esteemed Dr. Gallo was galloping off in the wrong direction and bringing the rest of the medical establishment with him. During the question-and-answer period that followed Montagnier's presentation, members of the audience, among them Max Essex, expressed a healthy skepticism about Montagnier's findings. The general consensus, however, was that the French were definitely on to something. One scientist later told Montaigner, "You've probably got it."

Then Gallo opened fire, infuriated that this obscure Frenchman was upstaging him—and on his own turf, no less. "Even given the rough-and-tumble give-and-take characteristic of American science," says Bernard Poiesz, who was in the audience that day, Gallo's critique was unusually harsh. He expressed serious doubts about the reliability of the Pasteur team's research, saying, "It was terrible science, that there was no way it could be true." Montagnier, who was accustomed to the polite Continental approach, was stunned by the viciousness of Gallo's scathing attack. Deeply disillusioned, he flew back to Paris the next day. And without Gallo's support, other scientists discounted Montagnier's findings; they returned to their labs and continued to waste precious time and money in a futile search for leukemia viruses rather than hunting for the real killer.

Privately, Mikulas Popovic, one of Gallo's top lieutenants at the LTCB, told Gallo that Montagnier's Cold Spring Harbor presentation was "very impressive. He has excellent data there. He was most advanced. There is no question about that. He picked out the correct virus." If Gallo had conceded defeat then and thrown his support behind the French virus at Cold Spring Harbor, a reliable blood test could have been widely available by the summer of 1984. Gallo wouldn't find *his* virus for another year, however. Consequently, the American AIDS blood test didn't reach the blood banks until the summer of

1985. Eminent British virologist Abraham Karpas called this "the lost year," during which thousands of people who received blood transfusions were infected with HIV.

Montagnier's Cold Spring Harbor report, Gallo later said, aroused his "competitive instincts." The two labs were still cooperating, but Montagnier wasn't quite so forthcoming. Gallo asked for another sample of the French virus. Again, the French complied but with one proviso. Attorneys for the Pasteur Institute had filed a patent application in London for an antibody test for LAV. In light of the patent application, Pasteur researchers extracted a written promise from Gallo that this virus sample would not be used for commercial purposes. With this fresh batch, which arrived in the LTCB on September 22, 1983, Mikulas Popovic, Gallo's chief virologist, was finally able to coax the pernicious virus into growing in the cell media. With the insights gleaned from the French virus, researchers were then able to isolate the same virus from other AIDS patients.

As convincing as the data Montagnier presented at Cold Spring Harbor was, though, few in the scientific community knew about it. They wouldn't hear about it for another four months, until February 1984, at a meeting held in Park City, Utah, a winter ski resort, where 250 of the world's top researchers met for the first large-scale scientific conference devoted to AIDS. Gallo, of course, was the keynote speaker, the glittery sought-after superstar whose research would be the centerpiece of the entire gathering. Montagnier, anxious to avoid another sulfurous confrontation with Gallo, dispatched his top lieutenant, Jean-Claude Chermann, a veteran virologist who had known Gallo for more than twenty years. Perhaps they would listen to him. Again, though, the French scientist was scheduled at the least advantageous time to make a presentation—just before lunch, when everyone was itching to hit the ski slopes. Worse yet, at the last minute Harvard's William Haseltine was added to the program ahead of Chermann.

During Haseltine's presentation, which droned on long after the ten minutes he had been allotted, restless members of the audience quietly slipped away. Those who virtuously remained behind to hear Chermann were astonished by what he had to say. French researchers had demonstrated that LAV targeted T cells, the very cells which AIDS patients were missing, and their blood test detected antibodies to their virus in about 75 percent of those infected. Chermann's evidence was virtually overwhelming that LAV, not HTLV, was the culprit behind AIDS. Later that day, a group of American scientists secretly met with Chermann in his hotel room. They wanted him to know that no matter what Gallo said, he had convinced them. "We grew the plant until it bloomed and we could see what kind of flower it gave," Dr. Chermann later said in describing the differences in the approaches of scientists at the LTCB and the Pasteur Institute. "The Americans kept examining seeds and shoots and trying to see if they would turn into the plant they wanted."[3]

Shortly after the Park City meeting, CDC officials sent tissue samples from AIDS patients to Gallo and Montagnier to determine the accuracy of the blood tests developed at their respective laboratories. On March 12, 1984, Gallo, along with his chief assistant, met with the CDC's James Curran in a restaurant in Bethesda to discuss the results of the CDC's head-to-head comparison of the test for the AIDS virus devised by the LTCB with the one developed at the Pasteur. According to Curran, in testing over 200 blood samples from AIDS patients, Curran told Gallo, the Pasteur test scored as well as the LTCB blood test in detecting antibodies to the virus that they thought caused AIDS; however, Gallo's attorney insists that the Pasteur test was not as acurate as the LTCB test.[4]

The Americans and the French would have to work together. While Gallo's underlings busily prepared the scientific papers to announce the LTCB's latest findings, he flew to Europe in the first week of April to negotiate the details of a joint announcement. At a meeting in Zurich on April 5, he told the audience that he heard the Pasteur Institute's blood test data are "almost as good as we have." The next day, he went on to Paris, where Pasteur scientists shared with him the computer printout of the CDC data. In a talk later that day announcing the discovery of HTLV-3, Gallo said it was "the same virus these guys [at the Pasteur] discovered last year."[5]

Then stories leaked into print about the Pasteur discovery of LAV and their development of an effective blood test. One front-page story in the Sunday edition of *The New York Times* on April 22, 1984, even extensively quoted Dr. James Mason, director of the Centers for Disease Control, who had collaborated with Pasteur researchers from the beginning. He said he "believed a virus discovered in France was the cause of the acquired immune deficiency syndrome."

Mason's "candid observations, entirely truthful, nearly cost him his job," according to one report. That Sunday morning, when *The New York Times* was delivered to the home of C. McLain "Mac" Haddow, chief of staff for Margaret Heckler, Reagan's Secretary of Health and Human Services (HHS), he went ballistic. He immediately called Mason's boss, Dr. Edward Brandt, the Assistant Secretary of Health. Brandt said Haddow "turned the air blue" complaining about Mason's interview with the *Times*, which he characterized as a "deliberate embarrassment" of the NIH, and heatedly demanded Mason's resignation.

The next morning, Brandt met with Mason in hopes of heading off an internecine warfare between the rival public health agencies. Mason convinced him that the French had indeed isolated the probable AIDS virus and had an antibody test that was quite effective in detecting the presence of this virus. Brandt quietly took Mason's side. They were, after all, physicians whose first allegiance was to the Hippocratic oath. This was a public health emergency that took precedence over bruised egos at the NIH. Brandt says he immediately ordered NCI director Vincent DeVita to compare the LTCB virus with the one from the Pasteur. If they were two distinctly different pathogens—and there was every reason to believe they were—they needed to know *now* in order to stem further infection and safeguard the blood supply. Brandt later told congressional investigators this comparison was a vital public health concern because, he said, "development of a blood test, of vaccines, and of potential treatments all might vary if there were two distinct viruses associated with AIDS." (Gallo, in contrast, told the same subcommittee that comparison of the viruses "did not affect public health.")[6]

According to Suzanne Hadley, who was the chief investigator for the NIH's later probe of Robert Gallo, Mason, along with James Curran and Don Francis, were also absolutely horrified at the prospect that the U.S. government was about to violate every sacred tenet of science by claiming all the credit for the discovery of the AIDS-causing virus, and destroy the collegial relationship between the two nations' scientists that CDC researchers had so assiduously cultivated. They furiously placed phone calls to HHS officials to persuade them to give the Pasteur scientists full recognition for their trailblazing work. To their immense relief, they were assured the French would be properly credited.

James Mason's own ordeal wasn't quite over, however. One of Heckler's senior public affairs officials called him in for a personal dressing-down and shrilly lambasted him for "demeaning the American contribution" to AIDS research and "embarrassing Secretary Heckler." A suitably chastened James Mason sat dejectedly in the back of the Hubert H. Humphrey Auditorium at the HHS headquarters on the afternoon of April 23, 1984, when the HHS held a press conference, which was hastily called to deflect attention from the spreading news of the French breakthrough.

AIDS had already claimed nearly 2,000 lives and more than 100 new cases were being diagnosed each week. The gay community was under siege. Outraged activists were holding candlelight vigils on the White House lawn. The Reagan administration, stung by charges of homophobia, was under enormous pressure to help stop the plague killing so many young men. HHS Secretary Margaret Heckler's announcement, which led off the nightly newscasts on all three networks that evening, was calculated to shore up her boss's flagging image. Robert Gallo, who had been summoned back to Washington from a trip to Italy to attend the press conference, shared the stage with Secretary Heckler.

Under the blinding television lights, with flashbulbs popping like champagne corks on New Year's Eve, Margaret Heckler, with the nation's top virus hunter by her side, faced the packed house of reporters. "Today we add another miracle to the long honor roll of American medicine and science," she said. "The probable cause of AIDS had been found—a variant of a known human cancer virus, called HTLV-3" by "our eminent Dr. Robert Gallo." "Today's discovery represents the triumph of science over a dreaded disease," continued Heckler, who added a thinly disguised swipe at the Reagan administration's legion of critics. "Those who have disparaged this scientific search—those who have said we weren't doing enough—have not understood how sound, solid, significant medical research proceeds."[7] The long national nightmare would soon be over, Heckler promised. Within six months, there would be a blood test for AIDS and within two years a vaccine would be available.

Then it was Gallo's turn at the microphone. Wearing a lightweight yellow sports jacket and tinted aviator glasses, the triumphant Gallo basked in the intense media glare. After years of being scorned by his peers because of discoveries that never quite stood up to scientific scrutiny, Gallo felt vindicated, his place in history assured. "When did you make the discovery?" one reporter asked. We've been growing quantities of the virus for at least six months, Gallo blandly replied, which would have been shortly after the Cold Spring Harbor meeting. This was the first indication, however, that he had isolated the virus by then; in fact, notes from his lab reveal that researchers were still struggling to connect AIDS with Gallo's leukemia virus. "Is your virus the same as the ones the French have?" another reporter inquired. Gallo responded that he didn't really know since he hadn't received enough of the Pasteur's LAV to make a clear comparison. This statement, too, was contradicted by his own lab records of experiments carried out with LAV.[8]

Hours earlier, Robert Gallo and his colleagues at the National Cancer Institute's Laboratory of Tumor Cell Biology, on behalf of their employer, the United States government, applied for U.S. patents on an antibody test and a method for propagating the AIDS virus, which Gallo called HTLV-3. A battalion of government attorneys had descended upon Gallo's lab in early April. They enlisted several of his top lieutenants, who worked late into the night and on weekends, to prepare the patent forms in time for Heckler's announcement. In the patent applications, Dr. Gallo and his colleagues swore, under penalty of criminal prosecution for perjury, that they were "the original, first and joint inventors . . . of the subject matter which is claimed and for which a patent is sought."[9]

French officials viewing the press conference in Washington were horrified. They had been assured by CDC officials their role in the discovery would be fully acknowledged. This was a breach of scientific protocol of the highest order—not to mention a flagrant disregard of their patent application for an LAV antibody test, which had been filed with the U.S. patent office on December 5, 1983, nearly five months earlier. Heckler's unconscionable failure to credit the French, which had been in her prepared text but left unread, was attributed to the fact that she wasn't feeling well that day. "She had a cold," one spectator recalled that Gallo later told congressional investigators, "and the cold medication clogged her head."

The press conference was the watershed. On that day, the research agenda for the assault on AIDS was set, based on government fiat rather than good science. Ethical protocol in science mandates that new discoveries are first published in scientific journals, which allows scientists to analyze the results before they are released to the media. But as had happened with HL-23 a decade before, the scientific community was bypassed in favor of a direct release to the press. Gallo's four separate papers reporting his putative discovery of the AIDS virus weren't published in *Science* for another ten days. By that time, the public euphoria over finding the cause of AIDS drowned out any serious discussion of what Gallo had written. "Getting one paper in *Science* is a lot," Gallo later crowed. "Getting two is fantastic. Getting three was a record. We had four at one time."[10] If researchers had been free to criticize Gallo's hypothesis publicly, they might have noticed that some of the AIDS patients were not infected by the virus. They even might have had the courage to point out that Montagnier's group had discovered this virus first.

And it was HHS Secretary Margaret Heckler, not the scientific community, who articulated the game plan that guided medicine's war on AIDS for the next decade. First, identify the pathogen, then develop a vaccine. It was no coincidence that this strategy, given the intellectual traditions of virology, was modeled on the successful conquest of an earlier viral scourge, polio. From then on, federal dollars for AIDS research funded only experiments that were in line with the prevailing hypothesis—that this virus is a lone assassin. Research on other possible causes, including Epstein-Barr virus, cytomegalovirus, and poppers, or a multifactorial approach was immediately abandoned.

On that day, the primacy of the NIH over the CDC was established, the full authority of the United States government was committed to protecting the U.S. patents on Gallo's AIDS test, and Robert Gallo was fixed in the nation's consciousness as the commander-in-chief of the research effort to combat this new plague. A strategy had been mapped out and a general anointed. There was no turning back.

There was only one problem in all of this. Little of what Margaret Heckler or Robert Gallo said that day would prove to be true. So from that day forward, money, ego, and American prestige, not good science, became the engines driving AIDS research.

CHAPTER 7

EL DORADO

Dr. Diane Pennica was Genentech's sixtieth employee. Tiny and delicate, with dark wavy hair that flowed down her back and expressive brown eyes framed by a thick fringe of eyelashes, Pennica looked like a fresh-faced high school cheerleader that day in May 1980 when she reported for work, not the scientist destined to develop a lifesaving drug that would transform Genentech into a biotech powerhouse. The struggling young company was still headquartered in a small, cramped warehouse on the tip of Point San Bruno in South San Francisco, a gritty, industrial town sandwiched between San Francisco and the swank enclaves of the Bay Area's affluent peninsula. Pennica, then twenty-eight, was assigned to work in a tiny, windowless laboratory under the supervision of Dave Goeddel, the cloning wizard who had led the Genentech team that synthesized human insulin.

Pennica didn't care about her surroundings. All she cared about was doing science. Her infatuation with biology had turned out to be a passport to adventure, an entree into the life of the mind universes removed from Fredonia, the farming community where she grew up in New York's Finger Lakes region. Pennica was the eldest of four girls, and her father, a carpenter, encouraged his brainy daughter to pursue a career as an elementary school teacher. As an undergraduate at the State University of New York College at Fredonia, she worked in a biology laboratory that was formulating a test for carriers of the cystic fibrosis gene. "This seemed like such an important thing to do and my teachers made science seem so exciting," says Pennica. "That's when I knew this is what I wanted to do with the rest of my life." After receiving her Ph.D. in microbiology from the University of Rhode Island in 1977, Pennica did her postdoctoral work at Hoffmann-La Roche in

New Jersey studying viruses until she was recruited by an unknown biotech company a continent away.

Pennica rented a spartan studio in nearby Foster City, a speck of a town built on the landfill that supports the San Mateo Bridge, a twelve-mile span crossing San Francisco Bay. It didn't matter where she lived—she spent every waking minute in the lab trying to clone urokinase, an enzyme secreted by the kidneys that dissolved blood clots. "I was young, naive, and unmarried at the time," she recalls of her grueling schedule. "This was a new challenge, the enthusiasm in the company was very infectious, and everybody else worked all the time too. Saturdays. Sundays. At all hours."

Less than two months after Pennica arrived in California, Genentech sent her abroad, to her first international scientific conference, the Fibrinolysis Congress in Malmö, Sweden, on June 12, where scientists doing cutting-edge research on clot-dissolving agents like urokinase would be presenting their latest findings. Her mission was to see if anyone had uncovered new clot busters or, in scientific parlance, thrombolytics—agents that lyse (dissolve) fibrin, the ropy-like material in blood plasma that forms a network of fibers that allows clots to congeal in the bloodstream (a process called thrombosis). Pennica was so anxious about making a good impression that she wanted to check out the conference site the day before the seminar. So she asked the hotel's concierge where the conference was being held. "Oh, the meeting of the doctors," the clerk airily replied. "That started today."

Pennica panicked. She must have confused the first day of the meeting because of the nine-hour time difference between California and Sweden. She was dressed in casual slacks and a hot-pink sweatshirt, which was hardly appropriate attire for a high-powered scientific gathering, but she didn't bother to change her clothes. She threw her suitcases into her room and literally ran to the conference hall. She found her way to a meeting room where about thirty men in suits were seated around a large table. When she heard someone utter the word "urokinase," she knew she was in the right place. Breathless, she sat down unobtrusively in the back, scribbling notes, horrified she might have missed something. She had barely composed herself when Désiré Collen, a professor of medicine at the highly respected Center for Thrombosis and Vascular Research in Leuven, Belgium, stepped up to the podium to report on his work with an obscure protein he called tissue plasminogen activator (t-PA). At that moment, Diane Pennica knew she had hit upon an exciting new area of research.

Scientists had known about the existence of t-PA since the late 1940s. In 1947, Tage Astrup, a Danish researcher, observed that the blood carried some type of clot-dissolving agent. The body secreted such minuscule amounts of this mysterious substance, though, that nearly three decades passed before scientists purified enough of it to be able to determine the role it played in the body. In the mid-1970s, scientists discovered that cells extracted from a woman who had died of cancer were secreting a clot-dissolving agent. In 1979, Désiré Collen, working with this melanoma cell line, succeeded in isolating the substance, which turned out to be an enzyme in blood plasma called plasminogen activator, and tested it on artificially induced clots in animals. Collen later received Belgium's equivalent of the Nobel Prize for this trailblazing work.

Earlier, researchers had identified other agents that were potent thrombolytics, like urokinase and streptokinase (SK), a protein produced by streptococci bacteria. Throughout the 1950s and 1960s, in fact, European researchers studied SK extensively. Highly effective in dissolving blood clots in the legs or in the chest (called pulmonary embolisms), it became the first thrombolytic agent to be used on patients. But streptokinase could induce serious allergic reactions, like fever, chills, nausea, and headaches, so drugmakers, such as Genentech, were constantly on the lookout for more potent thrombolytics that had fewer side effects.

The search for superior clot-busting agents intensified to a fever pitch in 1979, when Peter Rentrop, a young German scientist, made an astonishing discovery that revolutionized cardiology—and vastly expanded the market for thrombolytics. Up until Rentrop's breakthrough, doctors didn't understand the mechanisms that triggered heart attacks, the underlying biological reasons why blood vessels ferrying oxygen to the heart suddenly constrict, stanching blood flow.

Once it's deprived of life-sustaining oxygen for more than twenty minutes, the heart muscle tissue starts to die of asphyxiation. Autopsies of heart attack victims reveal the process in stunning clarity: when you slice open the heart, you can see how the tissues progressively turned a sickly gray from lack of oxygen, with death penetrating down to the deepest layers of heart muscle. Doctors use neutral medical terms to describe this horrific process of cell suffocation, talking blandly about how myocardial infarctions—heart attacks—cause tissue necrosis.

There had been hints over the years as to what triggered this phenomenon. Researchers knew clots formed when too much plaque built up on the arterial walls, but they thought that when the heart seized up, the spasms ruptured the plaque, freeing chunks that floated through the blood like giant ice floes hurtling downstream. "Cardiologists didn't believe the clots were the *cause* of the heart attack," Désiré Collen recalls. "There were some studies but there was no enthusiasm for the idea."

Ironically, researchers like Anthony Fletcher and Sol Sherry at New York University reported encouraging results in treating heart attack patients with streptokinase as early as 1958. "At that time, their thinking was that acute myocardial infarction was caused by a blood clot in the coronary artery," says Peter Rentrop, who's now a cardiologist at St. Vincent's Hospital in New York. "In fact, since the turn of the century, the terms 'coronary thrombosis' and 'myocardial infarction' were used synonymously. The problem at that time, though, was that there was no way to prove that the drug [streptokinase] really worked." And the results of other studies were contradictory, so this treatment strategy never gained converts among the mighty cardiology contingent.

Conventional wisdom shifted virtually overnight after a series of experiments provided conclusive evidence that heart attacks were provoked by clots obstructing blood vessels. In 1978, Peter Rentrop, along with colleagues at the University of Göttingen in Germany, threaded guide wires inside catheters that were then inserted inside the arteries of patients in cardiac shock. The notion was to use the wire to open the blocked blood vessels the way a plumber's snake clears a clogged drain. "But the mechanical interventions were cumbersome and unreliable," Rentrop recalls. So they began to use the guide wires in combination with streptokinase. On one sweltering day in the summer of 1979, however, an elderly patient, a woman stricken with a serious heart attack, was in such a precarious condition that there was no time to tease the guide wire through her artery. "Let's try just using streptokinase," Rentrop suggested, in a last-ditch effort to save her life.

Once she was infused with the clot-busting agent, Rentrop and other members of his team dashed into an adjoining room to watch what was happening inside her body on a monitor. An angiography, which beams images of the inner workings of the heart, revealed that there was, in fact, a clot completely blocking the blood flow in a key coronary artery, cutting off oxygen to the heart. Suddenly, almost miraculously, the vessel began to clear, and the blood slowly seeped through. Within fifteen minutes, the artery was opened, blood circulated freely, the heart resumed its normal rhythm, and the excruciating pain that accompanies acute coronary distress subsided. The heart attack had literally been stopped in its tracks. "Ladies and gentlemen," one of Rentrop's colleagues announced to everyone assembled in the room, "you have just witnessed medical history."

They certainly had. That fall, in November 1979, Peter Rentrop requested time to present his startling findings at the American Heart Association's annual convention. As a young researcher unknown to the cardiology mainstream, Rentrop, then thirty-eight, was granted only ten minutes, but it was enough. When he showed his dramatic films, jaws dropped. Here was incontrovertible proof not only that clots trigger heart attacks but that a clot-dissolving agent could limit the damage. The thunderstruck audience leapt to its feet and gave him a standing ovation. Cardiology would never be the same. His talk electrified the 40,000 cardiologists in attendance, and sparked a transformation in how heart attacks are treated that eventually slashed mortality rates, enabled victims to resume their normal lives quickly, and generated billions in profits for the drugmakers that later dominated the thrombolytic market.

Which is why Diane Pennica was energized when she heard Désiré Collen's talk about the thrombolytic potential of t-PA in Sweden seven months later. Streptokinase, which had been around for decades, was locked up by a handful of pharmaceutical companies. And behemoths like Burroughs Wellcome, a British-based drugmaker, had staked out a claim on urokinase, which was more expensive to produce than streptokinase but produced fewer side effects. Even the cloning work Diane Pennica was assigned to do on urokinase was merely a contract job for Grünenthal, a German pharmaceutical.

Tissue plasminogen activator (t-PA) was something entirely new, and possibly more effective, than the available clot busters. Collen, working with Burton Sobel, a cardiologist at Washington University in St. Louis, had given human t-PA harvested from Bowes melanoma cells to dogs in which they had induced clots in the coronary arteries. PET scans revealed that the heart muscle recovered quickly and the arteries themselves opened up much faster than they did with strep-tokinase. "There was every indication," Burton Sobel recalls, "that this might be a promising drug."

What's more, t-PA homed in on the clot-inducing fibrin in the blood with the precision of a heat-seeking missile. In contrast, streptokinase and urokinase were less selective, and dissolved not just fibrin but other plasma proteins essential to blood coagulation, like factor V and factor VIII. Consequently, these two agents can sometimes cause life-threatening hemorrhages. T-PA could be a magic bullet, a miraculous therapeutic agent directed only at the clot, leaving the protective plasma proteins intact. And since t-PA was an enzyme made by the body, not a foreign substance like streptokinase, there was also less chance of allergic reactions. "T-PA is promising," said Collen, conclud-ing his remarks to his colleagues in Sweden, "but there is too little of it for meaningful research."

Diane Pennica knew a way to produce large quantities of t-PA—through recombinant DNA techniques. By determining the sequence of the amino acids that comprise the t-PA protein, it was possible to clone the stretch of DNA encoding t-PA. The t-PA cDNA (complementary DNA) could be inserted into an expression plasmid, and then implanted into *E. coli* bacteria. Then these microbial workhorses of the genetic engi-neering revolution obligingly churn out—or express—large amounts of the t-PA protein. Over dinner in a nearby restaurant, which was located in a medieval castle, where the scientists convened after the meeting, Pennica forced herself to overcome her natural shyness and approach the imposing Désiré Collen about collaborating with Genentech.

A powerfully built man who towered over Pennica, Collen was dubious. "This is a huge protein," he told her, eying her skeptically. "I think it would be impossible to synthesize t-PA by cloning." "Oh, sure we can," Pennica rashly responded, and proceeded to jot cloning strategies on napkins to show him exactly how she would do it. Collen was convinced, persuaded as much by her evident enthusiasm as by her grasp of this wondrous new science of gene splicing. He agreed to give Genentech samples of t-PA and the melanoma cell line, and to act as a consultant.

Ironically, Pennica learned later that she had inadvertently stumbled into a special preconference session for the top researchers in the field. "They thought I was one of the speakers' daughters just waiting patiently for her dad," she recalls. "I was an intruder. They said if I had been a guy, they would have thrown me out. It was sheer luck and fate that I was at that meeting. If I had only attended the regular conference, I might not have picked out Désiré or recognized the importance of his research."

When she returned to Genentech, however, she had another skeptic to win over—Robert Swanson. "Don't waste any time on something peripheral," Swanson cautioned her, and insisted she continue to work on the urokinase contract, which would generate guaranteed income for the struggling company. "Why don't we do both?" she countered. "We could probably do the work side by side, and anything we learned from one project we could apply to the other." Swanson reluctantly relented.

Pennica's collaboration with Collen instigated more than nine months of nonstop work, fifteen hours a day, seven days a week. She was driven, in part, by rumors that other drug companies had teams of researchers that were attempting to clone t-PA too. "Sometimes, I'd come in at midnight to set up an experiment at 1 A.M. just to keep things going," says Pennica. "I don't know if I could ever work that hard again—it was so draining and so exhilarating at the same time. But that's how you beat the competition—you work harder than anybody else."

News of her research spread throughout the company, and t-PA was deemed a top priority. Bob Swanson—even, on occasion, Herb Boyer himself, who no doubt felt a certain kinship with this young woman from a working-class family who had come out of nowhere to scale the scientific citadel—would stop by her cubbyhole to cheer her on. "They would come into the lab and ask me what step I was on today," she remembers. "It was nice to have everybody so excited about a common goal." Behind the pleasant banter and encouraging words, though, Pennica could feel the heat.

And for good reason. Genentech's recombinant form of human insulin, which had been its first great scientific achievement, had been licensed to Eli Lilly. T-PA could be Genentech's ticket to the big time, demonstrating to an increasingly disenchanted investment community that biotechnology could fulfill its early promise.

Cloning the gene for t-PA, a twisted chain of 527 amino acids that looks like a string of pearls arrayed in haphazard loops, was daunting, far more complicated than Pennica ever imagined on that memorable day when she first met Désiré Collen. Using the t-PA protein samples sent by Désiré Collen as a starting point, Pennica worked backward from there to decipher the genetic code. Initially, William Kohr, an outstanding protein chemist at Genentech, determined some stretches of the sequence of amino acids on the t-PA protein. Pennica then designed DNA probes that corresponded to those amino acid sequences, matching them up like two complementary, interlocking puzzle pieces. Exploiting the double helix property of DNA, which dictates that complementary strands of genetic material are attracted to each other like magnets, she then used the probes to sort through a melanoma cDNA library of about 5,000 clones searching for a match. "It was overwhelming," she recalls. "But there's more failure than success in science and you can't be discouraged. You just have to keep going."

On the afternoon of October 25, 1981, Genentech's sequencing group returned the DNA sequence from another of Pennica's potential t-PA clones. They told her the protein sequence encoded by this clone hadn't matched any of the stretches of t-PA protein sequence in Genentech's computer. Again. "I was very disappointed," remembers Diane, who had looked at so many clones over the preceding year that the t-PA sequences were practically burned into her memory. "I took the sequence and went back to my desk. Suddenly, I looked at the sequence in my hand that they had returned. Then I looked at a portion of the actual t-PA sequence in my notebook from William Kohr. They matched. The DNA sequencing group just didn't have the stretch of sequences in their computer that I had in my notebook. My hands started shaking holding that piece of paper. I had done it. I had cloned my first gene."

But it was only a partial clone. One key loop (known as the 5 prime end, or beginning of the clone) was still missing, and it took another five months of herculean work to clone the end. "We had such a hard time getting this missing part of the clone. We thought the molecule might have a number of kinks, or secondary structures," she recalls. "We tried four or five different approaches to bypass that potential kink, and *finally*, after five months more of nonstop work, one of the approaches worked." Intriguingly, this is the point at which Pennica's rivals at Genetics Institute and at KabiVitrum in Sweden hit a roadblock.

In July 1982, after two years of exhausting work, Diane Pennica returned to Europe and announced at a conference in Switzerland that a Genentech team had cracked the genetic code for t-PA, and produced it in genetically modified bacteria and animal cells. When she was done, her colleagues gave her a standing ovation, which is extremely rare for scientific talks. It was a spectacular triumph for a young scientist who a scant two years earlier had been mistaken for someone's daughter at the Malmö conference. Shortly afterward, two researchers from KabiVitrum stopped by her lab. "Well, you beat us," they told her. "How did you do it? This project almost killed us. We worked nonstop." Pennica just smiled.

Al Meyerhoff was furious. A public interest lawyer with the Natural Resources Defense Council (NRDC), Meyerhoff was built like a football linebacker, but he had a wild mane of curly hair framing his freckled face that made him look positively cherubic. He was feeling anything but cherubic, however, that sparkling clear Saturday morning in March 1982 when he sped down Highway 101 to Pajaro Dunes, a ritzy beachfront resort on the Monterey Peninsula, a good two-hour drive from his office in San Francisco. Earlier in the year, Meyerhoff had spearheaded the successful fight to convince California officials to impose strict conflict of interest disclosure rules on University of California faculty. Now he was on a similar mission.

Stanford University president Donald Kennedy had invited leading scientists and the presidents of America's top research powerhouses—Harvard, MIT, Caltech, the University of California, and Stanford—for a two-day meeting at Pajaro Dunes with executives from eleven corporations—including Du Pont, Eli Lilly, Genentech, and Gillette—to hammer out guidelines for industrial links with academia. What was attracting the most attention about this scientific summit—and raising Meyerhoff's hackles—was who *wasn't* on the guest list: the meeting was closed to the press and public, and critics of the commercialism of scientific research like Meyerhoff were as welcome as civil rights marchers at a Klan picnic.

"It's not Yalta West," insisted one of the organizers of the Pajaro Dunes meeting in response to carping from journalists and consumer watchdog groups, which were incensed that they were excluded from this high-powered conclave. Considering that these five universities were showered with $600 million in federal research grants, roughly 15 percent of *all* the money the government dispensed for medical research in 1981, that's *exactly* what it was, Meyerhoff thought grimly, an intellectual Yalta where the heads of America's premier research universities were meeting with their industrial brethren to carve up what promised to be an enormously lucrative territory: the industrial applications of genetic engineering discoveries in academic labs. Stanford's Donald Kennedy, a respected biologist and former FDA Commissioner, who had convened the conference, had been calling for "a second Asilomar" for more than a year, in response to the nasty controversies that had erupted over the commercial intrusions on campuses across the country. With "the introduction of strong commercial motivations and conflicts of interest on the part of faculty members," Kennedy warned in testimony before Congress a year before, "there is the prospect of the significant contamination of the university's basic research enterprises."[1]

Underwritten by a $50,000 grant from the Henry J. Kaiser Foundation, the closed conference was light-years removed from the labored openness of the fabled scientific assemblage at Asilomar, and served only to underscore how much the expectation of riches from genetic engineering had altered the scientific ethos. The participants themselves exemplified how much the boundaries between commerce and academia had blurred. Three of the university presidents were on the boards of directors or were well-paid consultants of several corporations while at least four of the industry CEOs were trustees of Caltech, MIT, or MIT-affiliated enterprises. Even the amenities at the secluded private club, where visitors stayed in well-appointed town houses nestled amid the scrub pines and salt grass of the majestic Monterey coastline, were in stark contrast to Asilomar, a no-frills state-owned facility where Nobel laureates bunked with postdocs in sparsely furnished rooms without telephones or TVs.

Al Meyerhoff had no intention of being elbowed aside. He pulled up to the main gate of the sprawling private club around noon, two hours before the Pajaro Dunes mandarins had scheduled a press briefing, with plans to subvert their carefully choreographed confab with a little dose of reality. With the impulsive inventiveness of youth, Meyerhoff hoisted his bulky frame up on the hood of his car, and held his own impromptu press conference for a cluster of reporters. "We are concerned that, if left unchecked, the ever-increasing influence of the business sector in establishing university research priorities will result in short-term commercial factors overwhelming other considerations," Meyerhoff told a largely receptive audience of journalists. "Pajaro Dunes should be the beginning of a debate, not the conclusion of a treaty between these university and corporate presidents."

The Pajaro Dunes participants, stung by accusations that they were conspiring to create "campus cartels" that would profit at taxpayer expense, issued a manifesto of their own to reassure the public they were preserving the integrity of the university. "It is important that universities and industries maintain basic academic values in their research agreements," their draft statement declared. "Agreements should be constructed, for example, in ways that do not promote a secrecy that will harm the progress of science, impair the education of students, interfere with the choice of faculty members of the scientific questions or lines of inquiry they pursue, or divert the energies of faculty members from their primary obligations to teaching and research."

Donald Kennedy's ambitions to elevate this gathering to the same lofty moral plane as Asilomar were crushed by the cynical media accounts, which dismissed their grandiose rhetoric as sheer claptrap dressed up in "hortatory language." Pajaro Dunes was "a smoke screen," Meyerhoff later observed.[2] Within a few years, every one of these supposedly sacrosanct tenets of "basic academic values" had been violated. They were trampled in the stampede to stake a claim in what science reporter Nicholas Wade called "the genetic El Dorado." "It's like the movie *Invasion of the Body Snatchers*," said one university scientist. "You look into the eyes of someone and realize it's too late."

The once pristine laboratory suddenly was a hotbed of commerce where an entirely different culture reigned, perverting the scientific ethos. "The temple is being taken over by the moneylenders," said one disgruntled scientist.[3] Whereas biologists who went commercial were once snubbed by their high-minded colleagues, now the biotech fever was so intense that even a Nobel laureate like Cesar Milstein felt diminished because he hadn't started a company. "In this society," he griped, "you're made to feel stupid if you can't make money."[4] Another senior scientist observed, "It's amazing how attitudes change toward technology transfer when that first red Ferrari shows up on campus."

Those who were vocal in their resistance to biotechnology's siren song found their careers sidetracked, or even permanently derailed. "I could give you a list of who said 'go slow,' and you'll see almost all of them ran into career problems," says Jonathan King, a biology professor at MIT and an outspoken critic of these industrial ties. "Academics who tried to speak up without a base of support never got tenure. They did not survive. Even [James] Watson was publicly attacked by members of his own faculty at Harvard. These were big stakes."

This sea change promoted the emergence of an entirely new breed: the scientist-entrepreneurs who straddled both worlds. Universities never had millionaire scientists in their midst before, and it gave rise to a virtually untouchable class of scientific Brahmins who enjoyed the perks and power of rock stars. The trappings of that power were enormously seductive, eroding the integrity of even the most virtuous. "One worrisome aspect of these ventures is that they inevitably change and confuse the relationship of the university to its professors," opined Derek Bok, president of Harvard University, which prided itself on being a model of rectitude. "The faculty member who joins with the administration in founding a new company is no longer valued merely as a teacher and a scholar; he becomes a significant source of potential income to the institution."[5]

Commercial pressures dashed the traditions of scientific cooperation and erected insurmountable divisions between those who joined the Gold Rush and those who didn't. Scientists bound by corporate contracts were expected to safeguard trade secrets, with data dispensed to colleagues on a "need to know" basis, which stopped the free exchange of information that was the lifeblood of the scientific process. At a meeting of the American Society for Microbiology in the early 1980s, for instance, an Exxon attorney advised scientists to have their papers notarized before presenting them at scientific symposiums to ensure they'd be able to obtain patent protection for their ideas later on. "I was chilled by that," said Jonathan King, who attended the meeting. "A few of my colleagues said it is a total change in the canon of what is proper scientific ethics and how science works."[6]

Training of the next generation of scientists also suffered. Postdocs in a lab at Harvard, which was run by a scientist who also helmed a biotech, were pitted against each other in a fevered contest to come up with fast results. The ones who were second, however, ended up with nothing to show for their fellowship, making it almost impossible for them to land a job elsewhere. Graduate students at the University of California at Davis doing research for a professor who headed a biotech complained they were doing little more than free contract work for his company. And this growing chorus of grievances from young scientists represented just the very tip of the iceberg—most remained silent, fearing they'd sabotage their careers if they went public with their beefs.

Secrecy replaced the openness that was once the hallmark of good science. Experiments were now routinely locked up to protect proprietary secrets, and relations soured even between scientists who had been longtime collaborators. A few stopped speaking, and passed each other in the hallways with curt nods. One of the more celebrated, but by no means isolated, cases was the acrimonious falling-out between Russell Doolittle, a molecular biologist based at the University of California at San Diego (UCSD) and the Salk Institute, and Richard Lerner of the Scripps Research Institute, a nonprofit, federally funded laboratory in La Jolla, California, just a few miles down Torrey Pines Road from the Salk. The dispute arose in 1981 after Lerner, a molecular biologist whom colleagues describe as persuasive, strong-willed, and abrasive, helped to engineer a lucrative long-term licensing agreement with Johnson & Johnson that gave the drugmaker first rights to results from Scripps research. And their feud exemplified the changes wrought in basic science by the infusion of corporate dollars.

Lerner and Doolittle were once friendly rivals who often dropped by each other's neighboring labs for advice or simply to hash out ideas. It was from one such conversation that a serious question of scientific protocol emerged that evolved into a multimillion-dollar patent dispute. Both research teams were trying to devise a vaccine from synthetic chemicals instead of using the disease-causing organisms to stimulate an immune response. This revolutionary approach would circumvent the chief problem with vaccines, which is ensuring that the virus or bacterium is inactivated. Otherwise, the vaccine can cause the disease it was intended to prevent—a tragic consequence which has happened more than once, most notably in the mid-1950s when bad batches of the Salk polio vaccine triggered an outbreak of polio.

Thanks to advances in gene-splicing techniques, scientists from the UCSD and the Scripps group isolated certain proteins, which are called antigens, on the surface of the microbes that would prompt the body's defenses to produce antibodies to repel the foreign invader. The next logical step was to synthesize these antigens in the lab—a problem Doolittle and Lerner were grappling with. Synthetic antigens held out the promise of being safer, purer, and possibly even less expensive than traditional vaccines.

One of Doolittle's colleagues, Gernot Walter, a virologist on leave from the University of Freiburg in Germany, devised an innovative way of detecting these antigen proteins. If Walter's method turned out to be reliable—and could be used to identify the structure of these proteins—it would represent a giant step toward formulating synthetic versions of these proteins.

In early March 1980, Lerner, along with two colleagues from Scripps, dropped by Doolittle's lab and asked him to do a computer search for them. Doolittle said he told Lerner about Gernot Walter's discovery and suggested that Lerner try using Walter's approach. At that moment, Lerner didn't respond. Throughout the summer and fall, Lerner stopped by Doolittle's laboratory several times, mostly to get some advice on how to isolate antigens on the flu and hepatitis viruses.

What Doolittle did wasn't out of the ordinary: aiding ostensible rivals is commonplace in biomedical research and is an integral part of the code of behavior among colleagues. Sharing information and exchanging scarce materials are absolutely crucial to the collaborative scientific process, where every new advance is built upon the cumulative knowledge gleaned from previous discoveries. What happened next, however, was highly unusual. Walter and Doolittle published their findings in September, while Lerner's group went to press with similar results a mere five days later. Scripps, on behalf of Lerner's team, subsequently filed a patent application to exploit the commercial value of the idea.

Doolittle was outraged. Independent researchers occasionally do make the same discovery at virtually the same time—witness Baltimore and Temin's simultaneous isolation of reverse transcriptase. Doolittle felt Lerner failed to acknowledge others' contributions. It was a violation of scientific protocol Doolittle was willing to overlook—until he heard about the Johnson & Johnson deal. "Bad manners in science was one thing," Doolittle told reporters, "but making money out of it was another."[7] Doolittle and his colleagues then filed their own patent application.

Richard Lerner stoutly denied these accusations. He claimed that the use of this novel technique came to him ten months earlier, while he was in New York with his lab team in May 1979, right after the annual Cold Spring Harbor conference on tumor viruses. "It was early twilight in Manhattan, and we were walking in Central Park, trying to come up with a solution to this problem," he recalled. No one had anything to write on, so someone fished a crumpled napkin out of his pocket. "We wrote the whole thing down on the napkin," Lerner maintained.[8] After a lengthy dispute, Richard Lerner emerged victorious. Scripps was awarded the patents, which enabled the Institute to enter into a $30 million agreement with Johnson & Johnson, while Lerner negotiated a $60,000 consulting contract with the drugmaker. By securing the contract with Johnson & Johnson, Lerner was anointed the heir apparent to ascend to the directorship of the Institute when Scripps founder Frank Dixon retired.*

Russell Doolittle won the high moral ground in the eyes of the scientific community, which questioned not only the way Lerner handled this dispute but his acceptance of a consultancy from Johnson & Johnson. After all, they wondered, how could Lerner impartially serve the interests of Scripps when he was on Johnson & Johnson's payroll? In a letter to the University of California's Patents Board, Doolittle wrote, "There used to be a good healthy exchange of ideas and information among researchers at UCSD, the Salk Institute, and Scripps. Now we are locking our doors. The threat to scholarship is serious, indeed."[9]

Similar scenarios were being played out at other key research centers, where an invisible threshold had been crossed, marking the end of an unparalleled era in biomedical research. Scientists were polarized into warring camps, transforming the long-standing ethos of cooperation into the cutthroat competition of the marketplace. In fairness, academic scientists were always connected to a commercial network, and many of our leading universities were founded by corporate barons

*Johnson & Johnson ultimately recouped its investment too. Among the products the drugmaker obtained from Scripps, which receives around $70 million annually in federal grants, are Leustatin, a treatment for hairy cell leukemia, and factor VIII, a clotting agent for hemophiliacs. Not a dime in royalties has been paid, however, to the American taxpayer who underwrote the research that led to the formulation of these therapeutics.

like Rockefeller, Mellon, Vanderbilt, and Carnegie. Faculty members in every discipline have done corporate consulting, and entire industries, such as electronics, evolved out of campus laboratories.

But biotechnology was different "in several respects," says Sheldon Krimsky, a public policy expert at Tufts University who's witnessed firsthand the rise of industrial genetics. "In electronics, people who commercialized [their discoveries] left the university to set up their own firms. In biotech, most stayed at the university. Secondly, the public perceived the social and ethical issues as more sensitive in commercializing biomedicine than in commercializing materials." There was also the sheer velocity, the speed at which ideas were transferred to the marketplace. Unlike other fields, where ideas incubated for several years before their commercial applications emerged, a biotech discovery in an academic lab could be turned into a product overnight. "The link between information and wealth in the field of genetic information—the distance between the test tube and the cash register, if you will," observed Representative Al Gore, Jr., a persistent critic of the commercialization of campus research, "is much closer than is normally the case."[10] Every conceptual breakthrough, every discovery, potentially was the basis of a new class of drugs, and enterprising researchers seized every chance to cash in.

This trend was fueled, in no small measure, by the prevailing political winds. Ronald Reagan's science adviser, George Keyworth, a physicist from Los Alamos, was of the opinion that the root cause of the economy's sluggishness was this nation's failure to bring new scientific discoveries into industrial use. And Reagan himself was ideologically committed to privatizing federally sponsored programs—the more, the better—and bullied the Democratic-controlled Congress to remove any remaining obstacles that might impede this process. Congress passed legislation in 1981 that gave corporations hefty tax credits for investing in university research as an incentive to boost R&D spending; in 1986, the Federal Technology Transfer Act was passed to augment the Bayh-Dole Act, and enabled government researchers at federal laboratories like the NIH to cut similar deals, known as CRADAS or Cooperative Research and Development Agreements. "Essentially, this privatized the whole research enterprise," says science historian David Nobel. "And to add insult to injury, all deals made under Bayh-Dole are secret. The public is denied even knowledge of it, much less scrutiny or oversight." "In the climate of the Reagan era," acidly noted Leon Wofsy, a prominent UC Berkeley immunologist who was deeply disturbed about the ethics of these arrangements, "there was little concern for social responsibility or public involvement in setting policy and priorities."[11]

By the time of the Pajaro Dunes meeting, more than 200 biotech firms had sprouted out of academic labs, clustered mostly around universities like Stanford, UCSF, UC Berkeley, MIT, and Harvard, which were home to genetic engineering's pioneers, with dozens more on the way. Harvard's Walter Gilbert was among the leaders of the campus exodus. Gilbert resigned his endowed university position in February 1982 to become the full-time CEO of Biogen, a biotech he founded with some Harvard colleagues in 1978. His 460,000 shares of Biogen stock made him a multimillionaire. Gilbert's colleagues at Harvard, biochemist Mark F. Ptashne and molecular biologist Thomas P. Maniatis, founded Genetics Institute, while his fellow 1980 Nobelist, Stanford's Paul Berg, overcame his initial antipathy to commercial involvement to put together the scientific advisory board for DNAX, which was later bought by Shering Plough for a cool $29 million. Cetus, another Bay Area biotech, boasted even more illustrious advisers, including a trio of Nobel laureates, Donald Glaser, Joshua Lederberg, and Francis Crick.

Giant corporations were also swept in with the entrepreneurial tide. Du Pont entered into a $6 million agreement with Harvard Medical School to study molecular genetics; Washington University in St. Louis inked a $3.9 million deal with Mallinckrodt for antibody research, and a $25 million agreement with Monsanto for work on genetics, while industrialist Edwin Whitehead established the $127 million Whitehead Institute for Biomedical Research at MIT, to list just a few.

Not coincidentally, some of the most high-profile defections were from Herbert Boyer's own department at UCSF: his boss, William Rutter, started Chiron across San Francisco Bay in Emeryville, an industrial town wedged between Oakland and Berkeley. In 1980, Boyer's longtime friend and collaborator Howard Goodman, decamped to Massachusetts General Hospital, the largest and oldest of Harvard Medical School's teaching hospitals, armed with a $70 million deal with Hoechst, a German pharmaceutical, to establish a molecular biology laboratory. Under the terms of this lucrative alliance, Hoechst would get first shot at patent rights for any inventions arising out of this research. The German drugmaker could also pick which projects it would fund, which meant, in essence, it was setting the research agenda for the department, and faculty members doing Hoechst research were prohibited from consulting with other companies. This highly controversial arrangement sparked an intense media feeding frenzy and a congressional inquiry by Representative Al Gore, Jr., chair of the Subcommittee on Oversight and Investigations of the House Committee on Science and Technology, into the possible misuse of government funds.

The staggering amount of money involved in these deals bred a peculiar myopia: academics so identified with their corporate sponsors that they completely lost sight of who was responsible for putting them into a position where they even *had* discoveries to exploit commercially—the American taxpayer. In this vein, a particularly heated exchange during the 1981 congressional hearings between Al Gore and Dr. Ronald Lamont-Havers, a former NIH director who now headed research at Massachusetts General Hospital, was starkly revealing.

"We provided $25 to $26 million a year in direct Federal aid to Mass. General," Gore said. "I think it's fair to say that the current biomedical research capabilities at Mass. General are indebted in part to Federal support of basic biomedical research over the last 20 years.

"Now, isn't it a little unfair to the American taxpayers after this 20-year investment that's ongoing at the rate of $25 to $26 million a year, to give the cream of the results to a foreign company that gets exclusive licensing rights?"

"Let's examine that rather inflammatory statement," Dr. Lamont-Havers responded.

The normally unflappable Gore was incensed. "Rather what?" he asked, his voice rising.

"Inflammatory statement, if I may say so," Dr. Lamont-Havers responded.

"Well, I view the agreement as inflammatory," said Gore.

"Well, I don't think you've read it very carefully, anyway," Lamont-Havers petulantly retorted.

"You haven't given it to me," Gore snapped, clearly taken aback by Lamont-Havers's attitude.[12] He immediately demanded a copy of the confidential contract, which he later asked the U.S. Comptroller General to audit for any improprieties. The Comptroller ultimately found no illegality in the contract; however, the Comptroller's report warned that "care must be taken . . . that no Federal funds directly or indirectly support the research leading to an invention if MGH is to claim that the terms of a [government] funding agreement do not apply."

Gore seemed floored by Lamont-Havers's insolence. The representative was, after all, head of an important congressional subcommittee that helped oversee funding for basic research. He was not a vindictive man and, as a second-generation politician, preferred the good-old-boy ways of Beltway insiders, where power is wielded quietly through persuasion and consensus building, not through a show of force. Gore could, if he chose, make life extremely difficult for someone like Ronald Lamont-Havers. It is a measure of how far removed from reality Dr. Lamont-Havers was that he would have the temerity to challenge the representative.

Gore believed technology transfer had turned into a free lunch for private corporations, enabling them to own the rights to breakthrough discoveries emanating from academic labs without paying the salaries of scientists, graduate students, and postdocs, and other overhead costs like buildings, support staff, and libraries. "These agreements allow companies to skim the cream produced by decades of taxpayer-funded work, blurring the distinctions between propriety and proprietary interest," Gore warned at the close of these hearings. "My gut feeling is that the taxpayers are not being given sufficient consideration," he later told reporters.[13] He expressed grave concerns scientists would become "double agents" whose allegiance would be to their corporate sponsors, not the public. His words proved prophetic.

Aside from a handful of lawmakers like Gore or consumer advocates such as Al Meyerhoff or Ralph Nader, who viewed the Bayh-Dole Act as "a watershed disaster which eroded the public's ownership or control over important technology," few were willing to honestly examine the consequences of the unfettered commercialization of academic research. There was legitimate concern that without technology transfer too many inventions by government scientists would lie fallow. However, activists like Nader were angry that there was no accountability once the public's intellectual property was turned over to the private sector.

And the issues were far more profound and complicated than just the corporate plunder of the fruits of decades of taxpayer-supported research. "The triad of government, industry, and academia consti-tutes a mutually reinforcing system of self-interest that brings to a close an important period of independence for basic research in the biomedical sciences," noted Sheldon Krimsky of Tufts University. "But the greatest loss to society is the disappearance of a critical mass of elite, independent and commercially unaffiliated scientists to whom we turn for vision and guidance when we are confounded by techno-logical choices."[14]

The scientists themselves, who bristled at the mere suggestion that their corporate ties influenced their thinking, were often naively unaware of how subtly they'd been co-opted. In the late 1960s, to cite just one example, a leaking offshore oil well dumped thousands of gal-lons of oil into the Santa Barbara Channel and left an oil slick spread over several miles of ocean that polluted the coastline, killed fish and wildlife, and threatened to destroy the pristine area's delicate ecologi-cal balance. Yet California state officials couldn't find a knowledgeable campus scientist to advise them on the cleanup or to testify against the oil companies. The reason? Every single expert they contacted was already the recipient of research money from the companies responsi-ble for the spill.

The case of Charles Hine, a professor of environmental medicine at the UC Medical School in San Francisco, even more graphically illu-minates what happens when academics are contractors for private industry. Even though Hine was an employee of the university, he was a paid consultant to Shell and his research was supported by the Shell Oil Company, which had given him more than $400,000 in grants over a twenty-year period. During the 1950s, he discovered that DBCP, a pes-ticide made by Shell, was carcinogenic and caused the testicles of lab rats to atrophy. Shell delayed publishing the results for several years, and safe human exposure levels were never established. Nearly two decades later, in 1977, when more than 100 chemical workers at a factory that made DBCP turned up sterile, the Environmental Protection Agency banned the pesticide. In the interim, DBCP was sprayed on farmland in Cali-fornia's Central Valley. Traces of the chemical were found on common fruits and vegetables, in wells throughout the San Joaquin Valley, even as far south as Disneyland, contaminating the drinking water of an estimated 155,000 Californians, and triggering a rise in stomach cancer among those who unknowingly drank the DBCP-laced water.

But probably the greatest casualty in the creation of this new order was the scientific process itself. The unfettered exploration of basic research, where scientists are driven as much by instinct and intuition as by reason, adds to our understanding of the underlying biological mechanisms of diseases, which eventually results in quantum leaps forward in prevention and actual cures. A 1976 study of ten key advances in medicine since World War II revealed that "basic research . . . pays off in terms of key discoveries almost twice as handsomely as other types of research and development combined."[15]

Yet the new commercialism has brought about an increase in mission-oriented research—applied rather than basic studies—which is skewed toward the interests of the corporate benefactors. The research culture is now geared toward investing in research with a quick payoff rather than toward learning something new that might generate rewards later. Key research areas that could generate significant breakthroughs over the long term are neglected. And with such a large pack stampeding down the same path, there are plenty of photo finishes, which have sparked dozens of lawsuits and patent disputes— just as Admiral Hyman Rickover predicted. "In the long run, commercialism undermines rather than advances medical research because super profits can only be made by selling the sick a product," says MIT's Jonathan King. "There is no private investment in identifying what did the damage in the first place. The whole notion that something is damaging your cells doesn't exist in the medical arena anymore. The distortion of research priorities is now so profound that it has become invisible to young scientists. When I ask them what actually *causes* diabetes, they have no idea of what I am talking about."

CHAPTER 8

DODGING BULLETS

Elliott Grossbard first heard about t-PA in 1979 while jogging around the reservoir in New York's Central Park with his colleague and running buddy, Dr. David Rifkin of the Rockefeller Institute. Rifkin had worked with the Bowes melanoma cell line during in the 1970s when interest was growing in thrombolytic agents. It was Rifkin, in fact, who originally furnished samples of the cell line to Désiré Collen, which led to the Belgian scientist's breakthrough research. But Grossbard had no inkling then that he would be the person most responsible for transforming this obscure protein into the wonder drug of the 1980s, what Harvard's Eugene Braunwald, the dean of American cardiology, called the "penicillin of the heart." And the story of how Genentech, the nation's foremost biotech, used a $20 million federally-funded study to establish the primacy of its flagship drug, t-PA, is an all too fitting paradigm for the biotechnology industry itself, which was built on hope, hype, and the goodwill of the American taxpayer.

Lanky and bespectacled, with dark spiky hair and the lithe body of a runner, Grossbard possessed a glossy résumé. He studied hematology at Columbia University's College of Physicians and Surgeons, where he graduated first in his class, did his internship at Massachusetts General, one of Harvard's teaching hospitals, and was assistant director of the marrow transplant unit at the prestigious Memorial Sloan-Kettering Cancer Center in New York City. During the late 1970s, however, Grossbard became disenchanted with medicine, and earned a law degree from Yale University before he realized being an attorney "was even more bizarre than being a doctor." He returned to medicine, but he retained a litigator's combative edge, thriving on adversity like a buoy bobbing in a storm-tossed sea. He had a sharp, sardonic wit and the ability to think fast on his feet, and enjoyed exploiting the flaws in his opponent's logic like a fighter pilot on a strafing mission. These traits would serve him well when he helped t-PA to navigate through the treacherous shoals of the FDA approval process.

After leaving Yale, Grossbard worked for Hoffmann-La Roche in New Jersey, where he pushed t-PA, but he couldn't spark any real interest. "It's almost impossible to get a company that size to do anything," says Grossbard. "You need eight committees to even think about it." His unalloyed enthusiasm for t-PA did not go unnoticed, however. In the summer of 1982, he got a call from Robert Swift, head of Genentech's clinical research program. Swift told him they had just cloned t-PA and wanted Grossbard to supervise the clinical tests of the drug in order to get FDA approval. Initially, Grossbard begged off. T-PA was intriguing but there was no way his wife would leave New York. Then Genentech made him an offer he couldn't refuse—a phenomenal salary, stock options in a growing company, and what turned out to be the opportunity of a lifetime. The next five years would prove to be the most intense and exhilarating of Grossbard's life, as nearly every day brought a new crisis or another triumph, and his life seemed, in his words, like the silent-movie cliff-hanger serial *"The Perils of Pauline."*

Earlier that year, Robert Swift had contacted Sol Sherry, the éminence grise of thrombolytic therapy, who had conducted the original experiments using clot busters to treat heart attacks in the late 1950s. Swift asked Sherry to assemble a panel of the biggest guns in thrombolytics to advise Genentech on the development of t-PA. This group included some of the nation's top hematologists and pioneers in the development of thrombolytics—Victor Marder from the University of Rochester, William Bell of Johns Hopkins, and Harvard's Arthur Sashara, the princes of hematology surrounding their acknowledged king, Sol Sherry. They met on July 1, 1982, in Arlington, Virginia, with representatives of Genentech, along with Désiré Collen and Marc Verstraete, his colleague at the University of Leuven.

"All of us had been excited about the potential of t-PA," noted Sherry in his autobiography, *Reflections and Reminiscences of an Academic Physician.*[1] The group was duly impressed by Collen and Verstraete's presentation of their latest findings, especially by t-PA's superiority over other thrombolytics in selectively targeting clots without provoking severe bleeds. But would this superiority in the test tube and in animals translate to humans? They all agreed that many issues needed to be resolved before they could test the drug in the large multicenter patient trials the FDA required. But the committee never met again.

Elliott Grossbard's first official act for Genentech was to attend the American Heart Association's (AHA) annual convention in November, which was held in Dallas that year. The AHA's yearly meetings are like grand tribal gatherings, where all the various clans, ranging from cardiologists, hematologists, and academic scientists to hospital administrators and pharmaceutical industry flacks, assemble to hear about cutting-edge research, network with colleagues, and swap the latest gossip. And that year, one word consistently floated above the buzz in the hallways outside of meetings, in the drug companies' hospitality suites, and in the bars and restaurants surrounding the conference site: thrombolytics. Peter Rentrop's trailblazing work had transformed cardiology, and the field was in the midst of a vast sea change that was comparable to how penicillin revolutionized the treatment of infectious diseases. The implications of this paradigm shift were just beginning to filter into the consciousness of the cardiology community. Pilot studies using streptokinase on heart attack patients were being conducted by Peter Rentrop and others in the United States and in Europe. The preliminary results, people excitedly told each other, were nothing short of amazing.

Elliott Grossbard didn't need to spend endless hours immersed in Cardiology Central to scent what was in the air everywhere. The real action—and the real money—in thrombolytics was in cardiology—not in treating pulmonary emboli. "What the company needed was cardiologists," Grossbard realized, "and I could use Désiré [Collen] for the hematology."

Sol Sherry's panel was unceremoniously abandoned, which bruised some powerful egos and left a residue of hard feelings that would have long-term repercussions. When Sol Sherry wrote to Swift a year later to find out what happened to the committee, he says, he never even received the courtesy of a reply. But the company's curt dismissal of Sherry and his associates would come back to haunt them. "A serious error was made," Sol Sherry noted, "in completely shifting from those most knowledgeable and experienced in the science of thrombolytic therapy to a group of novices in this field, who were apparently unfamiliar with the previous literature and were loath to seek advice and not interested in learning from others."[2] Dumping the hematologists, who had an instinctual understanding of the balletic interplay of the chemicals in the blood system, would prove to be a big mistake.

Elliott Grossbard didn't think he was making a mistake, however. Muscling into the cardiology market could catapult Genentech into the big time—and generate piles of money. Heart disease is the number one killer in the industrialized world, which meant cardiologists were medicine's heavyweights. Nearly 7 million Americans suffer from heart disease and 1.5 million are felled by heart attacks annually. Nearly 550,000 of them die each year. Consequently, any lifesaving treatment that can reduce this horrendous toll has blockbuster written all over it. Wall Street analysts, salivating over the prospect of a breakthrough heart medication, estimated that annual revenues from the thrombolytic market could top $1 billion by the turn of the century. There was a revolution going on in cardiology, and Grossbard correctly sensed t-PA could place Genentech at its epicenter.

Grossbard spoke to about half a dozen cardiologists in hopes of putting together a team to do the first clinical testing of the drug, which is a protracted, nerve-racking—and occasionally futile—process. Testing a new drug takes many years and costs upward of $50 million—with no guarantee of success. There's a vast difference between the way a drug behaves in a test tube and how it acts in the crucible of the real world, in patients. New drugs normally go through three phases of clinical trials to pass FDA muster. Phase I, which usually involves a few dozen patients, determines whether the drug is safe to use, and at what dosage. Phase II entails testing a larger number of patients, anywhere from 200 to 500 people, and evaluating the treatment's effectiveness. The final phase normally involves 1,000 or more patients in order to gather enough data to convince the FDA the drug actually works without triggering serious side effects.

Many once promising drugs have foundered at any one of the checkpoints in the testing pipeline because of a myriad of unforeseen glitches. These run the gamut from the mundane—not being particularly effective or problems getting patients to enroll in the studies—to the truly catastrophic, such as discovering unexpected toxicities in patients that provoke grave side effects or even death. Which is why developing a new drug, from its discovery in the laboratory to delivering it to a patient's bedside, can eat up a staggering $300 million. Big drugmakers routinely absorb these kinds of losses when treatments don't perform as expected, writing them off as part of the cost of doing business, but the tiny biotechs like Genentech or Cetus or Chiron often have only that one drug.

Consequently, Grossbard knew that picking the right team of principal investigators (PIs), the physician-scientists at university teaching hospitals around the country who actually recruit patients and test the drug, to guide t-PA through the gauntlet of clinical trials could be crucial. For the initial tests, Grossbard settled on three PIs he felt could work together: Herman "Chip" Gold of Massachusetts General, Myron "Mike" Weisfeldt, chair of the department of cardiology at Johns Hopkins, and Burton Sobel at Washington University in St. Louis.

Ironically, the previous year, Weisfeldt had sent Grossbard's predecessor, Robert Swift, an elaborate proposal about how to study t-PA. "Weisfeldt had just gotten a postdoctoral fellow, Eric Topol, who had been exposed to t-PA while he was at UCSF," Grossbard remembers. "Eric had tremendous initiative. Even though they had no rep in thrombolysis, he sold Weisfeldt on the value and wisdom of working on t-PA."

Burton Sobel was also a natural choice. Intellectual and erudite, Sobel possessed a bracing, analytical mind. Sobel had worked with Désiré Collen since 1980, using t-PA harvested from melanoma cells, first in dogs and later in a small pilot study in humans. In the animal experiments, PET scans revealed "a beautiful recovery of the heart muscle while the chemical assay showed no change in the plasma protein, which indicated that there was no perturbation of the protective mechanisms," recalls Sobel. Later studies on humans demonstrated that t-PA opened blocked arteries with "a remarkable rapidity," says Sobel. He was intoxicated by t-PA's wondrous potential, and his staunch advocacy of the drug was almost messianic.

Harvard's Herman Gold, whom colleagues describe as "mercurial and quirky," rounded out the triumvirate. In April 1983, Gold, Sobel, and Weisfeldt, along with two of his associates at Hopkins, Eric Topol and Bernadine Healy, who would later be the first woman to head the NIH, convened in San Francisco to devise a protocol for a multicenter test of t-PA. "We wrote a protocol in one afternoon," Sobel reflects. The grateful company offered several of the PIs options to buy Genentech stock at a discount at a later date. Gold, for one, declined the offer, suggesting that he be compensated in some other way. Though he felt that the stock options wouldn't compromise his scientific judgment— if the drug didn't work, he had no qualms about saying so—it could appear improvident, and possibly tarnish the reputation he had carefully cultivated. And in the rarefied world of high-stakes academic science, appearances count more than reality. Most of the others apparently didn't think the stock options posed any ethical dilemmas, although Sobel and others ultimately returned them.

In the midst of getting clinical tests of t-PA off the ground, Grossbard says he received a call from his boss, Bob Swanson, Genentech's CEO. Eugene Kleiner, head of the venture capital firm that had provided the original seed money to bankroll Genentech, had a cousin who was a cardiologist. "He wants to work on t-PA," Swanson told Grossbard. Grossbard rolled his eyes, until he heard who the cousin was—Harvard's Eugene Braunwald, one of the giants of modern cardiology.

"Have you heard of him?" Swanson asked.

"Of course I've heard of him," Grossbard replied. "But if I try to get him involved in this study at this late date, it will be disruptive, because he will try to take it over."

"Do what you think is best. But *please*," Swanson emphasized, "call him." Grossbard did contact Braunwald. He was cordial and understood Grossbard's position. Braunwald, however, didn't rise to the pinnacle of medicine's most fiercely competitive field by being a shrinking violet. If t-PA turned out to be a wonder drug, Eugene Braunwald was going to make damn sure he was driving that train. Grossbard, who was well aware he could be arrogant and brusque, was savvy enough to be diplomatic and accommodating toward Braunwald and paid him a courtesy call. That small act would pay off in unforeseen dividends. Even though Braunwald didn't participate in the early tests of t-PA, he later became an immensely powerful ally who midwifed the birth of t-PA; his unqualified support legitimized and positioned the drug in the cardiology community in a way that even the most imaginative marketing campaigns never could.

The first in a long series of crises that plagued the development of t-PA was brewing behind the scenes, however. At Genentech's request, William Bell had been testing t-PA's effect on the plasma proteins in the blood in his laboratory at Johns Hopkins. Studies like this would eventually have to be submitted to the FDA as part of the company's approval application. Bell's research revealed that t-PA wasn't as fibrin-specific as they had originally thought, which had been one of the drug's key selling points. T-PA was demolishing other key plasma proteins, which meant it wasn't any more precise than streptokinase. "One of the things Genentech was putting forth was that t-PA did not lower plasma fibrinogen, that it was specific for thrombus formation [clots]—target-specific and fibrin-specific—and therefore wouldn't alter fibrinogen," says William Bell. "But we conclusively established there *was* systemic activation."

Bell, who has the looks and tenacity of Winston Churchill, chaired the session on thrombolytic agents at the AHA convention, which was held in Miami in 1983, where he reported his findings. "When I revealed the plasma fibrinogen was way down, Grossbard refused to pay my transport to the meeting," Bell recalls, even though Genentech had originally agreed to cover it. "Several weeks later, as I got to thinking more and more about this, I called up Bob Swanson," Bell continues. "He and I had become pretty good friends because [a close relative] has two children who are hemophiliacs and I take care of patients who are hemophiliacs. I told him this whole story and very soon after I got a check in the mail plus something extra. Grossbard later came to our laboratory and apologized, though he claimed that the way we made measurements of fibrinogen in the presence of t-PA was all wrong. Our laboratory at the Johns Hopkins School of Medicine, where some of the original discoveries about fibrinogen were made, has been measuring fibrinogen for more than forty years." Grossbard, however, tells a different story. Apparently, Bell's request that Genentech pay his way to the meeting in Miami was unusual. Normally, scientists pay their own way, using grant money. Initially, though, Grossbard agreed. "But when he went to the meeting and basically dumped on t-PA and then submitted a paper to *The New England Journal of Medicine*, the combination brought out my vindictive side," admits Grossbard. "And yes, I did refuse to pay his airfare. But it wasn't because he said bad things about Genentech. It was because he showed remarkably poor grace."

Bell also claims that when he submitted his research to *The New England Journal of Medicine,* he was suddenly under, in his words, "big-time pressure" to retract the paper. One of his superiors came down to talk to him. "Is there any way that's humanly possible that there might be a mistake?" he asked Bell.

"Well, I'm a human being," Bell responded. "Sure, I can make one. But I don't really think so. These are standard pedestrian-type assays that we're doing—and it's certainly not the first time we've done this."

"Do you think there's even a possibility that these things are wrong?" he pressed.

"Well"—Bell shrugged—"I'm not God."

"Then I think you'd better withdraw this," he was curtly informed. Bell did as he was told, but he wasn't happy.

Meanwhile, Elliott Grossbard was having his own doubts about t-PA. There were problems in Genentech's labs. The first attempts to produce recombinant t-PA (rt-PA) in *E. coli* with the gene so painstakingly cloned by Diane Pennica were a dismal failure. The bacteria would churn out t-PA proteins, but the proteins didn't work—either they weren't folded correctly or they didn't have the proper sugars on the surface, which were essential to provoking the proper biochemical reaction. Grossbard wondered whether Genentech's gene-splicing wizards could devise a method of making enough of this fragile protein to test it on patients, let alone scale up production enough to market it commercially.

This went on for several agonizing months until Arthur Levinson, who was later named Genentech's CEO, figured out how to smuggle the gene inside Chinese hamster ovary cells, and then coax the cells into producing functional rt-PA proteins that were indistinguishable from naturally occurring t-PA. Genentech scientists proceeded to do toxicology studies on the rt-PA, while Désiré Collen and Burton Sobel teamed up to study the effects of rt-PA in dogs, in preparation for human trials. By the end of 1983, the FDA gave them the green light to test rt-PA in humans.

On the morning of February 11, 1984, a Saturday, Elliott Grossbard's phone rang. "We did our first patient," Mike Weisfeldt excitedly told him. "Eric [Topol] has been pacing around like an expectant father. It was a woman in Baltimore City Hospital suffering from a mild infarction. The artery opened in about thirty minutes. We are ecstatic."

In the meantime, the NIH was gearing up to sponsor its own research into thrombolytic therapy, under the auspices of the National Heart, Lung, and Blood Institute (NHLBI). In 1982, the government funded a small trial of streptokinase conducted by Peter Rentrop, who had since moved to New York City's Mount Sinai Hospital, one of the nation's premier clinical cardiology facilities. Then, in 1983, a second trial of streptokinase was conducted by Ward Kennedy at the University of Washington. A Data and Safety Monitoring Board was formed as a watchdog group to oversee the trial and to deal with safety problems that might crop up. Among the members of the board was Victor Marder, Sol Sherry's protégé and a member of the committee that Genentech had so cavalierly disbanded.

Buoyed by the success of the Rentrop and Kennedy studies, which indicated that streptokinase was effective in opening up occluded arteries, the NHLBI established the Thrombolysis in Myocardial Infarction (TIMI) Study Group in July 1983. The group was responsible for launching a large trial of thrombolytic agents, which would be conducted at thirteen of the nation's top research facilities, including Brown University, Columbia University, Harvard, Yale, Cornell Medical Center, George Washington University, Washington University, and the Mayo Clinic. The chair of the steering committee that supervised this vast undertaking was none other than Eugene Braunwald, head of Harvard University's department of medicine and the undisputed dean of American cardiology. The point man for the NHLBI was Eugene Passamani, a cardiologist who had done his postdocs at Washington University, Burt Sobel's domain. Genell Knatterud represented the Maryland Medical Research Institute, a subcontractor that would supervise the actual operation of the trial and gather the data.

As originally conceived by the TIMI investigators, the TIMI trials would be a randomized double-blind placebo controlled study, which is the gold standard of drug testing. What this means is that patients chosen at random receive the drug, while others get no treatment. But since the trial is blind, the doctors don't know who is actually being treated, which prevents any subjective biases from creeping in that could skew their findings. This was the time-honored method of testing new drugs. The treatment would be streptokinase (SK), an old drug that researchers had plenty of experience working with, so there'd be no unexpected surprises, no extraneous variables to muddy up the data.

Within the insular world of academic cardiology, however, the tom-toms were beginning to beat for t-PA. Burton Sobel lobbied the NHLBI's Eugene Passamani to use the recombinant version of t-PA in the TIMI trials. After all, if rt-PA was better than streptokinase—and early experiments indicated there was a striking difference—they'd be wasting time testing an inferior agent. The recombinant form of t-PA was an as yet untried drug, however—it wasn't tested in humans until 1984. Besides, Genentech was having problems scaling up production. If the TIMI group did go with t-PA, they'd lose precious time waiting for the completion of pilot studies in humans. If they used SK or uroki-nase, TIMI could be up and running right away. Passamani, who was in charge of millions of taxpayer dollars, was facing a tough dilemma. He felt a study of SK or urokinase "might have been rendered moot by the development of a much more effective new thrombolytic agent." On the other had, using an untried new agent might be "an enormous waste of time" if it was "ineffective or, worse, dangerous."[3]

William Bell, for one, was increasingly impatient with Passamani's delays. "Look, if we want to find out whether these thrombolytic agents work, we can do this right now," he told him repeatedly. "Streptokinase is available. Urokinase is available. They've both been available for seven or eight years." Bell couldn't understand "why Passamani was waiting, waiting, waiting. There's nobody who's done this before in the history of the NIH. If a human health problem comes up, and you can answer a question, they've gone right ahead and done it. But Pas-samani kept saying we have to wait for this other agent, because it's probably going to be superior."

Finally, after much deliberation, the TIMI panel decided to test t-PA, which meant postponing studies of thrombolytic agents in patients for nearly a year. "We were very concerned as a group of investigators that we were about to embark on a multimillion-dollar study, spend a great deal of the taxpayers' money, and we were very concerned that we might study the wrong drug," Eugene Braunwald later told an FDA panel. "We felt it was our obligation, our first oblig-ation to determine which of the two drugs is superior, and we, there-fore, set about to study streptokinase and t-PA."[4]

In February 1984, Passamani invited Elliott Grossbard to Washington to discuss a possible collaboration. Genentech had just commenced tests of rt-PA on heart attack patients and had done extensive studies in animals. Grossbard and Burt Sobel brought the TIMI Data and Safety Monitoring Board up to speed on the status of their research. When Sobel characterized the drop in fibrinogen levels of the plasma proteins caused by t-PA as insubstantial, however, he inadvertently touched off a land mine—Victor Marder, the sole hematologist on the board. "*Any* drop in fibrinogen is significant," said Marder, echoing what William Bell had observed earlier. "The fact that it was affected is very significant, because it means the drug is *not* fibrin-specific and it does have an effect on the blood, if you give enough of it." No one else on the board, though, seemed to share Marder's concerns.

Ironically, Grossbard had considerable reservations of his own about hooking up with the NIH. Colleagues at Genentech had warned him to avoid working with the NIH—"they'll screw it up." Désiré Collen was even more adamant. "If you do this with the NIH I cannot take responsibility for what happens," he informed Grossbard. Genentech was gearing up to perform its own tests of t-PA, which would give the company complete control (pharmaceutical companies normally do their own testing of new drugs in preparation for product licensing). That way, if problems arose, or any fine-tuning was required, these fixes could be done in private, away from the prying eyes of the press and the investment community. Working with the NIH meant that any mistakes would be subjected to intense public scrutiny and place the fate of t-PA—and Genentech as well—into the hands of a capricious and often glacially slow bureaucracy.

So the TIMI steering committee made a Solomonic compromise that hopefully would satisfy everyone's demands. They would do an open label pilot study, a "rehearsal" for TIMI, Passamani noted, with a few dozen patients comparing t-PA and streptokinase before ramping up to a full-scale trial. Under these conditions, Grossbard decided to take the chance. "We were prepared to participate in studies that were properly done and were completely independent," says Grossbard, "as long as I was satisfied that there was a fair chance it would be good for the company."

Grossbard's decision to participate in the TIMI trials proved providential, however. In the spring of 1984, another crisis erupted that once again threatened to sidetrack t-PA. FDA officials discovered Genentech was using Chinese hamster ovary cells as a production medium for t-PA. Defective type C virus particles, fragments of known tumor-causing viruses, had been detected in the cell line. FDA officials feared the cells were contaminated with virulent retroviruses which could be inadvertently transmitted to patients. They ordered Genentech to stop testing the drug immediately. In August, the FDA planned to have a symposium with representatives from industry, academia, and the government. Until some consensus emerged from this group about the safety of the cell line, FDA officials told Grossbard, they didn't want any more patients studied.

Grossbard knew Genentech couldn't wait until the end of summer to resume tests. If news of the delay leaked to the press, it could be a public relations disaster that could send Genentech's stock into a terminal tailspin. Worse yet, while the FDA deliberated about potential problems with the cell line, Genentech's competitors, like Burroughs Wellcome and Eli Lilly, could catch up with cloning and expression. "The FDA had never gotten their arms around this cell line," recalls Grossbard. "We thought we'd have a problem getting the FDA up to speed and getting the cell line certified." The FDA didn't care that their actions were spawning big problems for Genentech, but Grossbard didn't think the agency would block the upcoming TIMI trials. He flew to Washington to plead his case with FDA officials. "You know, this NIH trial is underway," he told them. "This will put a real damper on their plans." Grossbard proved to be quite persuasive. "Because it was the NIH and it was this big operation, they backed off," Grossbard recalls. "We had this tremendous gift of being able to dodge bullets."

Pilot studies of rt-PA and streptokinase went ahead as planned. Then in December 1984, shortly after the first phase of the TIMI trials was launched, Grossbard got a call from Eugene Braunwald, asking him to come to Boston. Braunwald was sworn to secrecy, so he couldn't tell Grossbard how t-PA was doing in the trials, but Grossbard says the thrust of the conversation told him everything he needed to know. Braunwald seemed to be trying to sound Grossbard out on Genentech's timetable for producing more of the drug when they moved into the next proposed phase of the TIMI trials. Grossbard interpreted the fact that they needed more t-PA to mean the drug was doing well. Otherwise, they wouldn't be wasting taxpayer money to continue testing it. "Gene Passamani couldn't communicate with me officially, so Braunwald basically leaks to me that the difference between the drugs is pretty overwhelming in terms of opening up the arteries," recalls Grossbard. "I was ecstatic. There had been resistance to working with the NIH because you lose control and if it doesn't work out, you are screwed."

Genentech had taken a calculated risk in working with the NIH, and it had paid off beyond their wildest expectations. On March 1, 1985, the TIMI safety board met. Early reports from TIMI-I revealed that t-PA was twice as effective as SK in opening up closed arteries, a difference so staggering the board voted to halt the trials earlier than planned—an occurrence that is practically unheard of in the maddeningly methodical world of science. Normally, studies are stopped only if a treatment is too toxic and patients are dropping like flies, or if it is such an earthshaking advance that withholding it from patients would be morally indefensible. Clearly, t-PA fell in the latter category. The lone dissenter on the board was Victor Marder. "I'm not convinced that the difference in patency [opening of blocked arteries] will be translated to clinical superiority," he argued. "They haven't demonstrated any advantage in ventricular function [in the heart muscle] or mortality. You're asking us to accept a black box. We want to know something more about the drug."

Marder was overridden, trampled in the stampede to jump on the t-PA bandwagon. Shortly afterward, the NIH disbanded the TIMI Data and Safety Monitoring Board, and "relieved" committee members of their duties, ostensibly because they were overworked since many of them were members of other boards. A new panel would be assembled for the second phase of the TIMI trials. Victor Marder strenuously protested his exclusion, and asked to be reinstated on the new board. His offer was politely rejected, though he felt it was too much of a coincidence that dismantling the board meant silencing some of the people who had expressed, according to Marder, "the most vigorous skepticism of t-PA." "I was somewhat surprised that three of us were shifted off that committee," agrees Eliot Rapaport, a UCSF cardiologist who also served on the original TIMI monitoring board. "I did wonder if it had any relationship to [to the fact] that we were the ones asking the most questions."

A few weeks later, preliminary results of the TIMI trials were unveiled at a meeting of the American College of Cardiology. The news was sensational. Eugene Braunwald, a reserved man who is not prone to hyperbole, crowned t-PA the winner, and hailed the Genentech drug as "a major advance in thrombolytic therapy."[5] When the study results were published in April in *The New England Journal of Medicine,* Genentech's stock shot up to $28 per share, up from $18 a few months earlier. TIMI-I promulgated a reputation for the drug that remains undiminished to this day. "That study propelled t-PA into orbit," says Grossbard. "And it was an orbit that kept them ahead of the game even when information mounted to the contrary."

Kirk Raab, Genentech's newly installed CEO and successor to Robert Swanson, who assumed the title of chairman of the board, was galvanized by t-PA's stunning success. He pushed hard for boosting production capacity in preparation for marketing t-PA commercially. A sizable chunk of the $100 million raised in a stock offering in March 1985, as well as $40 million generated through the sale of a 4.9 percent stake to Boehringer Ingelhein, a West German pharmaceutical, bankrolled construction of a massive production facility. The four-story plant, which Raab bragged was "as big as two football fields and contains 10 miles of steel piping,"[6] was expected to turn out enough protein for at least three years. Raab, bursting with almost parental pride, excitedly told reporters they were already talking about building a second plant.

In preparation for producing t-PA commercially, Genentech's cloning wizards were experimenting with ways of making the protein in high enough volumes to meet the anticipated demand. They formulated a new preparation of predominantly single-chain rt-PA, which had distinct advantages over the more cumbersome two-chain form of rt-PA and was easier to synthesize. The second phase of the TIMI trials continued with the new batch of t-PA, which was administered at the same 80 milligram dose. A serious problem developed right away. Grossbard received an urgent conference call one afternoon in September 1985 from Eugene Braunwald and Gene Passamani. "We've done six patients and only two have worked," Passamani told him. "We're worried."

Grossbard thought fast. He knew the pharmacokinetics of the new batch were different—the t-PA produced by the new process had a shorter half-life. That meant the drug was cleared out of the bloodstream faster. "Let's try giving more earlier," he suggested.

"How about 150 milligrams?" asked Braunwald.

Grossbard backpedaled. He knew it would be impossible to scale up production to make enough t-PA to complete the trial if they used dosages of 150 milligrams. "How about 100 milligrams?" Grossbard countered.

"Elliott," Braunwald weighed in, "we're not going to have a lot more chances to do this. Claude Lenfant [the NHLBI director] is not going to want to know we're doing drug development for you."

But Grossbard prevailed and his luck held. The 100 milligram dose proved effective. In fact, the new version of t-PA was vastly superior, and cleared blocked arteries in about 80 percent of patients, compared with 65 percent for the old t-PA. T-PA was becoming an unstoppable juggernaut, and ongoing studies in Europe would stoke the engines even more.

In October 1985, Grossbard stopped in to see Peter Rentrop while he was in New York. Urbane and handsome, Rentrop exuded the Continental charm and looks of a Teutonic Dirk Bogarde. The pioneering cardiologist had left Germany because his trailblazing work generated so much professional jealousy. In the rigid hierarchy of German research, the *Übermeisters* who headed the laboratories don't like being upstaged by underlings. Rentrop had committed the cardinal sin of surpassing his superiors—though landing at Mount Sinai could hardly be called an exile from Eden. Rentrop told Grossbard he had very exciting news about GISSI (Gruppo Italiano per lo Studio della Streptochinasi nell' Infarto Miocardico), a 12,000-patient trial using streptokinase on heart attack victims conducted by an Italian research team. "I just came back from Italy and there's been a major development," Rentrop told him. The study had been completed in June, but the results were still confidential since they hadn't been written up in a scientific journal or presented at a meeting. Rentrop heard through colleagues in Italy that streptokinase slashed death rates from 15 percent to 8 percent for patients treated within one hour of a heart attack's onset. This was an astounding advance, the first tangible proof that thrombolytics actually improved survival in heart attack victims.

Grossbard was elated. Since streptokinase reduced mortality rates, and t-PA was perceived as being twice as effective as streptokinase, then logic dictated that using t-PA should reduce mortality even more. Consequently, Grossbard was confident t-PA would be rushed through the FDA, which normally rules on what it considers break-through drugs within six months, instead of their normally glacial two to three years. In the calculus of the marketplace, t-PA was shaping up to be a grand slam home run that would wow Wall Street, and rocket Genentech into the stratosphere. When he returned to California, he pushed for applying for FDA sanction to market the drug.

A few weeks later, Gene Passamani from the NHLBI called, and the tenor of his conversation confirmed what Grossbard already knew. Information from GISSI was trickling in, Passamani told him, which made it impossible to conduct the second phase of TIMI trials as they had planned. The original study design had called for testing t-PA and streptokinase against a placebo, but now that there was convincing evidence SK improved survival, it was unethical to withhold a lifesav-ing drug. Passamani suggested that they simply compare SK with t-PA in terms of improved heart function and mortality rates.

"I think that's a terrible idea," Grossbard told a surprised Pas-samani. "I'll present this to Kirk [Raab] and Jim [Gower, Genentech's vice president]. But I'm going to tell them not to do it. Thanks to you almost every cardiologist in America is convinced that t-PA is so good that you had to stop the study. We don't know how another trial would turn out. And if we don't come out ahead, we would have a tremen-dously self- inflicted wound. So why should we do it?"

Raab backed Grossbard, though the decision not to test how t-PA affects mortality rates would have unforeseen consequences, and became a key stumbling block in FDA approval of the drug. The American Heart Association's annual convention was slated for the following week in Washington, D.C. Braunwald, Passamani, and Knat-terud took the opportunity to meet with Grossbard in a private room at the Bethesda Hyatt, near the NIH. They spent more than two hours trying to persuade Grossbard to allow them to use t-PA in a head-to-head shoot-out with streptokinase. Grossbard stood firm. It might be better for patients to see which drug worked better. But that wasn't whose interest Grossbard represented. He worked for Genen-tech, and the fate of the company was inextricably linked with the for-tunes of the drug. He had no intention of jeopardizing the company's future by taking such a chance. "This could be a good thing for Amer-ica," said Grossbard, "but it wasn't going to be a good thing for us." Finally, Braunwald said in frustration, "Look, there are other compa-

Suzanne Hadley, former deputy director of the National Institutes of Health's Office of Scientific Integrity. Dr. Hadley was the chief investigator for the OSI's two most controversial cases: the probe into whether a colleague of Dr. David Baltimore falsified research results in a paper he co-authored, and most notably, the investigation into whether Robert Gallo of the National Cancer Institute committed scientific fraud.

(Olan Mills)

Dr. Max Tishler was one of the architects of the golden age of medical research during post-World War II era and played a key role in developing a method of mass producing penicillin. During the late 1950s and 1960s, he was president of research at Merck.
(Merck & Co., Inc.)

Dr. Tishler in his lab at Merck in the late 1950s. Besides playing a role in the mass production of penicillin, he held patents on more than 100 top-selling drugs. When this photo was taken, he was president of research at Merck.
(Merck & Co., Inc.)

Victor Marder, M.D.,
is a professor of medicine
at the University of Rochester.
A pioneering hematologist,
Dr. Marder was a vocal critic
of Genentech's clot-busting
heart medication, t-PA.

Jay A. Levy, M.D., a professor
of medicine at the University
of California at San Francisco,
is one of the nation's top virologists.
He was among the first to identify
HIV as the cause of AIDS.

(UCSF photo by Karen Preuss, 1996)

Robert Gallo, M.D., the former chief of the Laboratory of Tumor Cell Biology at the National Cancer Institute. Dr. Gallo has long been a controversial figure in scientific circles and some believe he exemplifies the changes wrought by introducing the profit motive into federally-funded research. (Bill Branson, 11/95)

Dr. Samuel Broder, former director of the National Cancer Institute, championed the approval of AZT for treating AIDS. (Bill Branson, 3/89)

Max Delbrück and Salvador Luria at the 1953 Cold Spring Harbor Laboratory Symposia on Quantitative Biology. Delbrück and Luria were among the wave of European émigrés who came to the United States fleeing Nazi persecution during World War II. The two scientists, who shared a Nobel prize in 1969, were architects of an infant discipline known as molecular biology, a discipline which has since come to dominate medical research.

(Karl Maramorosch, Cold Spring Harbor Laboratory)

Dr. James D. Watson is the co-discoverer of the double helix structure of DNA, a feat in scientific importance comparable to Einstein's Theory of Relativity. Watson, who also served for more than twenty years as director of the prestigious Cold Spring Harbor Laboratory, has been in the forefront of medical science for nearly half a century.

(Margot Bennett, Cold Spring Harbor Laboratory, 3/95)

Dr. Peter Rentrop is a German-born cardiologist. His breakthrough discovery that clots cause heart attacks and that naturally occurring substances could dissolve the potentially deadly clots revolutionized cardiology.

Dr. Diane Pennica, a senior scientist at Genentech, is considered one of the world's premier gene cloners. Dr. Pennica's synthesis of tissue plasminogen activator—t-PA—helped transform Genentech from a struggling start-up into a biotech powerhouse.

Harry Rubin, a professor at UC Berkeley, is a pioneering molecular biologist. Many of the key discoveries he made during the 1950s and 1960s paved the way for many of today's breakthroughs.

(Dennis Galloway/UC Berkeley)

Peter Duesberg, a professor at UC Berkeley, is one of the world's top virologists. Dr. Duesberg has also been a vocal critic of AIDS research, which he believes is driven by greed, not good science.

(Saxon Donnelly/UC Berkeley)

nies that are making t-PA. If we don't get it from you, we'll get it from them."

"We can't stop you from working with other companies," Grossbard quickly cut in, refusing to be bullied. "But these companies may say they have t-PA, but I doubt if they really can supply it. And even if they can, you'll have to do your pilot study all over again to be sure [it's safe]. And even if you do that," Grossbard continued, staring directly at Braunewald, "we think we have a patent and we think we're going to win. And if we do, we'll sue and stop the study, and then you'll be left with a half-completed study. So you *have* to work with us."

Grossbard was being incredibly brazen. In the superficially genteel world of academic cardiology, he was like Dirty Harry at High Noon. He did have them over a barrel—and everyone in the room knew it. The game was going to be played by Genentech's rules. Grossbard, shrewdly sensing he had the upper hand, pressed his advantage. He knew the TIMI trials were supported by $20 million in federal grants, which pays lots of salaries, helps to support eminent academic institutions, and makes the people who control these studies, like Braunwald, immensely powerful. The money had been approved, and they had to spend it—or risk losing it, which would tarnish their illustrious reputations and embarrass the NIH officials who had been instrumental in obtaining the funding in an era when federal grants were being mercilessly cut.

Genentech could be the spoiler that toppled this mammoth enterprise. So Grossbard suggested a face-saving alternative. "Why don't we test angioplasty in combination with a thrombolytic versus using just a thrombolytic?" he asked. "And forget streptokinase. Just give everybody t-PA, which is, after all, the state-of-the-art therapy."

Angioplasty, which had been introduced in 1977, is a procedure which entails inserting a balloon inside a blocked artery. Studies in the early 1980s had demonstrated that using angioplasty in combination with streptokinase kept blood vessels open. And from the very beginning, even the most optimistic proponents of thrombolytic therapy understood its limitations. Clot busters could only open blocked arteries and put patients back to where they were before they had a heart attack. But these agents couldn't open blood vessels permanently, while angioplasty could—which was Grossbard's rationale in advocating a test of a combination of the two treatments. There was some grumbling on the TIMI monitoring board about what to do, but eventually investigators adopted Grossbard's proposal. "There was a big difference in the reperfusion rates—two-thirds for t-PA versus one-third for SK, which is a difference you seldom see in biology," says Dr. Passamani. "The presumption was that this would translate into a much higher difference in mortality rates." TIMI-II was launched—and so was t-PA. "By dropping SK for all the subsequent studies," Victor Marder observes, "they essentially dropped SK from all usage. So t-PA became the law of the land."

To maximize the impact of t-PA, the TIMI group wanted to test a higher dosage of t-PA in the second phase of the TIMI trial, and increase the dosages from 100 milligrams to 150 milligrams. Grossbard initially resisted. "It's hard to make this stuff—this is going to increase the demand on our ability to produce it," Grossbard told them. "On the other hand, this is science. I'll agree to testing 150 milligrams but I won't agree to using it in phase two unless I agree it is better." When Grossbard told William Young, who was in charge of t-PA production at Genentech, about hiking the dosage, he went ballistic. They were having a difficult time producing enough for 100 milligrams; 150 milligrams would stretch their resources to the absolute limit—possibly even beyond the breaking point. However, when they used a 150 milligram dose of t-PA on another batch of patients "the arteries appeared to open much faster," recalls Grossbard. "This made a compelling case for doing 150 milligrams in phase two." Since the original Data and Safety Monitoring Board had been disbanded, though, and a new one had yet to be formed, there was no real safety review of this dosage change. A reconstituted Data and Safety Monitoring Board did review the protocol in February and July 1986, but the failure to have an experienced group review the dosage level would prove to be a grave oversight that almost derailed t-PA. "Their inexperience," says Victor Marder, "meant they had to start over at ground zero with the learning curve."

In April 1986, Genentech filed an application for FDA clearance to market t-PA commercially, a little over two years after the drug had been tested in the first patient, which is considered warp speed in the often sluggish drug development process. Once again, though, problems emerged almost immediately in TIMI-II. Grossbard, a newly minted father, was home with his wife and baby when he received an unsettling phone call from Burton Sobel.

"I am a little worried," Sobel told him. "I had two cerebral hemor-rhages. Maybe that's anomalous. But I'm afraid this dose is too high."

Grossbard immediately called Passamani to sound him out. Pas-samani assured him there were no problems. By July, however, there were more cases of cerebral hemorrhage. Dr. Francis Klocke, the chair of the Data and Safety Monitoring Board, as well as FDA officials, was alerted. Concern escalated to genuine alarm by the summer's end, when it was stunningly clear this wasn't a transitory phenomenon. All told, there was intracranial bleeding in 5 of 311 patients in a pilot study, three of whom died; major bleeding was observed in 41 other patients.

The board began the arduous process of sifting through a host of known variables in order to identify the culprit behind the sudden incidence of life-threatening bleeds. First, a telegram was fired off on August 15 ordering PIs to stop using aspirin in conjunction with t-PA. Perhaps aspirin, which had been added to the regimen, was what had tipped the scales. In September, Eugene Braunwald met in Boston with a group of hematologists to analyze whether there was anything suspicious about the current regimen. The only conclusion they reached was that a certain number of strokes may be inevitable with any thrombolytic agent.

On October 4, an emergency meeting of the Data and Safety Mon-itoring Board was held in Bethesda. The atmosphere in the NIH con-ference room was tense. People were dying—and no one quite understood why. The worst-case scenario was that t-PA was killing them—which happens very rarely, but often enough to give researchers plenty of sleepless nights when they're testing new drugs—but no one wanted to contemplate this nightmarish possibility. After a long day of scrupulously reviewing the available data, they still had no definitive answers as to what was inducing these stroke deaths.

Grossbard knew they had to figure out the problem. Fast. Other-wise, the board would halt the study—which would make the TIMI investigators look very bad and be an absolute disaster for Genentech. Grossbard instinctively sensed the higher dosage was the source of the increased incidence of bleeding. It seemed the most logical explana-tion. It was a new variable, and a law of diminishing returns was prob-ably in operation here as well. At a certain level, any clot-dissolving agent, no matter how fibrin-specific, was going to start affecting other plasma proteins. He decided to push for lowering the dosage back to 100 milligrams, but it was a gigantic gamble. If he was wrong, it could be catastrophic—and not just for the patients. "We were sitting on a volcano," Grossbard recalls. "Seventy-five percent of our stock price was based on the wildly hysterical projections of stock analysts on t-PA sales. We had to convince the safety committee the 100 milligram dose of t-PA was safe."

Grossbard was right. The dosage level was the source of the trouble: 150 milligrams of t-PA triggered three times as many cerebral hemorrhages as the 100 milligram regimen. When they went back to the lower dosage, the bleeding rates dropped dramatically. However, one key fact was lost amid everyone's relief about stanching the fatal hemorrhages: t-PA, which had been touted as a magic bullet, was turning out to have all the finesse of a bazooka. It had the potential to do as much damage to the protective mechanisms of the blood as streptokinase—where the risk of strokes is between 5 and 10 per 1,000—just as William Bell and Victor Marder had predicted. Neither scientist ever had the satisfaction of being a vindicated prophet, and their dire warnings were once again forgotten in the mad scramble to get t-PA on the market.

In the fall of 1986, Genentech officials requested a meeting with the top guns at the FDA to iron out any last-minute problems with their drug application. Kirk Raab and Elliott Grossbard attended the meeting, accompanied by Gene Passamani, Burton Sobel, and Herman Gold. The meeting seemed to go off without a hitch. Genentech officials left the meeting confident of clearing FDA hurdles to licensing t-PA, which would be sold under the trade name Activase. The company beefed up its sales force, stockpiled inventories of the drug in preparation for the anticipated avalanche of sales, and even brashly took out full-page ads in medical journals to announce: "Activase is coming soon."

The first indication of trouble occurred in January 1987. Elliott Grossbard received a detailed letter with a long list of questions from Abraham Karkowsky, a researcher in the FDA's Office of Drugs, which were sharply critical of Genentech's research methods and results. Grossbard was totally blindsided by the correspondence. Throughout the FDA review process, Genentech had worked closely with reviewers at the Office of Biologics, a relatively new division that oversaw drug approval of biologically derived therapeutics like t-PA. Now, suddenly, the Office of Drug Review, which had different drug-approval criteria and scant experience in dealing with genetically synthesized proteins, was muscling in on their territory. It was not a good sign, and the drift of Karkowsky's pointed queries raised Grossbard's hackles. "They were like the instructions a judge gives to a jury," Grossbard recalls, "clearly leading the witnesses in a direction we didn't like."

Grossbard knew something must be going on behind the scenes. Why else would the FDA capriciously change the rules at the eleventh hour when Genentech thought it was on the fast track for quick approval? Suddenly, t-PA was being shuttled to the Office of Drug Review, which wanted data about survival rates and enhanced medical benefits. "For the preceding two years working with Biologics, we had used coronary thrombolysis as our end point, not mortality," recalls Grossbard. "But I thought: 'Braunwald is on our side. Sobel is on our side. What can these guys do?'"

On Friday, May 29, promptly at 8:40 A.M., the FDA convened its Cardiovascular and Renal Drugs Advisory Committee, which was composed of eleven prominent academic physicians, to review streptokinase and t-PA. The panel didn't have the last word on whether a drug would be licensed, but the FDA usually followed its advice. Outside the packed auditorium on the NIH campus, securities analysts were frantically running around the hallways monopolizing pay phones, trying to gauge the mood of the panel.

The presentations of Sweden's KabiVitrum and Hoechst-Roussel Pharmaceuticals, the U.S. subsidiary of West Germany's Hoechst, AG, manufacturers of streptokinase, were models of Teutonic efficiency. Dozens of studies in thousands of patients demonstrated that SK opened blocked arteries, improved survival rates, and enhanced heart function significantly. At around 1:30, the committee unanimously agreed to recommend approval for intravenous administration of SK for patients "with suspected or presumed myocardial infarction [heart attacks]."

It was a tough act to follow, and Genentech's inexperience in dealing with the FDA was painfully evident. And it didn't help Genentech's case that *The Wall Street Journal* had run an editorial the day before insisting that the FDA approve t-PA. Dr. Raymond Lipicky, of the FDA's Office of Drug Review, passed around a copy of the editorial to other FDA staffers. "Well," he said dryly, "it looks like we don't have anything to do."

The studies they presented weren't nearly as encompassing as those done on SK, and seemed embarrassingly thin in comparison. As the afternoon wore on, the atmosphere grew more contentious. Panelists had serious reservations about the incidence of bleeding, about the change in dosage levels from 150 milligrams to 100 milligrams in the second phase of the TIMI trials, and about the change in the method of production of t-PA. Finally, the panel chair cut to the crux of the problem. "Is clot lysis a suitable surrogate for a mortality end point?" he asked. In other words, does dissolving clots automatically translate into improved survival rates? The evidence, the other panelists agreed, really wasn't there that it did. At 7 P.M., more than ten hours after they had started, with only half an hour off for lunch, they took a vote. Eight panelists voted for nonapproval while two abstained. The only saving grace for Genentech was that the stock market had already closed.

This was a staggering setback and there was no way to put a positive spin on it. A disheartened Raab and Gower met with the analysts, who predicted that as the news spread over the weekend, Genentech's price would plunge, from $50 a share to around $33 or $34 the following Monday morning. They were uncannily accurate: Genentech's stock dropped more than 11 points to $36, and brought the price of other biotech stocks down with it. The victory celebration that had been planned at a nearby hotel suite after the hearing deteriorated into a wake. Though there had been some hints that t-PA wasn't going to sail through the hearing unscathed, no one had expected such a complete shutout. Sobel, for one, was extremely agitated and thought something was going on behind the scenes.

In the grim postmortems that followed what one scientist called the "Friday afternoon massacre," FDA staffers admitted as much. They told reporters Genentech was caught in the cross fire of a turf war between the agency's Office of Biologics, whose domain was genetically engineered therapeutics, and the more experienced Office of Drug Review. "Because of the importance of these new, biologically derived drugs and the publicity surrounding them, everybody wanted in on the act," one FDA staffer said. "Coming so late in the process, many of us in Biologics felt we were being sandbagged."[7] FDA Commissioner Frank Young, a Reagan-appointee who was under tremendous pressure to accelerate the pace of drug approval, conceded, "The company may have received signals that were mixed. There was so much focus on lysis [clot dissolving] that they may not have heard clearly the concerns about mortality and ventricular [heart muscle] function. [But those concerns were expressed] in ways they should have heard."[8] Nevertheless, Young bowed to a White House request and ordered a review of what had transpired.

Complaints from patients and cardiologists all over the country poured into the FDA. There was an enormous media outcry that couldn't have been more favorable if Genentech had orchestrated it itself. FDA Commissioner Frank Young, in an effort to distance himself from the panel's ruling, held a press briefing in which he blamed the failure to approve t-PA on the lengthy meeting, rather than on insufficient data. "They probably should have knocked off at five o'clock and reconvened Monday morning," he told reporters. Popular TV talk show host Larry King, a heart attack victim who was treated with t-PA, blasted the FDA on his program. The following week, the first in a series of scathing editorials appeared in *The Wall Street Journal* lambasting the FDA advisory panel for its decision to "sacrifice thousands of American lives on an altar of pedantry." Subsequent editorials execrated the FDA panel as "The Flat Earth Committee," whose recommendations were "absurd" and were guilty of the worst kind of "sophistry."

But others weren't quite so charitable toward Genentech. Karl Mettinger of KabiVitrum, for one, blamed the company's failure to win the committee's endorsement on taking scientific shortcuts and on attempting to ride on the coattails of streptokinase's mortality data rather than accumulating their own. "Genentech tried to steamroller the committee even when it was obvious it wouldn't work," claimed one analyst. What's also intriguing, noted Sol Sherry, the father of thrombolytic therapy, is that while *"The Wall Street Journal* published several editorials and articles decrying the FDA's foot dragging on approving t-PA and claiming that thousands of lives were unnecessarily being lost because of this delay, [n]othing was said about the unnecessary delay in approving streptokinase and that it had been shown to save lives."[9] And *The Wall Street Journal*'s continued hectoring of the FDA prompted an angry letter rebutting their charges, and decrying the newspaper's "ad hominem attack" on Robert Temple, a highly respected FDA official. The letter was signed by eight former FDA commissioners or deputy commissioners, including Charles Edwards and Donald Kennedy, in a rare display of bipartisan solidarity. "One wonders whether the *Journal*'s editorial vehemence might have been directed against an advisory panel decision (which is not binding on the commissioner) if it had concerned a product submitted by an established pharmaceutical company with a wide range of products," Dr. Robert Bazell, NBC's science correspondent, tellingly noted. "Genentech needed that approval badly"—like so many other struggling biotechs, whose future often hinges upon approval of a single drug—"and thousands of Americans own stock in Genentech."[10]

Meanwhile, Genentech staffers had shifted into crisis mode. Streptokinase was headed for a swift FDA approval. Several other companies, including well-capitalized leviathans like Beecham and Burroughs Wellcome, had their own clot busters in the pipeline, but the real 800-pound gorilla, as far as Elliott Grossbard was concerned, was Eli Lilly. "I was always afraid Lilly would get the momentum to catch us," he recalls. Whatever competitive edge Genentech had was quickly being eaten up by these bureaucratic delays, and if they were beaten to the market by streptokinase, which was priced at $200 per dose, there was no way they could justify t-PA's proposed $2,200 price tag. "If you come out a year after someone else, forget it," one Genentech scientist said. "You'll have 10 percent of the market, and he'll have 90 percent." Grossbard could feel the sharks circling, closing in for the kill, and he knew the fate of Genentech hinged upon t-PA's speedy approval.

The following Tuesday, Kirk Raab, Robert Swanson, and Elliott Grossbard met in Eugene Braunwald's office at the Harvard Medical School in Boston, to brainstorm on how to recover from this setback and satisfy the FDA. The meeting wasn't all that productive, though. Every time Braunwald would make a suggestion, Grossbard would veto it. Swanson got impatient with Grossbard. After all, here's America's foremost cardiologist proposing various options and this jerk is saying, "It's not going to work," over and over like a broken record. Even though Grossbard wasn't a cardiologist, he felt he had really learned the field. The inescapable fact that gradually emerged over the course of the meeting was that Grossbard was right—they really didn't have any surefire strategies for turning this around quickly enough to retain their competitive edge. Finally, "we decided to act on many fronts," says Grossbard, "because we didn't know where salvation would come from." They knew that research being done outside of the United States, in Europe and in Australia, might generate promising results.

They decided to apply political pressure as well through Senator Ted Kennedy, the Senate's most powerful proponent of health care and who also, quite conveniently, represented Massachusetts. Kennedy's former chief of staff, Lawrence Horowitz, who was a physician, told them that Senator Kennedy would be interested in receiving a communication from his cardiology constituents asking him to look into this situation. According to Grossbard, Braunwald composed the telegram and helped draw up a list of a dozen or so prominent cardiologists who were sympathetic to Genentech, but he couldn't be the one to approach them. Still, Braunwald's implicit support carried enormous weight. When Grossbard called one cardiologist and read him the proposed telegram, the physician asked, "Is Gene Braunwald going to sign that?" "Yes," Grossbard answered. "Well," the doctor immediately responded, "if Gene Braunwald is going to sign that, then I'll sign it too."

Slowly, the pieces fell into place. The telegram was duly sent to Kennedy, several of the senator's staffers met with representatives of Genentech, and Kennedy reportedly talked to Commissioner Young. Two studies, in the United States and in Australia, were completed and they both demonstrated the heart's ability to pump blood improves after administration of t-PA. The studies weren't perfect—few ever are—but they satisfied the FDA's requirements. "It was a very exciting time," Grossbard remembers. "Everyone pulled together—inside the company and our friends outside of the company like Burt Sobel who helped us navigate through the FDA's objections. Alan Guerci [at Johns Hopkins] took three to four weeks out of his life to write up his data. He had nothing to gain from us—he believed in the drug and he wanted to help."

As the weeks ticked by and there was still no word from the FDA, however, Genentech officials grew nervous. "It's coming to the end of the year—if you don't get through the FDA before the end of the year, you might as well forget it—and the American Heart Association meeting is coming up in November," Grossbard recalls. "So I decided to try one more heroic thing to move this along." Grossbard called Burt Sobel and asked him what he thought about holding a press conference at the AHA meeting to discuss the delay in approval of t-PA. Sobel thought it was a good idea. "Well, see what you can do," Grossbard told him. Then he called Gene Morano, the medical reviewer at the FDA's Office of Biologics. "Gene," said Grossbard, "I just heard a rumor that some cardiologists are going to have a press conference about t-PA at the AHA. So if it's at all possible to get this done before the AHA conference, it would be much better." Morano thanked him for the information.

Grossbard has no idea whether his ruse succeeded, but on Friday, November 13, the day before the AHA was scheduled to begin in Anaheim, California, FDA Commissioner Frank Young, flanked by Genentech executives, held a press conference to announce the licensing of Activase as an emergency treatment for heart attacks. Ironically, a week earlier, with absolutely no fanfare, the FDA quietly approved streptokinase for the same clinical indication. And the $64,000 question that has never been answered was why the approval of streptokinase was held up for six months, until t-PA's was imminent. It certainly looked as though the fact that this was the first drug from America's biotechnology industry played a key role, and the lives that could have been saved by streptokinase in the interim apparently didn't enter into the FDA's calculus. "The timing and method of announcement raises questions about whether pressure on the FDA leadership from Genentech or *The Wall Street Journal* influenced the decision to approve t-PA at approximately the same time as SK, and to hold a press conference to announce the approval,"[11] congressional investigators later noted. "The controversy was so great that members of the FDA Advisory Committee published an article in the *Journal of the American Medical Association* to defend their actions and to publicly state, 'The acrimonious debate over t-PA that was aired in the press did nothing to hasten its approval.'" Reaction from proponents of streptokinase was even more pointed. "The real scandal," maintains Karl Mettinger, "is that under pressure from the White House, the FDA delayed our approval for six months. Otherwise, we could have been in the marketplace before Genentech had a chance."

Across the continent, a huge tent was erected in Genentech's parking lot. Inside the billowing tent, the biotech's 1,300 employees, most of whom owned shares in the company, congregated for a huge after-noon blowout celebrating t-PA's approval. In the midst of the revelry, controllers at San Francisco International Airport in nearby San Bruno stopped air traffic for ten minutes for a spectacular fireworks display, a gesture which underscored San Francisco's considerable civic pride in Genentech's victory.

Elliott Grossbard left the party early to catch a plane bound for Los Angeles and for a triumphant homecoming at the AHA. At the edge of the tent stood a tiny woman, barely five feet tall, who was quietly drinking in the intoxicating euphoria of the crowd. It was Diane Pen-nica, the cloner extraordinaire who started the t-PA juggernaut on that crisp June day in Sweden more than seven years before.

One afternoon a few days later, Pennica, clad in her usual work uni-form of jeans and sneakers, was dashing down the hallway when she was intercepted by one of Genentech's marketing people. "Diane," he said, "there's somebody I'd like you to meet. This is Steve Birnbaum. He's the first heart attack patient to receive t-PA since it was approved by the FDA. Steve, this is Dr. Diane Pennica, the scientist who cloned t-PA."

Birnbaum threw his arms around her. "Thank you, thank you," he told her. "Your drug saved my life."

CHAPTER 9

EXILE FROM
THE KINGDOM

Peter Duesberg had watched Margaret Heckler's 1984 press conference proclaiming the discovery of the putative culprit behind AIDS in stunned disbelief. "Science by press release," he snorted to colleagues, referring to the fact that research is always reported first in scientific journals so it is verified by other scientists—not announced to the world. What was even more surprising to Duesberg, a top virologist at UC Berkeley, was how quickly the notion that HIV causes AIDS became accepted. Yet the HIV theory contradicted everything Duesberg knew about retroviruses—and Duesberg, a protégé of Wendell Stanley's at UC Berkeley, was one of the world's experts on retroviruses. HIV was supposedly gobbling up key building blocks of the immune system, known as T cells, triggering the immune collapse that leads to AIDS. But retroviruses don't kill cells, Duesberg would peevishly argue with colleagues, they *need* the genetic machinery of cells to reproduce. If they kill cells, they'd doom themselves—and retroviruses are wily survivors, not assassins.

"Here Gallo was saying HIV is a virus that promotes the growth of leukemia tumors and yet it is also killing cells," recalls Duesberg. "So which one is it going to be, Bob? The more I looked into it, the more it seemed like my old friend Gallo all over again—big claim, but hardly anything to it. But no one else seemed to notice. All my virologist friends who enlisted in Nixon's War on Cancer haven't had much to do since we realized viruses don't cause cancer. They were leaping onto the AIDS bandwagon. Suddenly, they had a new virus to study—and a chance to justify their big grants, their Mercedes, and their frequent flyer cards. So they pulled their old uniforms out of the closet and dusted off their medals."

Privately, many scientists agreed with Duesberg, and were disturbed by the absence of clear proof of how the HIV virus triggers such chaos. "Peter passionately believes the orthodox view is dead wrong," observes John Maddox, the former editor of *Nature*, the esteemed British science journal. "My view is the orthodox view has some explaining to do." Others were outright disdainful of AIDS research. "They're mostly second-raters who've jumped on the AIDS gravy train because they couldn't get funding elsewhere," says Gunther Stent. Publicly, though, no one dared dispute the HIV theory for fear of losing their grants. Philip Abelson, the former editor of *Science*, evocatively described what happens to scientific whistle-blowers who air their grievances publicly. The scientist who questions "the wisdom of the establishment pays a price and incurs hazards. He is diverted from his professional activities. He stirs the enmity of powerful foes. He fears that reprisals may extend beyond him to his institution. Perhaps he fears a shadow, but in a day when almost all research institutions are highly dependent on federal funds, prudence seems to dictate silence."[1]

But Peter Duesberg, an energetic man with a leonine mane of wavy gray hair, relished his renegade status. He had no idea that what would happen to him would make Philip Abelson look chillingly prescient. The German-born scientist, whose slight accent and rapid-fire delivery made him sound like Colonel Klink on speed, was known among colleagues for his humor and iconoclasm. Possessed of a caustic wit and a galactic-sized ego, Duesberg even seemed to derive perverse pleasure in making rivals squirm. It's a trait that hadn't won him any Dale Carnegie awards in a world populated with egos of equally gigantic dimensions. Almost everyone tolerated his pointed barbs, however, like indulgent parents of a precocious little Mr. Know-it-all. He may have been a maddening twerp, but he was a twerp with an impeccable pedigree.

Duesberg's admission into what he calls "the club" was based upon groundbreaking research he did in the late 1960s and early 1970s. In 1969, he and Peter Vogt performed an experiment that discovered DNA which coded specifically for a virus. For this to happen, the virus must have somehow embedded itself into the genetic machinery of the

174

cells. But how? "Whatever DNA it was," recalls Duesberg, "it must be transcribed from RNA to DNA"—which was an absolutely heretical view at the time—"so we suspected the existence of some type of reverse transcriptase enzyme," which would invert the normal transcription process of DNA to RNA. "An enzyme that makes DNA from RNA doesn't exist in the cell," says Peter Vogt. "So if it's not in the cell, it's got to be in the virus—but we never did that experiment." Sure enough, six months later, Howard Temin and David Baltimore unveiled their discovery of reverse transcriptase in viruses. A few weeks afterward, in June 1970, Baltimore ran into Duesberg at one of the Gordon Conferences. "Your experiment inspired me," he told Duesberg. "It prompted me to test for reverse transcriptase in the virus."

Duesberg didn't care that he and Vogt were scooped on the discovery of this enzyme, because they were in the midst of performing the experiments that would clinch their careers. In 1970, he and Peter Vogt discovered the first oncogenes, the mutant genes believed to prompt the unchecked cell growth that characterizes cancer, and helped map the genetic structure of retroviruses (of which HIV is one). "Vogt was the biologist and I was the biochemist—we were truly very complementary," Duesberg recalls. "We suddenly became very popular." Invitations to elite conclaves poured in, and graduate students clamored to get in his lab. One year, an astonishing one-third of graduate students entering UC Berkeley, one of the top molecular biology programs in the country, requested to work under Duesberg—out of a possible ninety people in the department with whom they could have apprenticed. "He was a good cheerleader," recalls Pamela Mellon, a professor at UCSD who did her graduate work under Duesberg. "While other scientists might use underlings' data for self-aggrandizement, he went out of his way to promote people's careers and make sure they got the proper credit. And most professors sit off in their offices. But Peter actually did experiments with me, right there on the bench. He never took off his lab coat. He loved doing experiments."

It was at one high-powered gathering, a 1970 symposium the Pasteur Institute convened on tumor viruses, that Duesberg met Robert Gallo, another former altar boy who wasn't part of the cadre of Ivy Leaguers who dominated the upper echelons. "He was an interesting guy, full of energy and fun to talk to," says Duesberg. "We both liked to joke around, so we became friends. There were two streams in virology at that time. I was part of the oncogene gang as opposed to the virus-cancer boys at the NIH, like Gallo."

Right around this time, he and Peter Vogt also were two of the architects of the fabled West Coast virology lab group, which included such luminaries as Inder Verma of the Salk Institute and UCSF's J. Michael Bishop, along with his postdoc, Harold Varmus. "The meetings were very exciting because the field was just wide open then—everyone was flying all over the state talking to each other, and we could ask all kinds of questions using the new techniques—but they were also very intense," recalls Professor Mellon. "You never knew if somebody else had finished what you were working on. That was threatening because your career and your science depended on it. But the meetings were designed to learn what everyone was doing so you can either leapfrog over their work or abandon unfruitful directions."

As a member of the scientific nobility, Duesberg felt his position was secure enough to challenge the AIDS hypothesis. From what he could see, HIV violated all the rules of retrovirology—many of which he helped formulate. At best, the presence of HIV showed a person had been exposed to lots of microbes. If this was a court of law, to Duesberg's way of thinking, the evidence implicating HIV as the cause of AIDS would be circumstantial: whenever AIDS appeared, HIV arrived first. In other words, the victim and the virus have been seen together. But no one had produced the smoking gun. If he could convince his colleagues HIV was a passive bystander, the AIDS edifice would collapse like a house of cards. Then researchers could uncover what was really destroying the immune system and halt the tragic loss of lives.

Or so he thought. A scientist of the old school, he had trained at Germany's prestigious Max Planck Institute, where it was instilled in him to be skeptical and to question accepted wisdom. And growing up in post-World War II Germany, in the shadow of the Nazi atrocities, had made Duesberg determined to prove that not all Germans were narrow-minded storm troopers. He had no inkling that challenging the AIDS orthodoxy, which he felt obligated to do, would derail his own career.

In the fall of 1986, Duesberg began a nine-month fellowship at the National Institutes of Health. Officially, his mission was to study oncogenes and cancer, but unofficially, he wanted to poke around in Gallo's lab and find out firsthand what was going on. Duesberg wasn't shy about voicing his doubts about HIV. Once, Duesberg even engaged Robert Gallo in a debate while they were riding the elevator up to Gallo's laboratory on the sixth floor. According to Duesberg, Gallo was so flustered by Duesberg's badgering that he got off on the wrong floor. Duesberg obediently trooped out after Gallo. "You are totally off the mark," Gallo finally exploded, his face pinched in anger. "HIV is like a Mack truck—it would cause AIDS in Clark Kent. You are an irresponsible troublemaker who's just looking for attention."[2] For Gallo, ridicule in his own realm was the final insult. Relations soured between the two men. Not long after, when reporters questioned Gallo about Duesberg's views, he said, "I cannot respond without shrieking."

Before he left the NIH, Duesberg gave a seminar to a group of about a hundred scientists where he publicly outlined for the first time his reasons for questioning the link between AIDS and HIV. HIV's behavior defied everything he knew about infectious diseases, he told them. How could one microbe be the culprit behind twenty-five different deadly diseases? And why is it so selective, triggering pneumonia in homosexuals and tuberculosis in drug users? "They all should be getting the same diseases," he said, glancing around the room.

He pointed out to the group a well-known principle in biology, known as Farr's law, which holds that a microbe's age is determined by changes in its incidence over time. When a microbe is first introduced into a population, it expands exponentially, but then the incidence declines as people develop immunity, a process known as equilibration. Ever since 1985, when scientists could detect the presence of HIV after blood tests for HIV were devised, a remarkably constant 0.4 percent of Americans have been infected with HIV. "The figure is so steady that it is safe to conclude HIV has long been in America," Duesberg told his colleagues at the NIH. "So how could it suddenly cause a new disease?

"We know the basic rules for infectious diseases," he continued, "all of which HIV violates. Infectious diseases do not discriminate between men and women—but 92 percent of the HIV-positive people in this country are men," he said. Then he paused, and with the timing of a seasoned stand-up, he added, "Picky, picky virus."

Suddenly, in the midst of his talk, Duesberg was overwhelmed by a burly man who was built like a football player long past his prime. Hobbled by age, the man slowly made his way from the back of the auditorium. An electric current of recognition shot through the room. This figure was Albert Sabin, the doctor who had defeated the last great scourge of the twentieth century, polio.

"I think the views of a person like Dr. Duesberg are terribly, terribly important," Sabin sternly lectured the assembled gathering, in a forceful, gravelly voice that age had not diminished, "and we must pay attention to them." One of the true pioneers in virology, Sabin was a venerated figure, his opinions respected. Sabin thought projections of a heterosexual epidemic were utter nonsense designed to panic the public into appropriating more money. "This is not the population where you find AIDS," he told the thunderstruck gathering. "We have known this for almost ten years and the pattern has not changed. I am astonished by the hysteria. This is absolute madness."[3]

Duesberg was elated to have such a formidable ally. "We talked afterward about having a press conference," Duesberg recalls. "I thought: 'Now we'll get to the bottom of this. They've got to listen to Sabin.'" Sabin did hold a press conference the following month, in June of 1987, at the Third International Conference on AIDS, held in Washington, D.C., and reiterated what he said at the NIH meeting. But after that, Sabin backed off. Disappointed but undaunted, Duesberg persisted, writing papers critical of HIV for scientific journals and staging guerrilla attacks in the popular press accusing AIDS researchers of intellectual bankruptcy and worse. Initially, the AIDS establishment responded by humoring him. But the goodwill evaporated in the face of Duesberg's kibitzing from the sidelines while they did the laborious grunt work in the laboratory. Eventually, though, mainstream AIDS researchers, ground down by Duesberg's incessant sniper fire, capitulated. Duesberg got his open forum.

On April 9, 1988, the American Foundation for AIDS Research, better known as AmFAR, flew AIDS experts in from all over the country to Washington, D.C., for a discussion of the cause of AIDS. In an auditorium at George Washington University, Duesberg took on the kingpins of AIDS research, including Harvard's William Haseltine, Anthony Fauci, director of the National Institute of Allergy and Infectious Diseases, Warren Winklestein of the UC Berkeley School of

Public Health, and Murray Gardner, a veterinarian by training who headed the pathology department at UC Davis. Only Harry Rubin, once the king of retrovirology and still a commanding figure, supported Duesberg, his colleague at UC Berkeley.

Speaker after speaker trooped to the microphone with intriguing evidence that countered some of Duesberg's arguments. Duesberg brushed them all off, however, making no effort to conceal his contempt for the proceedings. He wandered around the room during the presentations or rudely interrupted the panelists with questions. Even the way he was dressed conveyed his disdain. While everyone else was somberly attired in a suit and tie, Duesberg showed up in khakis and an Oxford shirt that was open at the neck with the sleeves rolled up.

The most revealing moment in the forum came during a heated exchange between Duesberg and William Haseltine, when the long-standing enmity between the two scientists erupted into open hostility. Earlier in the year, Duesberg mentioned to a reporter that Haseltine's ties to Cambridge BioScience rendered his research suspect. "How can he be objective?" Duesberg wondered. "I deeply resent the implication that my business investments have affected my work," Haseltine bristled in response, and accused Duesberg of "serious confusion and misrepresentation of fact." When Duesberg's arguments don't hold up, Haseltine fumed, he "resorted to personal attack; he had impugned the motivations of individuals and institutions."[4]

Initially, Haseltine studiously ignored Duesberg, who was pacing around the back of the room, when he presented his first slide to the group. One of Duesberg's contentions was that during the later phases of AIDS, there isn't much HIV circulating in the blood. Consequently, if HIV wasn't being circulated throughout the body, how could it be provoking so much mischief? The graph in Haseltine's slide was designed to contradict this argument and demonstrate that there were, in fact, high levels of HIV present in the bloodstream during the end stages of the disease. "This gives us a summary of the virology," Haseltine said matter-of-factly, gesturing toward the slide. "During the latter phase of the disease" the amount of circulating virus rises. "That rise is concomitant with the period when T cells fall."[5]

Duesberg immediately spotted a problem. "Why are there no units on that slide?" he asked, referring to the fact that normally graphs have numbers on each axis; this one had numbers on only one side.

"Don't interrupt me," Haseltine shot back.

"I merely asked why the slide has no units on it," Duesberg retorted.

Haseltine stared sullenly, refusing to respond. The two men glared at each other like petulant schoolboys. Then the panel's moderator, sensing the acrimony in the air, hastily intervened by putting a halt to further questions from the floor, and managed to circumvent a nasty confrontation.

Duesberg's suspicions proved to be grounded in reality, however. That evening at a private party, Dr. Robert Redfield, an AIDS researcher at the Walter Reed Army Research Institute, admitted the graph was merely demonstrating a theoretical possibility. Which is why there weren't any units on the slide—it wasn't based on any real data. So Duesberg's criticisms weren't prompted by personal animosity or intellectual quibbling. He had good reason to question Haseltine's credibility. "It is difficult to think of an innocent explanation for Haseltine's behavior," one observer later noted. "Haseltine presented the slide as though it represented scientific findings, whereas it really represented speculation."[6]

When his turn at the podium came, Duesberg was oblivious to the deepening chill in the room. "HIV requires an average of a thousand sexual contacts to be transmitted, and then it supposedly kills its host," he said, peering over his wire-framed aviator glasses. "Even a virus has to make a living. How can it stay in business by committing suicide?" No one in the audience cracked a smile. He continued to reel off his arguments like a croupier dealing cards. Finally, one exasperated panelist took Duesberg's theory to its logical conclusion: if HIV has nothing to do with AIDS, then is it okay for a person who is HIV-positive to have unprotected sex with uninfected people?

Duesberg backpedaled, and quickly surveyed the room with his steely blue eyes.

"Well, is it?" the scientist pressed.

Duesberg hunkered down, defiant. "What difference does it make?" he responded finally. "You don't use a gas mask to protect yourself from bullets. AIDS is not an infectious disease."

The silence was stunning. Then, suddenly, the audience erupted. Warren Winkelstein jumped up and grabbed the microphone. "I can't let this last statement by Dr. Duesberg go by," Winkelstein said. "It's more than irresponsible to encourage transmission of HIV. It's *highly* irresponsible."

Duesberg was raising important questions, though his style annoyed many people. Worse, his intractable position that AIDS was not caused by an infectious agent made it easy to dismiss him as a reckless crank whose arguments weren't worthy of serious scientific scrutiny. After this, Duesberg's expulsion from the inner circle was swift. He was no longer invited to scientific meetings, his grants were cut, he couldn't get his papers published, friends and associates stopped talking to him because of his stance on AIDS, and graduate students refused to work in his laboratory. "No red-blooded graduate student would go to his lab," says Gunther Stent. "It's the kiss of death now." Duesberg was transformed into an obsessive pariah who was forced to mount his increasingly shrill attacks on AIDS research from any pulpit he could find.

Clearly, then, Duesberg suffered from his own form of myopia, a victim of his own hubris. He later commented that what he failed to see then was that too much money was already at stake, in grants, in consulting contracts, in patents, and in licensing agreements, to have a meaningful scientific debate. "This is what one is up against," he ruefully realized when it was much too late. "In view of the large personal and commercial investments in big science, it is virtually impossible to admit a fundamental mistake. Big science can respond to errors no better than the *Titanic* to icebergs."

Dissent was stifled, replaced by a dogmatism that was the antithetical to honest scientific inquiry. The notion that HIV is a lone assassin became incontrovertible, and evidence to the contrary was dismissed—even when it was championed by Luc Montagnier himself. According to Duesberg, it was easier for AIDS researchers, many of whom were tied to companies devising vaccines and therapeutics or making AIDS-antibody tests, to portray him as an arrogant crank who was out of his league than to admit they might be on the wrong track. After all, if HIV didn't trigger AIDS, or if other factors worked in concert with the virus to trigger the collapse of the immune system, they'd be out of business.

"We see a wave of devastating disease approaching," William Haseltine told a Senate appropriations committee in September 1985, a few months after Rock Hudson's death shocked a complacent America.

"For every case of reported AIDS in the United States there are about 100 or more carriers. . . . Unless sexual practices change dramatically in this country, it seems likely that infection of our young population with the AIDS virus may reach" the epidemic proportions of other sexually transmitted diseases, which infect a staggering 20 to 30 percent of young adults. His prognosis was chilling and his rapt audience in the crowded Senate hearing room was suitably horrified by what the eminent Harvard scientist said. Then Haseltine switched direction with the assurance of a Southern preacher, and held out the tantalizing promise that salvation was at hand for all these presumably doomed souls. Science was on the brink of astonishing breakthroughs in the fight against AIDS, he boldly predicted. *But*, he cautioned, again swiftly changing course and playing upon the fears of his audience, we need more money to make these possibilities a reality.

Other leading AIDS researchers were not nearly as confident as Haseltine. HIV was a retrovirus that embedded itself into the genetic machinery of the cell, which meant it was a wily, elusive—and perhaps even an intractable—foe. The war on AIDS, in the opinion of most, was going to be a long siege and heavy casualties would be sustained. Haseltine's virtuoso performance helped open the floodgates of federal funding for AIDS research and catapulted him from relative obscurity to national prominence, transforming him into a genuine media star almost on a par with Robert Gallo himself.

Suddenly, William Haseltine was everywhere, consulting with presidential hopefuls, testifying before other congressional committees, serving on dozens of AIDS-related panels, and glowingly profiled in *The New York Times Magazine,* along with his colleague and business partner, Max Essex. The two scientists were strategically positioned at the center of a small clique of colleagues and friends who sat on the peer review panels that determined who got federal funding for AIDS research. And controlling the purse strings meant they exerted enormous power over the direction of *that* research. As one health-care administrator put it: "It becomes like getting into college or getting into a country club. It's not a cabal, but a good-old-boy network. These guys work together and they're friends. So when your friends are in charge of the right agency, the circle begins to close."[7] Even one of Essex's and Haseltine's chief collaborators at Harvard, Jerome Groopman, candidly conceded that a small number of closely allied people controlled

AIDS funding, but there was some type of system of checks and balances. "I submit [for funding], I get reviewed, and I sit on the panel. It's not the best system, but it's better than most. And understand, when I come up for NIH review, my application doesn't go to my own committee. No one in my own university can review my work. I must file statements about my consultancy. Anyone who has published with me in the last five years cannot be reviewed by me."

By fiscal year 1986, Congress, in response to Haseltine's persuasive appeals, earmarked $244 million for AIDS,[8] up from virtually nothing less than three years before. At a time when grants for research were sharply slashed, it was remarkable to generate any money, much less hundreds of millions of dollars. A lot of this funding was dispensed to the institutions with which Haseltine, Essex, their friends, and their colleagues were affiliated. By 1989, in fact, Harvard and its affiliated hospitals were recipients of $32 million a year in AIDS research grants, which represented a hefty slice of the total AIDS funding pie. Normally, most areas of science—molecular biology is just one notable example—evolve over decades. The leaders in the field gradually rise to the top based upon an informal consensus as to who is doing the most significant work, and who has the best political connections. But AIDS sprang up overnight, like Athena bursting fully formed from the head of Zeus. The emergence of Haseltine, along with Gallo and Essex, at the pinnacle of the AIDS hierarchy, was as much a matter of fortuitous timing as it was based upon the quality of their science.

Essex didn't possess Haseltine's brazen braggadocio, but he certainly shared his penchant for unabashedly promoting his own work. "The science of creating a vaccine for AIDS is within our grasp," he told *The New York Times* in March 1986.[9] "How long it will take depends on what Federal officials will permit by way of testing and what kind of financial backing they give it. We *could* have a vaccine in three to five years if they would get behind it." His colleagues didn't share his optimism. Many felt his pronouncements were ill-advised because they boosted public expectations that were impossible to meet. What Essex didn't mention when he made such sweeping statements to the army of reporters who slavishly jotted down his every word was that a fair share of this financial backing most likely would be funneled into his laboratory. Nor did he mention his own vested interest in pushing vaccines, rather than other therapeutic strategies.

In 1985, Essex discovered gp 120 (glycoprotein, molecular weight 120), a protein that protrudes from the surface of HIV. Essex believed this protein was the probe HIV used to attach itself to healthy cells. But what was even more significant was that the gp 120 protein might provoke the body's immune system to produce protective antibodies to the virus. "We may be able to make a vaccine from it that will cause little or no illness in human beings but will give them immunity from the AIDS virus, just as cowpox vaccine protects against smallpox," he said.[10] For Essex, this discovery was a major scientific coup which thrust him into the same ranks as Robert Gallo and Luc Montagnier, with whom he had shared the 1986 Lasker Award.

For Cambridge BioScience, which held the licensing rights for the gp 120 protein, this breakthrough was a bonanza. The protein was pressed into service as the basis for Cambridge BioScience's inexpensive AIDS-antibody test, which could be administered in five minutes in a doctor's office, and for virtually all vaccine development in the United States. On the strength of this discovery, Cambridge BioScience forged lucrative alliances with SmithKline Beecham, the giant pharmaceutical company, and the Institut Merieux, France's leading vaccine maker, and generated $20 million through a stock offering. By April 1988, Haseltine's and Essex's stock in the company was worth $4.7 million and $2 million, respectively.

William Haseltine angrily rejected notions that the profit motive influenced their research. "A strength America has is translating its knowledge and skills from academia to business," he said. Besides, he added, "you could pick anybody in AIDS research, bigger than me, and find worse so-called conflicts of interest."[11] Haseltine was certainly right on that score: AIDS was fast becoming a *billion*-dollar business.

Even Jonas Salk jumped into the act. The diminutive silver-haired scientist was revered as a genuine hero by Americans, but among some of his colleagues he was considered a lightweight, a glorified lab technician, who had contributed little scientifically to the conquest of polio. Salk, who entered the polio field in the late 1940s, formulated his vaccine based upon techniques derived from the work of giants like Harvard's John Enders. Along with his two young associates, Thomas Weller and Fred Robbins, Enders devised a method of growing the polio virus in a test tube, which paved the way for producing enough for vaccines. The three men shared a 1954 Nobel Prize for their break-through. Salk's critics maintained that he simply took the next logical step. "You could go into a kitchen and do what he did," snorted Albert Sabin, Salk's archrival, who had begun studying polio during the 1931 epidemic. "Salk didn't discover anything." By the 1960s, Sabin's live-virus vaccine, which was easier to administer and conferred a more lasting immunity, supplanted Salk's vaccine as the preferred method of immunization throughout the world.

Despite the honors that were heaped upon him over the years, Salk was trapped by his own celebrity, which he felt undermined his scien-tific reputation, and his research was dismissed by his colleagues. The Nobel Prize eluded him and he was elected to the National Academy of Sciences late in life. So in 1962, with funding from the March of Dimes, he launched the Salk Institute in La Jolla, California. Salk envisioned it as "a cathedral to science," where researchers could freely pursue their muses amid the rugged splendor of the Pacific coast. "The Salk," as it is known, is now a renowned mecca for the world's top scientists. Salk himself was painfully aware they didn't willingly include him in their rarefied ranks. "I couldn't possibly have become a member of this institute," Salk once said, with some poignancy, "if I hadn't founded it myself."

In AIDS, however, Salk apparently saw one last chance to earn the respect of his peers. In 1986, Robert Gallo visited the elder statesman of vaccinology, who was now in his seventies, in La Jolla to discuss pos-sible strategies for an AIDS vaccine. That meeting sparked Salk's interest in devising his own AIDS vaccine. In 1987, Salk declared his intention to produce a therapeutic vaccine that would neutralize the deadly HIV and transform it into a benign infection. Unlike conven-tional vaccines, which prevent infections, therapeutic vaccines bolster the immune system's ability to fend off disease when a person is already infected. Salk's idea wasn't outlandish—French scientist Daniel Zagury had concocted a therapeutic AIDS vaccine a year ear-lier. Salk proposed using an inactivated HIV, rather than synthetic fragments of the virus—a strategy that was reminiscent of the approach he employed in his polio vaccine—to stimulate an immune response. His plan was immediately denounced by other scientists as outmoded and risky, and FDA officials branded this scheme down-right dangerous.

Salk shrugged off these criticisms by offering to inject himself with the vaccine to prove its safety, and formed a company, Immune Response, to finance this undertaking. An estimated 15 million people were infected with HIV worldwide and that number was expected to double by the turn of the century. So the potential market for a vaccine—or any effective therapeutic, for that matter—was phenomenal. Well-heeled benefactors, dazzled by the association with the most celebrated name in vaccines and the chance of raking in astronomical profits with a successful AIDS vaccine, excitedly ponied up $20 million almost overnight. Colgate Palmolive, for one, purchased a 12 percent stake in the company while the Institut Merieux paid $7.5 million for the rights to market the proposed vaccine in Europe, Africa, and Latin America.

Once the putative cause of AIDS was identified, ranks closed and researchers proceeded in lockstep to commence the search for a cure. Immediately after the publication of Gallo's 1984 papers in *Science* describing his discovery of the AIDS-causing virus, his laboratory was inundated with requests from investigators all over the country for samples of HTLV-3, for uninfected cell lines in which to grow the virus, viral clones, and a host of other reagents that researchers need to conduct experiments.

Scientific etiquette dictates that researchers share their data and materials unconditionally to advance progress as quickly as possible. But Gallo did the unthinkable: he hoarded the reagents. To withhold information from other qualified investigators is a serious breach of protocol.

Robert Gallo's behavior in the interferon dispute, when UCLA's David Golde accused researchers at Hoffmann-La Roche of stealing a cell line, demonstrated that he was well aware of these principles—he had even reportedly offered to "punch out" David Golde to defend his smeared reputation. According to Congressional investigations, though, in this instance, Gallo violated this sacred tenet. Repeatedly. Gallo freely supplied pals like Robin Weiss, Duke University's Dani Bolognesi, and Max Essex with as much material as they wanted. Others, however, like the NIH's Malcolm Martin, and Michael Gottlieb, the Los Angeles physician who identified the first AIDS cases, were refused outright. And still others had to sign onerous agreements that severely restricted the kinds of experiments they could perform with the reagents before Gallo would send them materials. With some, Gallo insisted that "work with HTLV-3 will not be published without prior approval by Dr. Gallo." Even more telling was his proviso, inserted only in his agreements with scientists who had access to LAV, that "reagents will not be used in comparisons with other viruses." This condition, notes one investigator, was presumably driven by his desire to keep independent researchers from comparing HTLV-3 with LAV, the Pasteur virus, and uncovering their "uniquely close genetic relationship."[12]

Gallo was particularly harsh toward CDC scientists like Don Francis, whom he stonewalled apparently because he felt they were in bed with the French. While Gallo furnished plenty of viral samples to his friends for free, the Cancer Institute charged its sister agency, the CDC, $75 a liter. The CDC was even forced to open up a charge account at the NCI's satellite facility in Frederick, Maryland. Relations between the two agencies reached such a low ebb that in June 1984, the CDC's Dr. Frederick Murphy felt compelled to visit Bethesda and smooth over Gallo's ruffled feathers. Apparently, Gallo was intransigent, and threatened to not provide CDC scientists with the research materials they required. A June 11, 1984, memorandum Murphy wrote to Dr. Walter Dowdle, the CDC's acting director, vividly recounted their confrontation:

"[I]t was a tense moment, fraught with the possibility of non-delivery. Our tack, stated orally in several different ways as we discussed the matter with Dr. Gallo, was that public health purposes were paramount. Dr. Gallo agreed. In our conversation, it became clear that comparison of his HTLV-3 prototype with the French prototype LAV occupied a separate niche—the comparison was seen as having both academic and public health purposes. Because of the latter, I offered, using several tacks, to have certain comparative tests between his HTLV-3 and the French LAV done at CDC; Dr. Gallo declined each time, stating that such would be done in his lab. It was quite clear from our discussion that this was the only subject which engendered such difficulty—when we switched to other themes . . . there was no problem." The reason Gallo didn't want others comparing the two viruses, according to Joseph Onek, Robert Gallo's attorney, "is because Gallo and the French scientists had already agreed they were going to do the comparison and they wanted to be the first to publish them. Both papers were prepared but it was Montagnier who decided not to publish them because he felt there was going to be better data available later."

Gallo later told congressional investigators that he withheld the cell lines from scientists he felt he "could not trust," who would "stab me in the back," or who "would embarrass me or call me dishonest if there was something wrong with the cells."[13] His bizarre behavior contributed to the growing undercurrent of rumblings about the integrity of his science, about what Harry Rubin characterizes as "the flummery that was going on in Gallo's lab." According to the staff report, Fischinger and DeVita gave Gallo license to give and withhold his materials at will. At the PHS level, noted the staff report, "Dr. Lowell Harmison institutionalized the selective withholding of research materials, as a matter of political and commercial policy." And when NIH director Dr. James Wyngaarden questioned Gallo about withholding research materials, Gallo "insisted he was sharing his samples as fast as he could." Nevertheless, numerous scientists complained about the hoarding of precious reagents. Gallo's efforts to control scientific scrutiny of his virus were ultimately futile, and the truth slowly but inexorably began to leak out.

In the summer of 1984, Martin Bryant, a physician with a Ph.D. in molecular biology, wanted to devise an AIDS blood test. A commercial test wouldn't be available for another year, so Bryant hoped to formulate an effective screening test to use at UC Davis's teaching hospital, where he was on the staff. The first step in the process was to determine the genetic sequence of the AIDS virus—and Bryant was in a unique position to do this. He had just received some samples of Robert Gallo's HTLV-3 AIDS virus. His boss, Murray Gardner, an eminent animal retrovirologist, had good relations with scientists at the Pasteur Institute, and with Jay Levy, a leading UCSF virologist who had also isolated a variant of the AIDS virus, which he dubbed ARV (AIDS-related virus). Gardner had obtained samples of the French's LAV when he was in Paris in April 1984, shortly before Margaret Heckler's press conference. Consequently, Bryant was perhaps the only scientist in the world with samples of all three known AIDS viruses.

To make the test as effective as possible and ensure that he didn't miss any extraneous variables, he felt compelled to compare genetically the French's LAV with HTLV-3 and ARV. Since Gardner had received samples of the Gallo lab's virus from one of their outside sub-contractors, Bryant hadn't signed Gallo's troublesome "no comparisons" agreement. But what Bryant saw when he peered through the microscope didn't make any sense.

Since most viruses mutate like crazy, even succeeding generations of the same strain of viruses are never identical; there is always some variance. It was clear the French virus and Levy's ARV were the same virus, but there were deviations in their respective genetic makeups that reflected their different origins. Similarly, Gallo's HTLV-3 and Levy's ARV were clearly the same virus, but again there were distinct differences. When Bryant matched up HTLV-3 with the French LAV, however, they were exactly alike, virtual carbon copies.

Bryant was dumbfounded. Either the virus mutated or it didn't. It couldn't do both. So in the fall of 1984, Bryant wrote up his results. In the paper's conclusion, he noted that in doing a molecular comparison of the three viruses, "ARV can be readily distinguished from the LAV and HTLV-3," but "LAV and HTLV-3 are identical." Perhaps someone else had noticed this phenomenon too and could come up with a plausible explanation as to why some strains of the virus mutated and others didn't.

As a professional courtesy, Gardner sent Robert Gallo a draft of Bryant's paper. When Gallo received it, he went ballistic. According to Gardner, Gallo appealed to Gardner's patriotism and "alternately harangued and pleaded with" Gardner "to delay or abort publication of the Bryant paper."[14] Subsequently, Gardner received a phone call from Dr. Peter Fischinger, the NCI associate director, who reportedly told him "you would be well-advised not to get in the middle of this."[15] An anguished Gardner complained bitterly to Jay Levy. Levy then called Dr. Malcolm Martin at the NIH. "At 4:30 today I received a telephone call from Dr. Jay Levy," Martin wrote in a November 28, 1984, memorandum. "He was quite upset because of pressure being put on Dr. Murray Gardner by the NCI staff not to publish [this] data. . . . He likened the situation to a 'Watergate coverup' and stated that all data pointed to apparent theft of the French AIDS virus."[16] Gallo's lawyer, Joseph Onek, says that Gallo wanted to delay publication because he and Montagnier had agreed to publish their comparison at a later date.

When Bryant's paper was published some months later, the genetic comparison of the three AIDS viruses was omitted. Bryant, an idealistic young postdoc, was "devastated" by this incident, his faith in the sanctity of science shattered. He left Gardner's laboratory soon after.

In the meantime, Malcolm Martin and A. B. Rabson, a fellow researcher at the National Institute of Allergy and Infectious Diseases, performed some comparisons of their own. They uncovered exactly what Martin Bryant had. There was about a 10 percent genetic variation between Levy's ARV and the French virus. The French virus and Gallo's virus, wrote Martin and Rabson in a subsequent paper, were "virtually identical." These similarities are "difficult to explain" and were "surprising in view of their independent isolation."[17] "We offer no explanation for the similarity of HTLV-3 and LAV," Dr. Martin wrote in another scientific article, "but informed virologists will certainly draw certain obvious conclusions."[18]

At a New York AIDS conference held on a bitterly cold day in February 1985, Dr. Joseph Sonnabend, a pioneering AIDS researcher, showed reporters slides of the French and American viruses, and explained the significance of the genetic sequencing Pasteur Institute scientists had performed on the three known AIDS viruses, LAV, HTLV-3, and ARV. Sonnabend knew Gallo's virus was identical to the one isolated by Luc Montagnier. Not similar, but *exactly* the same. To the eyes of a veteran researcher, it was like looking at copies of the same photograph. He also realized there was only one explanation for these two viruses' striking similarity: HTLV-3 *was* LAV. It was not something the diffident scientist felt comfortable revealing to the press, though, so earlier he had queried fellow scientists as to how to handle this issue. David Baltimore's response, said Sonnabend, was typical. "When I told him I thought it was important to tell reporters the truth—that Gallo's and Montagnier's isolates were the same—he said 'Joseph, please don't do this,'" Sonnabend recalls. "My only interpretation of this was that he felt we should clean our own dirty laundry."

The underground war that was brewing over priority for the discovery of the AIDS virus was "important for reasons other than to glorify its discoverers," noted one esteemed British science journal. "The total U.S. market for diagnostic kits alone, to screen blood for the presence of the AIDS virus, is estimated at $80 million. Who receives the money from patent rights obviously depends on who first patented the procedure for isolating the AIDS virus."[19] Even the august *Financial Times* of London weighed in. "Much more than scientific prestige is at stake," the *Times* noted. "Patent rights on the soon-to-be-marketed diagnostic tests—as well as on an eventual vaccine for the disease—will be worth a fortune both to the research institute and to the individual scientists who can prove they were first in the AIDS field."[20]

In the midst of this growing controversy, on May 28, 1985, the U.S. Patent and Trademark Office approved the U.S. government's patent application for an HIV-antibody test devised by Robert Gallo. The normally glacially slow agency had moved at warp speed in granting approval in less than a year. Because of the public health emergency, patent officials boasted, the application was pushed through in a near-record seven months. Of course, no one had an explanation as to why the patent for the Pasteur test, which had been filed in December 1983—roughly four months before Gallo's, during which time hundreds of people were infected with AIDS-contaminated blood—was still languishing at the agency.

Earlier in the year, the NIH had solicited competitive bids for licensing rights to the lucrative test. More than twenty companies applied for licenses but only five were picked: Ortho and Abbott Laboratories, among the major pharmaceuticals, and three small companies which did contract work for Gallo's laboratory—Electro-nucleonics, Litton Bionetics, and Biotech Research Laboratories. Intriguingly, the latter two firms were owned by none other than Gallo's longtime colleague and mentor, Robert Ting. It was a cozy arrangement. Government officials saw nothing wrong in awarding contracts that were potentially worth millions to three companies so closely allied with Robert Gallo, one of the patent holders on the test for antibodies to the AIDS-causing virus. After all, they noted, the contracts were awarded based upon a point system and those three companies certainly had a leg up on their rivals since they had been working with samples of the virus furnished to them by Gallo for many months. But what was "rigged," says one informed source, "was that the HHS limited the number of licensees to five in order to create an incentive for these companies and protect their market share."

Officials at the Pasteur Institute watched this sideshow unfold with a growing sense of outrage. On August 6, 1985, Pasteur Institute director Dr. Raymond Dedonder, accompanied by a phalanx of attorneys, flew to Washington for a meeting with a group of high-level HHS officials. Tall and distinguished, with a thick shock of white hair, Dedonder had studied in the United States and was quite fond of the brash, casual Americans, who had embraced him when he was a young scientist. It pained him greatly to be forced into a distasteful confrontation with his scientific compatriots.

Dedonder didn't flinch from what he had to do, however. The atmosphere at the meeting, which was chaired by Dr. Lowell Harmison, science adviser to the Assistant Secretary for Health, was tense. The "basic claim" of the Pasteur delegation was that Robert Gallo ". . . either knowingly or mistakenly appropriated Dr. Montagnier's invention," according to a memorandum of the meeting. Pasteur officials, the memo continued, "made three oral *demands* which they say are necessary to avoid litigation over who should be credited with the HTLV-3 patent and who should derive the commercial benefits." These included *"recognition* that Dr. Montagnier of the Pasteur Institute was the true inventor of the HTLV-3 test kit and diagnostic method of detecting AIDS," and *"reissuance* of the HTLV-3 patent previously issued to Dr. Gallo" with Dr. Montagnier listed as either inventor "or, at least, joint inventors with Dr. Gallo's group."[21] Gerard Weiser, Pasteur's patent counsel, left no doubt that the Pasteur had every intention of pursuing their claims to the fullest extent of the law, including filing for an interference with the Patent and Trademark Office based upon "derivation." According to the memo, this was "a polite way of claiming theft." The Pasteur requested a written response to these allegations within the month, by September 6.

NIH officials were equally incensed by the Pasteur's claims, which they felt had no merit whatsoever. "At the time, everyone in the system thought the French were trying to take credit for Bob's work, that they were putting more credit on Montagnier than was warranted," said Dr. James Wyngaarden, who was then director of the NIH. "Everyone up and down the line felt that."[22]

Gallo even intimated to NIH officials that Montagnier may have inadvertently stolen *his* virus. By June 1984, Gallo knew LAV and HTLV-3 were genetic twins. But his explanation was that a contamination occurred in Montagnier's laboratory, and that colonies of LAV growing in petri dishes in France had been contaminated with samples of HTLV-3 the Gallo group sent to the Pasteur in May. Gallo even called Montagnier that June to tell him of his suspicions. The French scientist responded with uncharacteristic fury. "If there were to be contamination, it could only be the other way round, HTLV-3 contaminated by LAV, since we had LAV long before and had sent this virus to other laboratories," Montagnier indignantly told Gallo. "I was shocked by Dr. Gallo's accusation," Montagnier later recalled, "and decided soon afterward to break off our collaboration."[23]

After the meeting with Dedonder, HHS officials were convinced the French charges were "outrageous." Harmison ordered Peter Fischinger to launch an internal investigation. Fischinger requested a number of key papers from Gallo's lab and interviewed Dr. Gallo and his top assistant, Dr. Mikulas Popovic, who worked directly with the virus and performed the seminal experiments. Based upon what he learned from Gallo and Popovic, Fischinger concluded that Pasteur's accusations were groundless. "There is no evidence that material from any outside laboratory, including the French, was used in generating the HTLV-3 virus," Fischinger wrote in a report to his superiors. "Dr. Gallo and his laboratory were the first to identify the virus and to describe the virus antibody test."[24]

However, as congressional investigators later concluded, "the documents generated by the LTCB scientists formed the framework for the entire U.S. Government defense. But many important facts were not revealed by the LTCB scientists . . . [and] many of the assertions contained in the LTCB scientists' submissions could not be substantiated. Thus, the entire U.S. Government defense was constructed on a false and defective infrastructure."[25] According to the investigators' report, revelations that contradicted what Gallo was telling them or threatened the American patent were ignored or actively suppressed. From the beginning, probers noted, "HHS officials had committed themselves to one thing only—defending the blood test patent of Gallo, and by extension defending the claimed international political and scientific preeminence of the United States and Dr. Gallo."[26]

As the United States geared up to battle the French, Don Francis, who had worked closely with Pasteur scientists and was one of the few people involved who genuinely understood what was at stake, sent a stern letter to James Curran, his boss at the CDC. "[T]here are really important ethical scientific issues that the Public Health Service should consider before putting up a strong defense," Francis wrote in his September 5, 1985, missive. "I am sure I am not alone in believing that Bob Gallo exceeded ethical bounds in his dealings with the French. If this litigation gets into open court, all of the less-than-admirable aspects will become public and, I think, hurt science and the Public Health Service. The French clearly found the cause of AIDS first and Dr. Gallo clearly tried to upstage them one year later."[27] But Francis's warnings went unheeded. The next day, HHS Secretary Margaret Heckler's top aide, Mac Haddow, on the basis of Fischinger's investigation, dispatched a curt letter to the Pasteur Institute informing them the United States had found no evidence "to support your position that [our AIDS test patent] is invalid."

This was tantamount to a declaration of war. The Pasteur began to prepare for their courtroom showdown, retaining Townley & Updike, an old-line New York law firm whose midtown Manhattan offices resemble an exclusive private club, with richly burnished wood-paneled walls, thick oriental rugs, overstuffed sofas, and wing chairs in autumnal colors. Then, in early December 1985, James B. Swire, a partner in the law firm, received the first in a series of anonymous phone calls he got over the next several years from angry scientists who were afraid to go public with what they knew. The caller in this instance would identify himself only as someone who was speaking for concerned scientists, but what he had to say was shocking. He told Swire that the reproduction of HTLV-3 that accompanied Robert Gallo's original *Science* articles announcing his discovery of the AIDS-causing virus in May 1984 was not HTLV-3—it was LAV. "There was not and there never was an HTLV-3," the caller insisted. "It was always LAV."

"Are you talking about this as the same *generic* virus?" Swire asked, trying to clarify what the man told him. "No, there *never was* an HTLV-3," the informant repeated. "There was always only one physical specimen and that is LAV."

Swire was stunned. If what the caller said was true, it was the first hard evidence that this dispute was more than just about sharing credit, and that maybe Montagnier should be in the spotlight all by himself. "It was like something out of Watergate," Swire recalls. "Up until that time, my assumption was that we would probably wind up finding that Gallo had studied the French virus and used it to advance his own development by whatever it would turn out to be—a month or two months or three months. And we'd wind up fighting for how much credit we'd get for helping him advance his work." Subsequent events confirmed the informant's seemingly outlandish story.

In the meantime, American officials were closing ranks. Assistant HHS Secretary James Mason, who, as head of the CDC, had told *The New York Times*, the day before Heckler's fateful press conference, that Pasteur Institute scientists had discovered the AIDS virus, appeared to have had a change of heart and was now an active supporter of the United States' interests. "Quite frankly," he wrote in a widely circulated October 1985 memo, "I believe our case to be strong should this issue be litigated." Justice Department attorneys, however, wanted to avoid any ugly courtroom battles, so they had offered the Pasteur a face-saving deal. The Americans would share credit with the French for the discovery of the AIDS virus, and the Pasteur Institute could sell its AIDS test kits in the United States without paying any royalties to Robert Gallo.

To Pasteur officials, this was no compromise—it seemed more like a patronizing slap in the face—and they rejected the offer. On December 12, 1985, the Institute filed the first of several lawsuits against the United States government. At the same time, the Pasteur requested copies of all documents relating to Gallo's discovery of the AIDS virus under the Freedom of Information Act. For the Pasteur, it wasn't so much the money or even national pride, but a matter of principle. "They were really outraged that what had happened was detrimental to the interests of science," recalls James Swire. "They engaged in a free exchange of laboratory reagents. They never tried to keep Bob Gallo or anyone else from studying what they were developing. All they wanted [in return] was an understanding that they would get proper credit and nothing would be commercialized without their approval or permission. Gallo's lab breached that understanding and [as a consequence] any scientific exchange between the two labs had been stopped" in the midst of a public health crisis.

As time went on, though, the U.S. government's staunch defense of Robert Gallo started to disintegrate as more startling evidence emerged that contradicted his story. In the April 18, 1986, issue of *Science*, under orders from NCI director Dr. Vincent DeVita, Gallo and his associates published a brief letter that admitted the photographs, known as electron micrographs, identified as HTLV-3 which appeared with his original *Science* articles were "inadvertently composed" from pictures of LAV. James Swire's anonymous informant had been right. But Robert Gallo dismissed the disclosure as inconsequential, and blamed the mix-up on a technician who had accidentally pulled out the wrong slide. *Nature,* however, described the acknowledgment as "acutely embarrassing." And Pasteur Institute lawyers told *The New York Times* that "the story the United States Government has put out is falling apart."

Despite the brave front put on by NIH officials, behind the scenes an intense debate raged about how best to proceed. Gallo seemed humiliated and wanted to resolve this affair as soon as possible. According to the staff report, he contacted David Baltimore and Lewis Thomas, another eminent senior scientist, and asked them to intervene. Gallo told them he was willing to settle and split the royalties and credit right down the middle. Then Thomas, whom DeVita had also asked to mediate the patent dispute, called François Jacob, a Nobel laureate at the Pasteur. But the U.S. government's lawyers, as Gallo put it, were "complicating it." They preferred to stall because they felt they had a better than even chance of beating the Pasteur in court. Besides, they persuasively argued, "how can we equate [a] payout as ... something other than [an] admission of culpability?"[28]

By the fall of 1986, however, with the Pasteur winning key legal decisions, President Reagan "personally ordered U.S. officials to seek a settlement."[29] So on a spring afternoon in March 1987, Robert Gallo and Luc Montagnier—with Jonas Salk, who had helped midwife the deal, patrolling the hallway—hunched over a small desk in a hotel room in Frankfurt, Germany, and hammered out a "definitive scientific history" of their "co-discovery" of the AIDS-causing virus. Their account, which was executed under intense pressure from their respective governments, halted more than two years of acrimonious battles, and formed the basis for an agreement between the French and American governments that was unveiled a few days later in Washington, on March 31, 1987.

Flanked by Vice President George Bush and Secretary of State George Shultz, with a grimly determined President Ronald Reagan looking over his shoulder, French Prime Minister Jacques Chirac declared to reporters gathered in the East Room of the White House the terms of their truce. Montagnier and Gallo would share the credit for the discovery and their governments would jointly patent the rights to the test for detecting the AIDS virus—a patent that would eventually generate ten of millions of dollars for the U.S. government and $100,000 a year in royalties to Gallo. Officially, the occasion marked the end of the controversy. But unofficially, many of the Pasteur scientists, who had signed the agreement under extreme duress, seethed with resentment.

There was a swelling tide of discontent at the NIH, as well. Researchers there were demoralized by the stance of government officials, who many believed had orchestrated a high-level cover-up, stonewalled the French, and deliberately withheld key documents. This sulfurous affair tarnished science's pristine image and violated everything they believed in—the rigorous pursuit of truth, science's much vaunted self-correcting mechanisms, and the international spirit of cooperation that was central to the scientific process. "The Pasteur had very strong suspicions about what really happened, but there's a big difference between having suspicions and having actual proof," says James Swire. "If we had gotten the documents we requested, we never would have settled."

But the ink wasn't even dry on the agreement—when its underpinnings began to crumble.

CHAPTER 10

PUSHING THE ENVELOPE

Gray-haired with blue eyes and patrician features, Victor Marder is a meticulous man. He believes good science is rigorous and deliberate, not rushed. Hastiness breeds sloppiness and haphazard thinking and vital elements that can have profound consequences may be overlooked or simply ignored. Marder felt that the TIMI-I study was a prime example of what goes wrong when science is hurried. In his view, the study was ramrodded through the Data and Safety Monitoring Board, it was halted prematurely, unfavorable data were disregarded in order to put t-PA in the best possible light, and Genentech had unprecedented influence over policy decisions—all of which was antithetical to the scientific method.

So on a crisp fall day in September 1988, Marder, a professor at the University of Rochester's Medical School, sat facing a panel of congressional investigators in a nondescript hearing room tucked away in a corner of the Sam Rayburn Office Building on Capitol Hill and shared his grave misgivings about the conduct of the TIMI trials. Seated behind Marder in a neat row were Eric Topol, Eugene Braunwald, and Alan Ross, a cardiologist at George Washington University and one of the original TIMI investigators, with their legs and arms crossed, not looking particularly pleased with Marder. Marder didn't care what they thought of him, though. In tandem with Sol Sherry, he had been a persistent thorn in Genentech's side. A group of prominent academic physicians—disgusted, one said, by how "American cardiology had been turned into a marketing arm of Genentech"—had coalesced around them.

Marder had plenty to get off his chest. "There was a lot of pressure to get things done," Marder testified. After the initial shoot-out between SK and t-PA "we were being pressed to stop the study short [because] . . . they found a very significant difference between the two [agents]," he told the congressional panel. There really was no difference: "the bleeding was the same in both groups, and there was no difference in mortality rates between both groups even though one drug was twice as effective as another in opening a vessel."

Marder's credentials as an expert in thrombolytics were impeccable. He'd studied medicine at Johns Hopkins University in the 1950s, where groundbreaking research on clot-busting agents was performed by the field's pioneers, and his formative years as a scientist were under the tutelage of Sol Sherry. From the time he was a medical student, the arc of his career paralleled the development of thrombolytics. Marder pointed out that there were considerable risks to using t-PA, but they were lost in the euphoria of discovering a breakthrough heart medicine that was the product of America's new biotechnology industry. Arteries tended to close up again (reocclude) quickly after using t-PA, which could be extremely dangerous.* When the arteries block up again, patients are rendered more vulnerable to a second heart attack. But the hematologists, for whom circulatory complications like this are numbing routine, were cut out of the loop when the original monitoring board was disbanded. The cardiologists who replaced them didn't understand the profound consequences of these side effects. Yet TIMI-I anointed t-PA as the superior agent—"heart Drano," as it was called in the press—and nothing that surfaced since altered this perception.

"It's easy to see how this happened," Marder reflects today. "T-PA was one of the first molecules made by genetic engineering. It's a new company, a U.S. company backed by a lot of venture capital with 'darling' status on Wall Street. So there's a lot of publicity and anticipation. And the Heart Institute wanted this study to work. It would be a big success and create a lot of glory for the Institute."

Congressional investigators' digging uncovered plenty of questionable practices. Among the more disturbing revelations was the cozy

---

*Even before the TIMI-1 trials in the 1980s, scientists were aware of reocclusion problems with t-PA (there were reocclusion problems with SK, as well, though they were not as serious). In some of the initial studies, says Victor Marder, "the dose of t-PA had to be escalated because of early reocclusion problems. This has always been a bugaboo with t-PA."

relationship that evolved between Genentech and government scientists, who seemed to be in a state of denial about just how that alliance was. During the study, dosage levels of t-PA had been changed to enhance the drug's effectiveness. "The producers of SK weren't close to the design of the trial," Marder says. "SK was simply dispensed as prescribed. So the TIMI trial really was designed to develop t-PA, and find the best dose and the best regimen." It also came to light that Genentech, for the second phase of the TIMI trials, would cooperate only with a trial of t-PA exclusively. NIH officials reluctantly went along with this scheme, which meant, in essence, that millions of dollars of tests of what would become Genentech's flagship drug were paid for by American taxpayers.

Nor did government officials see anything wrong with the fact that at least thirteen of the researchers involved in the NIH-funded studies, including principal investigators and members of the TIMI steering committee, owned stock in Genentech or options to buy the stock at discount prices later on. Among them were four Johns Hopkins researchers, Drs. David Bush, Nisha Chandra, Bernadine Healy, and Myron Weisfeldt; Dr. Eric Topol received options for 6,000 shares of stock, though he later returned them. When a *Newsday* reporter, who heard rumors that federally funded researchers owned Genentech stock, started checking around to confirm this, the TIMI operations committee immediately alerted the researchers that they might be contacted by a reporter. "You are, of course, not obliged to reveal confidential information," read the March 18, 1987, memorandum.

When Congressman Ted Weiss, who chaired the NIH oversight subcommittee probing Genentech, read this memo, he was outraged. Clearly, these researchers, whose careers had been nurtured for years at great public expense, had conveniently forgotten who signed their paychecks. "There was no suggestion that such disclosure was a reasonable thing to do?" he asked the NHLBI's Eugene Passamani in a particularly heated exchange during his committee's hearings. "Why didn't NIH encourage disclosure of conflicts of interest?"

"Mr. Chairman, it would be applying a rule that does not exist," Dr. Passamani blandly replied, in a circuitous bureaucratic obfuscation. "It seems to me that for me as a Federal employee to insist upon that sort of disclosure without backup would be more than I should attempt."

"Except that one could interpret your instructions of advice as suggesting that people not disclose that information and to keep it from the public," snapped Weiss, obviously irritated by Passamani's moral opaqueness.

"That was not intended," Dr. Passamani shot back. As far as legislative investigators were concerned, though, Passamani missed the point. "It is not possible to determine whether or not stock ownership clouded the judgment of scientists who helped determine dosage levels and other treatment decisions," a congressional report later noted. "However, potential conflicts of interest were present for at least three members of the TIMI Committee that made such decisions."

The scientists themselves, however, bristled at the implication they'd compromise their integrity—and hurt their careers—for a few shares of stock. "I don't believe this was ever driven by a desire to make money," maintains Elliott Grossbard. "These people are driven by ego. That's what makes them tick. If they don't believe that SK is better than t-PA, it's not because they have stock options. It's because they made up their mind that t-PA is better than SK."

Grossbard was right on one score: the American cardiology community was sold on the superiority of t-PA, which Genentech claimed justified the staggering difference in cost. Once it was approved, t-PA exploded out of the starting blocks, posting sales of $56 million in the last five weeks of 1987, and roaring past the $100 million mark within its first six months on the market, on its way to first-year sales of $188 million, the most spectacular drug debut in history. In February 1988, Elliott Grossbard's stock options converted, making him another of Genentech's paper millionaires. By any yardstick, even his detractors grudgingly admitted, Grossbard earned every penny.

T-PA dominated the clot-busting market, gobbling up a 66 percent share despite its steep $2,200-a-dose price tag. Genentech's gross profit was about $1,800 on each $2,200 dose of t-PA, according to industry estimates, far in excess of even the whopping 70 to 80 percent profit margins common with successful new drugs. The price, Genentech CEO Robert Swanson insisted, "reflects the enormous investment we've made in the development of this product and in developing a whole new technology to manufacture it." Genentech did plow $200 million into t-PA, an expense that was pumped up by the phenomenal cost of genetically synthesizing a protein as large and as intricate as t-PA. T-PA's molecular weight was one to two *hundred* times that of conventionally produced drugs like Tagamet, the ulcer medication—comparable to the difference between crafting a tugboat and building an ocean liner. "There has never been another product of this size and complexity," opined Swanson, "made through this kind of manufacturing."[1]

Genentech managed to retain its stranglehold on the thrombolytic market even in the face of mounting scientific evidence that t-PA wasn't any better than its rivals. In early 1988, Sol Sherry, weary of all the unsubstantiated hype about t-PA, agreed to debate Eugene Braunwald about the streptokinase–t-PA controversy at the upcoming meeting of the American College of Cardiology, which was scheduled to be held in March in Atlanta. Sherry was the first to raise questions about t-PA, starting in 1985 with a sharply critical editorial in *The New England Journal of Medicine*, which was followed by a steady stream of other papers in leading scientific publications. "It appears that strongly expressed opinions, rather than scholarship and open-mindedness," Sherry sourly noted, "make for leadership in academic cardiology."[2]

It promised to be quite a match-up. In medicine's intricate pecking order, Braunwald was the ultimate insider, the undisputed king of cardiology. And Sherry's primacy in thrombolytics and encyclopedic knowledge of the field was unquestioned. However, Braunwald refused to go head-to-head with Sherry. Since none of the cardiologists would debate the immensely powerful Braunwald, he agreed instead to a match with Victor Marder, who proved to be a worthy adversary.

The Marder-Braunwald debate was a bracing intellectual slugfest. Some of those who actually listened to the arguments of each scientist awarded the win to Marder, who had the advantage of knowing some inside information about the results of upcoming studies, which undercut t-PA's claims of superiority. As in the Kennedy-Nixon debates, however, appearance counted more than substance. Positions had polarized on either side of the question, based as much on ego, politics, and personality as on merit, so few minds were changed that day.

But the cracks really began to show in May 1988, when results of a forthcoming British study were leaked to the press. The Nottingham University Medical Center study, which compared t-PA with a placebo, revealed that the Genentech drug reduced mortality by about

20 percent, which was about the same as streptokinase's 18 percent mortality reduction. Genentech's stock plummeted more than 8 points. Then in November 1988, a researcher in New Zealand found the same thing—no significant difference between t-PA and SK. Genentech kept up a brave face and downplayed these findings, insisting that a "true test" would be available when GISSI-2 (Gruppo Italiano per lo Studio della Streptochinasi nell' Infarto Miocardico), a gargantuan match-up between SK and t-PA of 20,000 patients from thirteen countries, was completed.

Behind the scenes, however, the company was in turmoil. Despite its record-setting launch, t-PA failed to meet Wall Street expectations, which had been inflated by Genentech's hype that this would be the first billion-dollar drug produced by gene splicing. The overzealous proponents of thrombolytics had drastically miscalculated the percentage of heart attack patients who benefited from agents like t-PA. Only about one in five—or about 200,000 Americans each year—could be treated with clot busters, which meant the market for the drug was far smaller than originally anticipated. By October 1988, sales of t-PA had slackened, slowed primarily by stiff competition from the cheaper SK, the drug's hefty cost, and difficulties administering it through an intravenous drip. With hospitals overstocked, the company was forced to halt production of the medication for the remainder of the year, and Genentech's stock plunged to 17 from a high of 53 a year before.[3] Investors lost millions.

Then, in November 1988, Genentech sustained another crushing blow when a British court rejected the company's broad patent on t-PA, which paved the way for Burroughs Wellcome to sell their version of t-PA. Rumors were rife of Robert Swanson's impending resignation, and headhunters shamelessly tried to poach Genentech's 500 stellar scientists, which the investment community viewed as the company's greatest asset. Once again, the beleaguered biotech's woes dragged down the entire industry: three-quarters of other biotech companies' stocks slipped below their initial offering price. By the fall of 1989, the marketing war ratcheted up another notch when the FDA approved Eminase, a clot-busting agent derived from blood plasma that was manufactured by SmithKline Beecham. Now three agents were available, and more were in the pipeline. It was only a matter of time before the competition loosened Genentech's hammerlock.

Genentech was confident, however, they'd score a decisive victory with GISSI-2, adding another powerful weapon to their marketing arsenal, and settling the streptokinase–t-PA controversy once and for all. Since so much was riding on GISSI-2, whose results were due to be released in March 1990, Elliott Grossbard felt compelled to attempt to uncover the study's findings before they were known to the public. "I had an agreement with [a member of the Italian team] that he would tell us a day or two ahead of time," says Grossbard. "But that doesn't give you a lot of time" to prepare a response if the results were unfavorable. At the American Heart Association meeting in November 1989, Grossbard buttonholed colleagues in hopes of eliciting some clues about the vast European trial. When he did get an idea of the outcome, his heart sank—there was no real benefit. He shared the bad news with fellow Genentech executives. It would take a miracle, he thought, for the company to rebound from such a staggering setback.

Four months later, in March 1990, at a medical conference in Florence, Italy, Dr. Gianni Tognoni revealed to the world what Genentech already knew: SK was as effective as t-PA in saving lives, even though t-PA cost ten times as much. Both agents had their downside risks: streptokinase was linked to a greater number of bleeding problems and allergic reactions, while the incidence of strokes and reocclusion was higher with t-PA.

Coming in the midst of an intense cost-containment drive in medical care in the United States, the GISSI-2 news should have been a mortal blow for Genentech's pricey wonder drug—but Genentech was ready with a dazzling counteroffensive. Over the winter, they had discovered what they believed was a deep flaw in the study's design. In the massive European trial, heparin, an anticoagulant that keeps arteries open after they're cleared of clots, was usually given to patients about twelve hours later. In the United States, however, doctors dispense heparin simultaneously with t-PA. A study by Alan Ross showed t-PA is most effective when heparin is injected at the same time. Consequently, the salutary effects of t-PA were dulled by the delay in administering heparin in GISSI-2.

A week after the GISSI-2 results were unveiled, Genentech persuasively argued its case at a company-sponsored forum prior to the American College of Cardiology meeting in March, which was held that year in New Orleans. There, thousands of cardiologists heard Italian scientists talk about GISSI-2, but immediately afterward, Alan Ross hammered home the critical importance of using heparin in combination with t-PA. The strategy worked. T-PA definitely took a big hit after GISSI-2, but many cardiologists dismissed the study as a blip on the radar screen, and t-PA continued to claim the lion's share of the clot-busting market, accounting for half of Genentech's annual revenues.

How Genentech kept t-PA afloat in the face of a mounting crescendo of bad news was, a *BusinessWeek* story noted, "a textbook case of medical marketing." Selling prescription drugs is unlike merchandising in any other industry because they're the only products in the world that aren't chosen by the people who use them. Doctors—along with pharmacists, nurses and hospital administrators—call the shots. In the rarefied world of drug marketing, the tools of the trade are drug trials and scientific forums, the lingua franca test results and papers in professional journals.

Drug companies spend more than $10 billion annually on marketing and promotion, which translates to about $13,000 a year that is spent *per doctor* to influence their treatment decisions. Doctors are bombarded by a barrage of information—at company-sponsored seminars, medical conventions, educational events, and in splashy ads in medical journals—and wooed by the battalions of salespeople drugmakers deploy to hawk their products. And drug companies aren't shy about using high-pressure marketing tactics to persuade doctors to adopt their medications. But the ways pharmaceutical companies are allowed to promote their products are very tightly regulated by federal agencies and the American Medical Association.

Genentech—despite its legions of ponytailed young scientists exuberantly high-fiving each other in the hallways, and the freewheeling intellectual atmosphere reminiscent of late-night college bull sessions—quickly earned a reputation as a bare-knuckles street fighter whose explosive growth was fueled in part by stretching the rules to the limit. Genentech's aggressive sales campaigns flattened the competition, sparked probes by Congress, the Federal Trade Commission, and the FDA, and prompted an indictment of its top sales executive on bribery charges. Kirk Raab, the company president and COO, was known for pushing the envelope. Raab's attitude, said one observer, was if you're not, "then maybe you're not close enough to the line."

Raab, who started out as a salesman in Brooklyn, New York, in 1959, was the bespectacled, buttoned-down product of an utterly different corporate culture, a throwback to another era. He always seemed out of place among the jeans-clad whiz kids at the company's Friday afternoon beer blasts—even when he and Robert Swanson showed up in blond wigs, with surfboards tucked under their arms, and warbled a few off-key duets. Yet Raab arrived in February 1985 amid much fanfare. Robert Swanson may have been a brilliant strategist and financier who, in less than a decade, had transformed Genentech from an idea hatched over a few beers into the darling of Wall Street. But he knew he didn't have the expertise to guide Genentech through the next crucial phase in its development, where many successful start-ups founder.

The longtime number two at Abbott Laboratories, Raab was a pharmaceutical industry veteran and seemed like an ideal choice to pilot Genentech through the difficult transition from a peerless scientific powerhouse to a fully integrated pharmaceutical company. "I like to describe Abbott as a wonderful battleship that as president I could steer across the Atlantic and could move one degree left or right after 100 meetings," Raab said. "So I wanted to come here [Genentech] to be on a PT boat."[4] Raab immediately set in motion strategies to speed Genentech's evolution. He recruited twenty top sales executives from leading pharmaceuticals, who formed the nucleus of what grew to be a 350-member sales force, stepped up marketing and promotional efforts, and scaled up their production capabilities to commercial volumes.

Genentech's first product was Protropin, a human growth hormone to treat dwarfism, which passed FDA muster in 1985. As the first drug created by recombinant DNA techniques that was marketed by a biotech company—Genentech had licensed its genetically engineered human insulin to Eli Lilly—Protropin enjoyed considerable cachet and its splashy debut signaled Genentech's emergence as a full-fledged drug company. The truth, however, was that they had produced the drug simply because they could use the new gene-splicing techniques. Now they had to justify all the money that went into devising this therapeutic and come up with a disorder that it could treat. The way Genentech's salespeople expanded the minuscule market for this drug established the swashbuckling style they used to push its other products, such as t-PA.

The FDA sanctioned Protropin only for treatment of the 7,000 children who suffer from pituitary dwarfism in the United States. The agency, though, had no control over how doctors prescribed the growth hormone once it had been approved. Genentech exploited this loophole in the law by legitimizing treatment of children who weren't hormone-deficient, and were merely short in stature, which exponentially swelled the market for the drug. "Of the three million children born in the U.S. annually, 90,000 will, by definition, be below the third percentile for height," according to a report in the *Journal of the American Medical Association*. Putting that many kids on Protropin could generate an $8 to $10 billion yearly bonanza for Genentech. Now that abundant quantities of the once scarce growth hormone could be made by Genentech's obliging bacteria, the next step was to transform the medical profession's perception of shortness and brand it a disease.[5]

First, Genentech identified potential "patients" through alliances with two charities, the Human Growth Foundation in Falls Church, Virginia, and the Magic Foundation in Oak Park, Illinois. The two organizations had for years sponsored "height screenings" for children at schools, shopping malls, and state fairs, and suggested kids who were very short for their age visit a doctor for evaluation. Both groups received the bulk of their funding from Genentech and from Eli Lilly, which sells a competing growth hormone. The foundations' connections with Genentech and Eli Lilly, however, were not revealed to school officials or to the parents who received follow-up letters (parents of "normally short" kids who did contact physicians were then faced with the agonizing decision of whether to allow their otherwise healthy and still developing child to consume an expensive drug whose benefits, to any except a tiny percentage, were unproven and whose long-term risks were unknown). Then Genentech funneled millions of dollars into research grants to pediatric endocrinologists, and to doctors and nurses for consulting, and for their participation in the National Cooperative Growth Study, which tracked the long-term safety and efficacy of Protropin. Said one leading pediatric endocrinologist: "Genentech co-opted the field."[6]

Within a few years, an estimated 20,000 to 25,000 American children used growth hormone—70 percent of whom were on Genentech's Protropin—at a cost of $20,000 to $30,000 a year, which was borne by parents and insurance companies. However, when a cluster of studies suggested growth hormone did nothing for children who were just plain short—the drug sparked an initial growth spurt, but the kids simply reached their adult height sooner and weren't any taller than they would have been anyway—criticisms mounted. "This year, Boston City Hospital ran out of money to immunize children," complained a pediatric endocrinologist at Harvard Medical School. "Can we afford, in this present climate, to squander this kind of money on an inch or two of height? For an esthetic problem?"[7] Yet Genentech's sales executives, in a spectacular show of their trademark ability to deflect any criticism, blunted the impact of these findings by promising that more studies that might yield different conclusions were on the way, which gave parents renewed hope and prevented sales from flagging. And, they maintain, over 90 percent of Protropin patients are hormone deficient (although a 1992 NIH study put the number at closer to 50 percent.) The height screenings have since been discontinued and a Genentech corporate spokesman says that the foundations have been prohibited from using Genentech funds for the screenings if they are even reinstituted.

So when t-PA was approved in November 1987, Genentech's resourceful sales team was ready with strategies reminiscent of the techniques they used to drive sales of Protropin past the $150 million mark, which was about *twenty times* the company's original projections. Genentech employed an array of tactics in its fierce battle to dominate the immensely lucrative thrombolytic market, winning physicians' loyalty with impressive scholarly presentations and educational forums featuring leading U.S. cardiologists like Drs. Eric Topol and Alan Ross, who spoke on behalf of the company.

The company also dispatched 350 doctors and nurses to promote the drug in videos and at medical conventions, and trained hundreds of nurses nationwide to instruct colleagues on the proper use of thrombolytics. Genentech insisted the 200 to 300 "nurse preceptors" they hired weren't doing sales pitches for t-PA, but many hospital officials complained the nurses acted like Genentech sales reps when they were supposed to be doing their jobs—a practice one former FDA Commissioner called "outrageous." "This has been one of the most aggressive campaigns I've ever seen . . . sometimes it gets a little oppressive," said Dr. Michael Eliastam, chief of Stanford's Emergency Medicine Department, where several Stanford nurses worked for

Genentech on the side. "They bring literature in . . . [and they] audit cases and point out which ones should have gotten t-PA."[8]

Genentech also established the National Registry of Myocardial Infarction, which collects confidential information on heart attack victims to track patient treatments and their outcomes. Genentech pays nurses and doctor's assistants from $10 to $50 for each patient about whom they submit information to the registry. Clintrials, Inc., of Lexington, Kentucky, a statistical analysis firm, then compiles the data. Genentech touts the registry as a useful treatment tool for hospitals, and more than 1,400 of the nation's 6,000 acute care facilities send names to the registry because it helps them pinpoint trends in care in their hospitals.

However, the registry is not a purely altruistic endeavor. Genentech's salespeople benefit too. The registry arms them with invaluable information about treatment practices by doctors and hospitals, so they know where to concentrate their marketing efforts and how to tailor their sales pitches. "This appears to be a marketing tool disguised as a serious study," concluded an FDA investigator in a report to his superiors. He noted that "one physician surmised that hospitals which used streptokinase or Eminase were targeted for Genentech sales pressure. Several hospitals refused to participate in the registry . . . [because] the use of patient identifying information was seen as being invasive to privacy, and [because of the] marketing overtones of the program."[9]

None of this is particularly unusual in the pharmaceutical industry, which, observed one health policy analyst, "spends more on trinkets, gifts, samples and [overall marketing] than it does on finding and carefully testing new drugs."[10] What is unusual is systematically savaging a competitor's product—which is exactly what SmithKline Beecham says Genentech did when SmithKline's clot buster, Eminase, was in the final glide path heading for FDA approval in the fall of 1989.

Genentech officials asked California's Senators Alan Cranston and Pete Wilson to contact the FDA about having an FDA advisory committee hearing to review Eminase before it was approved. "We were concerned Eminase [wouldn't] have to go through the same [approval process] as t-PA," said a Genentech spokesperson. The FDA, however, had decided a hearing wasn't necessary for Eminase and didn't appreciate Genentech's unwelcome intrusions. "I don't remember ever seeing congressional letters asking an agency to slow down" the approval of another company's product, said an FDA spokesperson, who described Genentech's unseemly offensive against Eminase as a "barroom brawl."[11] Genentech also polled doctors about whether they would rather use a product formulated through genetic engineering like t-PA or one derived from human blood plasma such as Eminase. This purportedly scientific survey subtly planted the seed in physicians' minds, charged irate SmithKline Beecham executives, that Eminase could carry blood-borne diseases like AIDS. Genentech argues that the company's tactics are "normal."

Even more egregious were Genentech's alleged attempts to sabotage tests of rival drugs that might undermine their hegemony in the American clot-busting market. In 1988, Dr. Cindy Grines, who is now a cardiologist at the prestigious William Beaumont Hospital in Royal Oak, Michigan, a suburb of Detroit, was trying to enroll patients in a study to test a combination of t-PA and SK, which would cut costs. According to Dr. William O'Neill, a cardiologist and Grines's boss at William Beaumont, the local Genentech representative spread false rumors about what she was trying to do, telling physicians half the patients would be treated with a placebo and the expense of the study would be borne by the patients. "[T]he Grines study [was] a potentially huge risk which would cut the total sale of t-PA in half," recalls Dr. O'Neill. "A lot of things were done so [doctors] wouldn't send patients. This was all a cold blooded calculation to keep up the stock price and their valuation on Wall Street."

Charles Hennekens, head of the Division of Preventive Medicine at Boston's Brigham and Women's Hospital, one of Harvard Medical School's teaching hospitals, encountered similar problems when he was the U.S. coordinator for another study, known as ISIS-3 (International Studies of Infarct Survival). ISIS-3, the largest treatment trial in the history of medicine, encompassed 46,000 patients from twenty countries who were randomly assigned to one of three thrombolytic agents, streptokinase, t-PA, and Eminase. Since Genentech refused to participate in the study, researchers used a version of t-PA made by Burroughs Wellcome. Hennekens says he had trouble recruiting patients because Genentech salespeople spread rumors and outright lies to discourage physicians from referring patients. Doctors were allegedly told streptokinase could cause cerebral hemorrhages and that Eminase was made from blood plasma, again raising the specter of AIDS. "I've never seen anything like it," said Dr. Hennekens, who's conducted numerous trials.[12]

The FDA dispatched a field investigator to look into numerous complaints from a dozen hospitals around the country. According to the FDA report, Genentech representatives told physicians and hospital administrators that Burroughs Wellcome's t-PA "was inferior or ineffective," that "using a product other than Genentech's t-PA would compromise" patient care, and that "malpractice was a distinct possibility if [the] center participated in ISIS-3." One Genentech-trained nurse even admitted to the FDA investigator that the studies and the journal references she quoted "were nonexistent." Apparently, according to the FDA report, the lobbying efforts were effective: enrollment was less than expected at more than half the sites, a nurse on Genentech's payroll prompted one hospital to withdraw from the study, and at two hospitals doctors with stock in Genentech suddenly refused to participate after they had originally agreed to do so. Genentech's scare tactics, however, didn't harm enrollment to any significant degree and ISIS-3 remains the largest treatment trial in medical history. Because the FDA field investigator concluded that there was "nothing in the regulations that relates to the interference in a clinical trial by outside influences," no action was taken against Genentech.

Genentech's tough tactics extended into the courtroom as well. In April 1990, after a seventeen-day trial, the company won a patent infringement suit against Genetics Institute, a Boston biotech that had developed a modified version of t-PA. In a highly controversial verdict, a Delaware jury awarded sweeping patent rights to Genentech. In essence, the company was now the exclusive owner of all synthetic variations of t-PA as well as natural t-PA, which included the sequence of amino acids invented by Mother Nature, not Genentech. Critics charged this was a perversion of the original intent of the *Diamond* v. *Chakrabarty* Supreme Court decision that extended patent protection to biological inventions.

This signaled the start of an entirely new and disturbing chapter in pharmaceutical history. In the past, drug companies routinely copied each other's products, merely changing a molecule or two in order to qualify for patents of their own. The Genentech victory meant the company had a monopoly on a natural chemical contained in the blood of every person on the planet, a precedent-setting decision that opened the door to patenting life itself, right down to every base pair on the human genome. This was good news for Genentech's legion of fans on Wall Street but bad news for heart patients. Genentech's aggressive defense of its exclusive rights to t-PA quashed the development of t-PA clones that might have been able to clear arteries faster and cause less bleeding. "Plenty of drug companies were working on such drugs until Genentech abruptly put an end to this research by suing companies that were developing new, improved clot-busters based on t-PA," noted *Forbes*. "Not wanting any threat to its market . . . it killed off potential rivals in the cradle."[13]

Ironically, Genentech officials had good reason to try to torpedo the ISIS-3 trials. When the results were unveiled in March 1991, they dealt t-PA a blow from which some industry insiders doubted it could recover. The ISIS-3 researchers discovered there was no meaningful difference between the three agents and that t-PA didn't save any more lives than Eminase or streptokinase. In fact, there was a slightly higher risk of strokes using t-PA. If U.S. doctors "began to use [streptokinase] routinely," said Oxford's Rory Collins, one of the British ISIS-3 researchers, "it would save more than $100 million each year."[14]

Genentech's spinmeisters immediately went on the offensive, poking holes in the study's design and insisting the Burroughs Wellcome version of t-PA wasn't the same as theirs. This time, though, as with Samson shorn of his hair, their legendary powers of damage control didn't work quite as well and the seemingly magical hold t-PA had on the American cardiology community diminished. Many doctors switched to the lower-priced drugs and Genentech's share of the market fell to 50 percent, a drop analysts laid solely at the doorstep of ISIS-3. The price of its stock plummeted from $64 to $15 a share, and morale at the company sank. Still, retaining half the market in the face of all this negative evidence was amazing, and a tribute to Genentech's sales acumen.

Kirk Raab was in a desperate quandary. T-PA's market share would dwindle to nothing if they didn't do something fast, and the fate of Genentech was in jeopardy. The group of scientists who had been intimately involved with the development of t-PA were frustrated too.

Beyond mere market share, they were confident t-PA was a wonder drug that saved more lives than its rivals when it was given properly. Yet it had never been tested in an accelerated dosage in combination with heparin, which they believed would demonstrate its considerable advantages. Perhaps Genentech should sponsor its own study. But that would be a phenomenal—and extremely expensive—risk. What if their own study demonstrated no benefit? A finding like that would be disastrous and many of Kirk Raab's closest advisers counseled against it. Raab nevertheless felt there was no other way to stem t-PA's continued market erosion. At the very least, the company needed to show doctors that they still supported the drug.

"Raab asked me if they should do a prospective comparison on mortality," recalls Burton Sobel. "I said, 'No, don't do that.' I didn't think it was necessary. ISIS got to be a tremendous circus—it was disgusting. All they wanted to do was make noises about how evil Genentech was, and criticize the excessive cost. To me, though, the data was very clear and I figured the American physician community would come to the right conclusions. But Kirk was very hard-nosed about what the company needed to survive. He decided from a business perspective that he had no choice, so he rolled the dice."

Raab's big gamble was a $55 million study—known by the acronym GUSTO, which stood for Global Utilization of Streptokinase and t-PA for Occluded Coronary Arteries—that was launched in 1990. It was, says one longtime industry observer, "a $55 million defense of a $200 million market share." To ensure there wouldn't be even the *appearance* of impropriety this time around, Genentech distanced itself from GUSTO by putting in place what one researcher called "draconian" ethical controls that established new industry standards. This was not the typical drug trial sponsored by a pharmaceutical company: Genentech wasn't involved in setting up the study, the steering committee overseeing the trial was independent, and researchers were forbidden to own stock or consult with Genentech for at least a year after the results were released. They even asked Victor Marder to serve on the committee overseeing the study. Eric Topol, a TIMI veteran who was now head of cardiology at the Cleveland Clinic Foundation, chaired the study, and Duke University, with its massive cardiac computer databases, was the nerve center and data clearinghouse. Duke was a natural choice to coordinate the massive study. Rob Califf, who headed the study, had been a postdoc at Johns Hopkins with Eric Topol, and Duke Medical School's chancellor, Ralph Snyderman, was a former Genentech executive. In 1987, Snyderman joined Genentech as director of research and development and shepherded t-PA through the FDA before returning to Duke in 1989.

On April 30, 1993, at a press conference in Washington, Eric Topol excitedly announced the GUSTO results, and declared victory for t-PA. "We have to put to rest this battle of the thrombolytics," Topol crowed to a gallery of reporters. "Accelerated t-PA was significantly better." After examining the medical records of 41,000 patients in fifteen countries, researchers discovered that 6.3 percent of patients die when given t-PA in combination with heparin, compared with 7.3 percent of those given streptokinase. The differences were slight—one more life out of every hundred patients—but statistically significant nevertheless, though the incidence of stroke remained higher using t-PA. Even more startling was the discovery that prompt use of t-PA within two hours after the onset of a heart attack slashed death rates even further, to 5.4 percent, which would save an additional 2,000 lives each year in the United States. The results made headlines and Genentech's stock jumped $4.75 a share to $37.50.

However, some scientists who took a hard look at the data didn't share Wall Street's enthusiasm. It wasn't a fair contest, critics maintained, because a hyped-up version of t-PA, turbocharged by the addition of heparin, was compared with a standard dose of streptokinase. And in the real world, patients deny their chest pains are a heart attack, so they delay getting treatment until four hours or more after their symptoms appear. The longer a victim puts off going to the hospital, the more irreversible damage occurs, so the differences in efficacy between the two agents narrow considerably. "The coda to this sonata is the naysayers began to say the differences in mortality are very small and it isn't worth [the difference in price]. But when you're the one laying on that gurney, and you don't know if you're the one in a hundred who'll survive because of t-PA," counters Burton Sobel, "believe me, it matters."

Jubilant Genentech executives faxed news releases with the results to hospitals across the country, while overheated sales reps used hyperboles like "greatest" and fastest" to extol the virtues of t-PA. Genentech also sponsored, either directly or indirectly, several educational forums to spread the word. In October 1993, Alan Ross, one of the GUSTO investigators, was paid $2,500 to conduct an hour-long teleconference with sixty-six hospitals. Eric Topol, who headed the study, also did a teleconference, for which he received $1,000. Genentech did not sponsor these teleconferences directly—the University of Texas Health Science Center did. The center, however, financed the forums with money from a $16,000 grant provided by Genentech (in fairness to Genentech, this is a typical practice in the pharmaceutical industry, where virtually all continuing medical education seminars are sponsored by drugmakers).

However, GUSTO investigators had pledged not to accept consulting fees from Genentech for a year after the results were released. When confronted with this seeming contradiction, Alan Ross huffily told a reporter, "I go and say what I believe, regardless of who is or isn't the sponsor. No company can buy my opinion." Eric Topol, however, insisted he never would have participated if he had known of Genentech's connection with the teleconference. "I've done everything I can to distance myself from this company," said Dr. Topol. "Our good research is clouded by their marketing practices that I think are atrocious."[15]

In the wake of GUSTO, William Ginsburg, a malpractice attorney in southern California, conducted lectures about how physicians can avoid being sued when treating heart attack patients. "Other than price, personally I don't think there's much difference between the two drugs," Ginsburg told doctors, in talks he delivered at five different hospitals near Los Angeles. "But now listen to me as a lawyer," he continued. T-PA may not be any better than its rivals, but the media has been saturated with so much publicity hyping the GUSTO trials that a "public expectation" has been raised that t-PA is better than streptokinase. Consequently, Ginsburg warned, if a doctor fails to use t-PA, the likelihood increases that he or she will be hit with a lawsuit. Grieving relatives think, said Ginsburg, that "if only Dr. So-and-so had not been so concerned with finances" and "had used what this patient really needed . . . Elizabeth would still have a father."[16]

This harsh scenario was pretty jolting to a group of professionals who must live with the constant fear that even their seemingly most innocuous decisions can provoke costly legal action. A few members of the audience were offended by what they perceived as the vaguely threatening tone of Ginsburg's remarks, which they dismissed as a thinly disguised sales pitch—even though Ginsburg wasn't paid directly by Genentech. Because Genentech wrote a check to each of the hospitals for a "continuing education" class, which included Ginsburg's fee, technically the attorney was paid by the hospital—not Genentech. Drug companies do sponsor educational classes at hospitals (though Genentech later halted these particular seminars) and Ginsburg says that his opinions were his own and were not influenced by Genentech. However, implying doctors might get sued for malpractice if they don't use a particular product struck some as a highly offensive tactic.

At least Representative John Dingell, chairman of the House Energy and Commerce Committee, thought so. In response to several complaints from doctors about Ginsburg's lectures, Dingell instigated a congressional probe of Genentech in 1994, focusing on the GUSTO trials and on the company's marketing practices.[17] Dingell's investigation was cut short by the November 1994 elections; the decisive Republican victory in both houses forced him to relinquish the chairmanship of his committee. Dingell's staffers' didn't find any improprieties in the conduct of GUSTO. But they found plenty to squawk about concerning Genentech's promotion of the GUSTO results, citing evidence that "Genentech's promotional activities involving t-PA . . . may have violated various provisions of the Federal Food, Drug, and Cosmetic Act." Dingell asked the FDA to step in.

The FDA had sent sharply worded warning letters to Genentech about its brazen marketing violations every year since 1989. Genentech officials either shrugged them off or placed the blame on individual salespeople by claiming the misdeeds were the work of isolated employees acting on their own. It became increasingly difficult to blame the consistent pattern of abuses on a few overzealous renegades, however. "Despite several communications with your firm regarding the advertising and promotion of your product Activase," a 1993 FDA memo testily noted, "Genentech and its employees have elected to willfully and flagrantly disregard the law and its applicable regulations." Finally, the agency, at Dingell's urging, initiated a full-scale investigation. On September 12, 1994, the FDA sent a letter to Genentech outlining its belief "that Genentech is engaged . . . in a continuing pattern of violative behavior."

At the same time, the agency requested a voluminous number of internal documents related to suspected abuses in the promotion of its three top-selling drugs, Activase (t-PA), Protropin, and Pulmozyme, a cystic fibrosis medication. Genentech made loud noises that it was "cooperating" with the agency's request, and sent over 120 boxes of materials. None of them were indexed or labeled, however. Since the FDA, which had been gutted during the antiregulatory 1980s, was notoriously short-handed, many months would pass before the staff could wade through all those documents. So much for "cooperation." (The woefully outflanked FDA has about forty staffers to police the advertising and promotional activities of the entire pharmaceutical and medical devices industries; as of this writing, the FDA had not concluded its investigation.)

A month before, on August 4, 1994, a federal grand jury in Minneapolis returned a fifty-one-count indictment of conspiracy and fraud against three executives of Caremark International, a home-health-care company, and Edmon R. Jennings, Genentech's top sales executive, for paying more than $1.1 million in kickbacks to Dr. David R. Brown, a Minneapolis physician, to induce him to prescribe Genentech's Protropin, which is distributed by Caremark. The indictments were the result of a three-year investigation of Caremark launched by the Justice Department, and assisted by the FBI and the Department of Health and Human Services' Office of the Inspector General. Government affidavits revealed the doctor treated over 350 patients, including some Medicaid patients, and racked up annual Protropin sales of between $3 million and $4 million. The indictment charged that kickbacks were paid under the guise of over half a million dollars in research grants, more than $100,000 for marketing and consulting fees, and another $224,000 for overhead expenses, such as office rents and nurses' salaries.*

All of this, of course, could be chalked up to being a fiercely aggressive little guy in a cutthroat industry. "We're not Merck," sniffs Elliott

*In June 1995, Caremark pled guilty to mail fraud in connection with its involvement in kickback schemes, and agreed to pay $161 million in fines and penalties to the United States. In October 1995, Dr. David Brown was convicted of two counts of receiving kickbacks. Charges against the Caremark executives and Edmon Jennings were dismissed because there was insufficient evidence they "acted willfully."

Grossbard. "When you are winning the competitive battles, as we have, you can't expect everybody to be happy about it," agreed Richard Brewer, Genentech's head of marketing. "Moaning and groaning is going to happen. It just gets blown out of proportion."[18] And Paul Leyland, Genentech's public relations director, insists that their sales force has maintained the highest ethical standards since he joined the company.

But what about the human casualties of this sales blitz? "These practices which place profits first may ultimately jeopardize patient safety," observed Representative Ron Wyden during an October 12, 1994, congressional hearing probing marketing abuses in the drug industry, "by unnecessarily exposing persons to potent drugs, or by denying patients more appropriate alternative care." In other words, what happens when a company like Genentech has so successfully elbowed aside the competition that a hospital pharmacy stocks only their drug?

The family of Elijio Uresti, Jr., says he found out the answer the hard way—and that it nearly cost him his life. In December 1991, the fifty-seven-year-old high school principal and father of four was suddenly stricken with such sharp, stabbing pains across his chest that he could barely breathe. Nearly seven hours later, when Uresti arrived in the emergency room of the hospital near his home in San Diego, Texas, a rural hamlet about fifty miles west of Corpus Christi, doctors immediately gave him an infusion of t-PA. It was as if a bomb had been detonated in his brain, blowing out all the circuits. Uresti started vomiting, and the monitors in the ER went berserk, which were danger signals that he was in the throes of a catastrophic brain hemorrhage. Doctors worked feverishly to save Uresti's life, but the bleeding gushed out of control. Uresti sank into a deep coma, lasting more than a month. When he finally regained consciousness, he had the mind of a four-year-old, and now requires round-the-clock care.

According to a lawsuit filed by his wife, in their haste, emergency room physicians had overlooked one crucial factor that Uresti's family believes was responsible for leaving him severely disabled: Uresti was acutely hypertensive, with blood pressure of 210/120. Anyone with blood pressure over 180/110 had been excluded from the t-PA clinical trials because of its risks for acutely hypertensive patients. However, even though streptokinase is much less likely than t-PA to cause strokes in individuals with high blood pressure, there was no other clot-busting agent in the hospital pharmacy. According to a lawsuit filed by Uresti's wife, Irma, a Genentech salesman had persuaded the hospital to stock t-PA to the exclusion of other thrombolytic agents by extravagantly extolling the medication's advantages and minimizing hazards.[19] Genentech salespeople "hustle the use of t-PA in acute-care facilities but they fail to adequately warn of the risks," says Randall Jackson, the Uresti family's attorney. "Then along comes Elijio Uresti with his first MI who is acutely hypertensive and these doctors' knee-jerk reaction is to hit him up with t-PA." Genentech has denied the family's claims and the lawsuit is proceeding.

So how good is t-PA? Is it heart Drano? Or is all the hoopla just marketing hype? Picking through the mountains of conflicting data, Charles Hennekens comes closest to knowing the answer. Hennekens—"Charlie" to just about everyone—is part of a breed that's nearing extinction—the independent academic investigator. The genial Hennekens, with his shock of white hair, cobalt-blue eyes, and disarming smile, acts more like a high school athletic coach than one of the head honchos at the Harvard Medical School and the majordomo of vast, trendsetting studies that have altered medical practices. Hennekens's landmark Physicians' Health Study, for example, revealed aspirin can reduce the risk of heart attack, elevating the lowly tablet to the status of a potent heart disease fighter. Because of this study, millions of middle-aged Americans consume baby aspirins each day, and 70 percent of heart attack patients are now given aspirin, which saves about 5,000 lives a year.

Hennekens himself still seems astonished that a mathematics whiz kid from Brooklyn who dreamed of being a baseball player—he nearly signed a contract with the Minnesota Twins—could have such a successful fallback career. His nice-guy persona masks an iron will that endowed him with a stubbornly independent streak that prompted him to adopt unpopular positions—some of which have put him at odds with his boss, Eugene Braunwald. Hennekens is beholden to no one, except the data, and he painstakingly weaves the threads of facts into a comprehensible tapestry like Rapunzel spinning flax into gold.

So which is better, streptokinase or t-PA? After all, the results of the original TIMI-I study, which established t-PA as "penicillin for the heart," were never duplicated—even though the same researchers conducted subsequent studies. Were the findings of TIMI-I just a statistical fluke? Even GUSTO concluded the overall difference in mortality between streptokinase and t-PA is less than 0.7 percent; statisticians dub this "a dead man's margin" because it's not considered statistically significant. So how is t-PA superior? Advocates on either side of the debate "look for every little nuance to support their case—they become more like lawyers than scientists," Hennekens observes one sunny summer afternoon, relaxing with his feet up on the desk at the end of a long day. His spacious office, which is crammed with sports mementos and squash trophies—he was once nationally ranked—is in a suite of offices over a video store on a quiet tree-lined street in Boston. The best way, indeed the only way, to settle this "is to retreat to the data," he says, ticking off the numbers with the ease of an insurance actuary.

"GUSTO randomized patients an average of 2.8 hours after their onset of symptoms," he continues. "Less than ten years ago, in the prethrombolytic era, these early-treated patients had a mortality rate of about 13.5 percent after 35 days. Which is a huge mortality rate. So let's give them all aspirin. Then we reduce their death rate by 23 percent. So now, instead of 13.2 percent, it's more like 10.3 percent. Now what? Let's give all these patients not just aspirin but streptokinase. That reduces mortality by 30 percent, to about 7.2 percent. Plus, streptokinase has the desirable property of one less disabling stroke per thousand treated patients. Now GUSTO is saying we should give them all accelerated t-PA. Then the mortality rate drops to 6.3 percent but you've increased the disabling strokes by two per thousand." Cost-wise, Hennekens goes on, "if you gave everybody t-PA instead of SK, it costs about $6,000 more to save a life—and that figure doesn't include the care of the excess number of disabling strokes. So if t-PA gives you a little better mortality when given earlier, that must be weighed against the sevenfold increase in cost and the clearly higher risk of stroke and cerebral hemorrhage, which is a special problem."

Which thrombolytic would Hennekens, whose father died of a heart attack when he was fifty-six, take? "I'd get myself to the hospital fast instead of sitting around wondering if I was having a gas attack," he says. "Getting treatment—any treatment, even aspirin—before damage is done to the heart is the real key."

There's a much larger issue, Hennekens insists, that's raised by the endless t-PA debate: ensuring that academia and industry are completely independent so the data that emerge don't even have the appearance of possible bias. However, in an era when nearly every prominent scientist is tethered to numerous corporations, that's going to be tough. "Increasingly, we're not going to be able to rely on federal funding to support important scientific research. But if we rely on industry funding, we're going to have to have a standard that deals with not just the absence of any real conflicts, but the absence of apparent, *even perceived,* conflicts," emphasizes Hennekens, his eyes flashing with a sudden intensity. "We have to establish that standard and get it to work. There is no other way."

CHAPTER 11

PIERCING THE VEIL

It took a Pulitzer Prize–winning investigative journalist, John Crewd-son, who was backed by the considerable resources of the *Chicago Tribune*, to pierce the veil of secrecy that shrouded what actually happened in Robert Gallo's lab throughout the winter of 1983. In 1987, Crewdson, who reported a wide array of stories ranging from Watergate and corruption among U.S. immigration officials to sexual abuse of children, was assigned by the *Tribune* to cover AIDS. Crewdson wasn't particularly happy with his new assignment—he knew nothing about medicine or AIDS and had no interest in changing that state of affairs. He wanted to go to Central America, which was riven by civil war. He dutifully swung into action, though, reading everything about AIDS he could get his hands on, meeting with federal officials, and nibbling around the edges of the AIDS research community to find any unreported stories.

In January 1988, he attended a conference on AIDS convened in London by the World Health Organization. There, people urged him to check out the patent suit settlement. He flew on to Paris to investigate their allegations, but Montagnier refused to meet with him; the French virologist had signed a confidentiality agreement and he intended to stick by it. Besides, the Nobel committee wasn't happy with unseemly disputes that tarred science, so Montagnier wisely refrained from stirring up any more controversies.

In clandestine meetings at nearby bistros, though, a couple of the junior researchers at the Pasteur, who feared losing their jobs if anyone knew they violated their oath of secrecy, vented their fury into the wee hours of the morning while the taciturn Crewdson quietly jotted notes. Unfortunately, a few disgruntled Young Turks weren't enough to substantiate the serious accusations they were making—that Robert

Gallo had stolen the French's AIDS virus, and the Americans had poached their patent rights. Crewdson spent the next month criss-crossing Europe, interviewing people in Germany, Sweden, Finland, France, and England, accumulating bits of tantalizing information from people who seemed quite sincere, and vainly trying to piece them together into a comprehensible whole.

It wasn't until Crewdson went on to New York City to meet with one of the Pasteur Institute's attorneys, James Swire, that he finally hit pay dirt. They were an incongruous pair—the bearded and burly Berkeley-bred Crewdson, and Swire, lanky and genial with the polished, under-stated style of a moneyed Brahmin. Swire was the type of source reporters dream about, the person who opens the door onto a corridor that leads to other corridors—and saves the reporter from spending fruit-less hours chasing down promising leads that end in one blind alley after another. He certainly had an agenda—many whistle-blowers do—but he was also genuinely interested in uncovering the truth. Swire shared with Crewdson the thousands of pages of documents he had obtained from the NIH through the Freedom of Information Act.

What Swire had was a veritable gold mine of information. Crewd-son spent the next month in the bowels of the Chrysler Building, where Swire's law firm was ensconced, poring through boxes of lab notes, correspondence, and memorandums. A picture slowly began to emerge, especially from the seemingly arcane lab notes. Crewdson instinctively knew that deciphering what was in those "hieroglyphics" would ultimately answer the question of who actually discovered the AIDS virus. Like a bloodhound sniffing the air, Crewdson nostrils were filled with the scent of scandal. High-level cover-ups, possible fraud perpetrated by government officials, frightened sources who insist on anonymity—suddenly, this had all the earmarks of the kind of story the persistent and methodical journalist excelled at doing. He was on his way.[1]

In November 1989, the *Chicago Tribune* published "The Great AIDS Quest," John Crewdson's 55,000-word exposé on Robert Gallo. It was a bombshell, a monumental work of journalism that observers say didn't earn Crewdson a rare second Pulitzer only because he never exposed a "smoking gun"—conclusive proof that Gallo's lab had stolen the French virus. He came tantalizingly close, however, and presented an avalanche of painstakingly documented—but ultimately circumstantial—evidence that strongly suggested Gallo's lab had isolated their version of HIV from cultures sent by Luc Montagnier's group at the Pasteur Institute. What he brought out quite clearly, though, was the reason *why* the French upstarts managed to beat out the more experienced and far better-funded Americans. Gallo was so obsessed with finding another leukemia virus that was part of the HTLV family that he missed obvious clues as to the virus's real identity and neglected to perform the appropriate tests—an embarrassing oversight that would banish a first-year graduate student to scientific Siberia.

"Gallo and his assistants spent the better part of 1983 surrounded by the AIDS virus but unable to see it—a pack of duffers searching for a lost ball in the high weeds, blinded by an improperly calibrated test and their mistaken belief that the AIDS virus *must* resemble Gallo's leukemia-causing retrovirus," Crewdson later wrote.[2] Crewdson believed that once Gallo realized his mistake, he used the French virus in a frantic scramble to catch up and make up for lost time. Crewdson's story sent shock waves throughout the AIDS research community, which reverberated through the halls of Congress and the upper echelons of the NIH.

"Have you seen this yet?" asked Robert Lanman, the NIH's attorney, holding up Crewdson's article to Suzanne Hadley, who was then the acting director of the NIH's Office of Scientific Integrity (OSI). Hadley's eyes grew big as saucers as she scanned the story. "Why didn't somebody let me know about this sooner?" she wondered aloud. After all, policing science was her job.

The OSI had been created earlier that year, in March 1989, to mollify members of Congress: a rash of scandals had rocked the scientific community, making it painfully clear science's much vaunted self-correcting mechanisms weren't working. Originally, each institute at the NIH had its own misconduct policy officer, who handled that Institute's investigations. And science took great pride in policing itself; researchers chafed at outside intrusions and insisted their system of internal checks was enough to catch any charlatans. Peer review panels scrutinized grant applications before any money was awarded. Editors of scientific journals sent articles submitted for publication to "referees," other experts in the field, to determine the significance and validity of the findings. Once articles were published, researchers attempted to replicate their results to double-check their accuracy.

Incidents of sloppy science, misconduct, plagiarism, manipulation or faking of data, and outright criminal behavior were now regularly front-page news, and congressional probes by Representatives John Dingell and Ted Weiss revealed that universities were lax about punishing miscreants. "Universities have a vested interest in not finding anyone guilty of fraud," explains Robert Bell, author of *Impure Science*. "Because if they do, they may have to return the delinquent researcher's grants. When someone blows the whistle, universities set up investigatory panels, which are almost inevitably kangaroo courts that cover up abuses." The OSI was created because science's internal policy had failed. "HHS realized if it didn't fix the system," recalls Dr. Hadley, "it was going to be fixed by Congress, which was not too pleased with the NIH's performance."

Suzanne Hadley was in the midst of investigating perhaps the most notorious of these cases, what became known as the David Baltimore case, which had dragged on for several years. In 1986, Margot O'Toole was a postdoctoral fellow in the MIT laboratory of Thereza Imanishi-Kari. That year, Imanishi-Kari co-authored with MIT's David Baltimore a scientific paper published in the journal *Cell*. The article purported to show that antibodies expressed by one mouse could mimic those of another mouse. O'Toole accidentally discovered laboratory notes and noticed serious discrepancies. "It was obvious from these records that the experiment had not yielded the published results," O'Toole says. O'Toole voiced her concerns to Imanishi-Kari and later reported her suspicions to Baltimore and MIT officials. Baltimore dismissed her claims, calling O'Toole a "discontented" postdoctoral fellow. Suddenly, O'Toole became a pariah. She lost her position and could not find another one. Finally, she took a job answering phones for her brother's moving company.

University investigators at MIT, where Imanishi-Kari had her laboratory, and, initially, at the NIH performed little more than a perfunctory probe of O'Toole's charges. (Imanishi-Kari moved to Tufts University in 1987.) As *The New York Times* wrote in a scathing editorial: "The initial investigations of Dr. O'Toole's complaints smacked of an old boy network drawing up the wagons to protect scientific reputations." The facts began to emerge only when the case fell under the noses of scientists Walter Stewart and Ned Feder, the NIH's self-appointed "science cops," and the House Subcommittee on Oversight and Investigations, headed by Representative John Dingell. It was David Baltimore's stubborn refusal to admit the possibility that a colleague committed fraud in a scientific paper he co-authored, however, that escalated this transgression into what was dubbed a "scientific Watergate." He even orchestrated a letter-writing campaign among his colleagues to stop Dingell's inquiry.

Hadley had been at the center of this maelstrom, patiently digging behind the scenes. When Robert Lanman showed her Crewdson's exposé on Gallo, they were on a flight back to Washington, after a discouraging meeting in Boston with attorneys for Dr. Imanishi-Kari and Dr. Baltimore. "We were getting nowhere trying to get her to cooperate with us," recalls Hadley. "We had gone to Boston to have a very frank discussion with her attorneys." Hadley doubted the NIH's candor did any good—in all likelihood, the case would drag on for many more months.[3]*

And now the nasty rumors that had circulated for years about Robert Gallo were wending their way into print, a disheartening development to those who still believed scientists were the lab-coated guardians of truth. The next morning, Hadley contacted William Raub. He already knew all about the *Tribune* story, he told Hadley, but he wanted to give the National Cancer Institute a chance to clean its own house. Over the next several weeks, there was a series of meetings during which NCI officials tried to respond to the principal points raised in Crewdson's story. In the meantime, Representative John Dingell fired off a letter to Raub asking whether he planned to investigate the disturbing charges raised by the *Tribune*. Raub informed the lawmaker he "recognized the need for an inquiry" and that one was getting underway.

Suzanne Hadley didn't think the NCI would do a thorough probe of its star scientist, however. As the NCI reports trickled in, her belief

---

*The Baltimore case went on for another ten years. In 1991, the Federal Office of Scientific Integrity, based on evidence derived from a Secret Service forensic analysis of her lab notes, determined that Dr. Imanishi-Kari *had* fabricated the data in her 1986 article. However, an appeals panel reversed that decision in 1996, and concluded that the Secret Service's evidence was based on erroneous assumptions and that there could well be innocent explanations for the inconsistencies they identified. But opinion remains sharply divided as to whether Dr. Imanishi-Kari was an innocent victim or the government simply failed to present a persuasive case.

was confirmed. She badgered Dr. Raub to turn the matter over to the OSI, which had the experience and the mandate to conduct such investigations. In February 1990, Raub relented. Hadley then notified Gallo that the OSI was opening an inquiry into the events that occurred in the Laboratory of Tumor Cell Biology (LTCB). Little did Hadley know that this would turn the next several years of her life into a Kafkaesque nightmare that nearly derailed her own career.

On the surface, Suzanne Hadley was an unlikely candidate to do battle with the biggest names in science. Tiny and soft-spoken, with a halo of short blond hair, translucent skin, and large eyes, Hadley resembles a fragile porcelain doll, but her delicate demeanor masks a constitution of titanium. Born dirt poor in a small town in West Virginia, she supported herself and her husband working as a secretary while attending college. After a brief stint as a social worker, she earned a Ph.D. in experimental social psychology at the University of Massachusetts and arrived at the National Institute of Mental Health in 1978 as a postdoctoral fellow. She quickly distinguished herself as an outstanding science administrator and shot up the ranks to deputy division director before being appointed the NIMH's misconduct officer in 1987. When the OSI was formed, the hardworking Hadley, who regularly put in twelve- to fourteen-hour days, was a natural choice to help launch the new department. She would need that internal fortitude to weather the storms that followed.

Robert Gallo proved far more intransigent than Thereza Imanishi-Kari. And what Hadley didn't know then was that the OSI's investigation into whether Gallo's lab stole the French virus was doomed from the start, stymied by the daunting complexity of the science and by the blind loyalty of many of Gallo's minions at the NCI. "We felt we should conduct this investigation the way we would for any other scientist by tape-recording the interviews and obtaining the original laboratory notebooks," recalls Dr. Hadley. "But these simple and routine things were appalling to the NCI and to Gallo, and they fought them. Their attitude was: 'This was all dealt with during the formal settlement [in 1987], so why stir it up again?'"

According to Hadley, Gallo stonewalled repeated requests for his original laboratory notebooks, which contained records of experiments conducted in late 1983 and early 1984, when researchers on both sides of the Atlantic were feverishly racing to identify the deadly

AIDS pathogen. "The lab notebooks were key to our investigation but Gallo dragged this out and kept putting us off," Hadley recalls. "First, we'd hear that Gallo was traveling and he took this material with him, which was highly unusual. Then, when Gallo was out of town, his underlings locked the laboratory and refused to let anyone in to get the notebooks"—even though, since he was a federal employee, Gallo's notebooks were government property. OSI investigators ultimately obtained more than sixty lab notebooks, and spent dozens of hours interviewing Gallo and his top aides, in an effort to expose what transpired during that time.

Under the wilting federal scrutiny and the unflattering media attention it generated, a pall settled over the lab. "After Crewdson's article," says one former LTCB scientist, "things got very bad in the lab. Everyone was being paid to sit around." Gallo's cooperation, however, was little more than perfunctory. "The way Gallo dealt with our requests was very smart," recalls Hadley. "If we asked him about HTLV-3, he'd put together a package of material on HTLV-3, including a summary and copies of notebook pages. But this distracted attention from the notebook pages that weren't copied. But how was one going to know them? What were we going to do? Search his lab? But I now understand that the practice of letting Bob prepare these packages of material misled us from what was really important." Gallo's attorney calls Hadley's contentions "utter nonsense. Any documents they wanted, they got. . . . There's never been any allegation that they didn't have all the documents they wanted."

In a highly unusual move—but perhaps not a surprising one given Gallo's status and the millions of dollars at stake—the NIH asked the National Academy of Sciences to appoint a blue-ribbon panel of scientists to oversee the OSI's inquiry. Chairing what became known as the Richards Committee was Yale University biochemist Frederic Richards, who was known among his colleagues as exceptionally ethical. Built like a bulldog, with the tenacity to match, Richards, with his thick head of snow-white hair and the rugged, square-jawed good looks of an outdoorsman, was a scientist of the old school. He and his fellow panelists were serious about their duties because the charges were very grave. "There's no doubt from the start that we were just window dressing to validate when the report came down that the right data and the right conclusions were drawn," says Dr. Richards. If this was the plan of the NIH officials, what they hadn't factored into their calculations was that the Richards Committee had no intention of simply rubber stamping the OSI's findings—and they were an unanticipated wild card in this investigation.

By June 1990, disturbed by what Dr. Hadley had uncovered, the members of the Richards Committee began clamoring for the appointment of an independent counsel; all their legal advice shouldn't be coming solely from the NIH, which they believed had a vested interest in concealing the truth. And during committee meetings held at the NIH, panelists started peppering Dr. Hadley with questions about the patents, which they instinctively recognized were at the crux of this controversy. "Patents and possible false statements are matters of potential criminal conduct and we don't do criminal investigations," Suzanne Hadley told them during her reports to the committee. "Several committee members came into this exercise angry," Hadley recalls. "They truly believed wrongs had been done. They challenged us from the very beginning about the adequacy of the NIH response. Because I was trying to play it by the book, I kept insisting on a tempered middle-of-the-road response."

Hadley herself certainly had growing suspicions that money, not just Nobel Prizes, was at the heart of the Gallo affair, but she wanted to stick to the OSI's mandate, which was to probe malfeasance in the lab. "Our investigation prematurely focused on a single paper, which was almost necessary to avoid being overwhelmed," explains Dr. Hadley. In retrospect, she realizes, "ultimately, it was a misguided effort because it narrowed [the investigation] down into obscurity and triviality while trees were falling all around. Had I examined the patents more carefully sooner, I would have comprehended the relationships between the papers and the claimed discoveries and the patents."

Despite their honest endeavors, Hadley's and Richards's panel were stumbling around in the dark. They had no idea, really, what they were looking for and even if they had, they didn't have the legal clout to compel a recalcitrant Gallo or the NIH to produce information that could jeopardize the United States' lucrative patent. Compounding these inherent problems was an almost palpable antagonism toward the OSI on the part of Suzanne Hadley's new boss, Bernadine Healy, who was confirmed as the NIH director in April 1991.

The directorship of the NIH had been vacant throughout most of the Bush administration after the resignation of James Wyngaarden in July 1989, who was forced out in part because he was not an abortion foe. Reputable scientists were reluctant to submit to the moral litmus test imposed by the conservative Bush White House, which banned scientific experiments using tissue from aborted fetuses. The intensely ambitious Bernadine Healy, a cardiologist who headed the Research Institute of the Cleveland Clinic Foundation, accepted the job no one else wanted. And President Bush reaped a lot of favorable publicity for appointing the NIH's first woman director. Privately, though, Healy confided to friends that it was only when they couldn't get a man that they were willing to hire a woman to do their dirty work.

Healy was sensitized to the issue of scientific integrity and conflict of interest through her involvement with the original TIMI trials of t-PA. Healy was one of the cardiologists who were roundly chastised for owning Genentech stock, which prompted her to institute strict ethical guidelines when she conducted a later study of another drug. According to Suzanne Hadley, however, Healy "hated the OSI. She had no use for us at all."

Some believe her feelings stemmed from a 1990 misconduct investigation Suzanne Hadley did of a scientist accused of falsifying a grant application at the Cleveland Clinic Foundation, while Healy was its research director and Healy's husband, Dr. Floyd P. Loop, was the clinic's CEO. An internal inquiry of the researcher, which was chaired by Healy, cleared the researcher of any intentional wrongdoing. Dr. Healy excused the scientist's overinflated portrayal of the status of his research as "anticipatory writing," rather than outright fraud. A subsequent OSI probe by Suzanne Hadley concluded he *had* stepped over the line; her report was sharply critical of Healy as well, whom she felt had glossed over the biochemist's false statements and ignored incriminating evidence. (Healy's nagging doubts about the flaws in the initial inquiry did prompt her to launch a second probe, which resulted in the termination of the disputed grant).

According to Hadley, from virtually the moment Dr. Healy moved into her office in Bethesda, she seemed hell-bent on dismantling the OSI. Her feelings reflected the widespread suspicion and animosity within the scientific community toward the office; the OSI's secretive information-gathering methods were viewed as little more than star-chamber proceedings where the accused were denied the due process of law. "The OSI did not have effective leadership for two years," Dr. Healy explained in a television interview. "I walked in and in the first few months I saw a series of horrendous management failures, sloppy performance, failure to abide by their own guidelines, a rogue satellite office that was created that had no supervisor, no attention to confidentiality . . . the sloppiness was appalling."[4]

The underlying tensions between Dr. Healy and the OSI that had roiled beneath the surface for weeks bubbled over when the OSI's draft report of the Gallo probe was finally ready in May 1991. Fred Richards, frustrated by an endless round of bureaucratic delays in an investigation that had now gone on for over a year, wanted first crack at the proposed report. There was a serious problem, however, with press leaks from the committee to reporter John Crewdson. "We'd meet," Fred Richards admits, "and before we got home, all the information would be transferred to Crewdson." So when Joseph Onek, Robert Gallo's attorney, got wind of this situation, he threatened to complain to Bernadine Healy. It was one thing for the Richards Committee to see an early draft of this report before Gallo had a chance to review it. It was quite another to have it plastered all over the *Chicago Tribune*.

According to Suzanne Hadley, an irate Bernadine Healy summoned Hadley, William Raub, and Robert Lanman to her office for what quickly evolved into an acrimonious meeting. "You are to have nothing more to do with this case and nothing more to do with the OSI," she curtly informed Raub. Then she leveled her sights on Hadley. "Call Fred Richards and cancel the committee meeting," she told Hadley. Raub told Hadley he was going to share the report with Healy. But Hadley resisted. The OSI was designed as an independent body and the NIH director wasn't supposed to be privy to the results of ongoing investigations. But Raub intervened, and insisted on giving Healy the report.

The next morning, Hadley says, Healy called her and ordered her to rewrite the report and delete all the "editorializing." "When I got off the phone with her I was speechless," recalls Hadley. "The main elements of the report were about falsifications in one of the original *Science* papers. But what got Bernadine were the general comments we made about Gallo as a lab chief, that his actions warranted significant censure."

Hadley and Jules Hallum, a former Oregon Health Sciences University virologist who had recently come on board as director of the OSI, agreed that obeying Healy's imperious command to revise the report would violate the independence of the OSI. They decided to commit to paper their concerns and write separate memos to Dr. Healy. They never got a chance, however. In the midst of this, Robert Lanman showed up at Hadley's office early one morning, dispatched by Healy to retrieve Hadley's telephone records. "She thinks you're talking too much to Margot O'Toole [the whistle-blower in the Baltimore case]," he explained. "He came into my office hanging his head—I could tell he didn't want to do this," recalls Hadley, who was still in charge of the Baltimore case, as well as the Gallo investigation. "I told Jules, who was furious. In his memo, he described it as a fishing expedition that was linked to her order to rewrite the report."

Hallum angrily defended his deputy. In a sharply worded confidential memo dated June 10, Hallum informed Healy that rewriting the Gallo report would not only "weaken the force of the findings" but be seen—and understandably so—as a "whitewash." What disturbed him most, though, was Healy's seizure of Hadley's telephone records. "I have given Dr. Hadley my complete trust in [the Baltimore] case," Hallum wrote, "and in my view that trust has been totally justified."[5] Healy finally backed down. As she later noted in a letter to the *Chicago Tribune*, "I did ask [Hadley] to revise the amateurish and poorly written report for style and structure, but when she complained that revision would change the meaning, I withdrew my request immediately."

The hostilities continued to escalate between the two women. Shortly after, Hadley discovered that a panel member advising the Baltimore case investigation had once written a positive letter of recommendation for Thereza Imanishi-Kari. When Hadley suggested that the scientist should recuse herself because of possible conflicts of interest, the NIH director went ballistic. Jules Hallum delivered the bad news to Hadley. "Dr. Healy has sent me to rein you in," Hallum told her, and confiscated her OSI files. "You are not to make any more decisions on these cases." The diminutive Hadley, completely shaken by this turn of events, was no match for the formidable NIH chief. Convinced Healy was out to destroy her and her work, Hadley felt she had no choice but to resign. "Jules," she told her boss, "I'm marked. I'm dead. I'm on her list."

John Dingell, as the self-appointed watchdog of scientific ethics, was enraged by Healy's "shabby" treatment of Hadley, and intervened on her behalf. On August 1, he summoned the embattled NIH director to Capitol Hill to explain herself. "These events raise again the question of whether NIH has the institutional will to investigate . . . when issues of misconduct arise," Dingell said in his opening remarks. In a widely publicized showdown, Dingell grilled Healy, intimating that her actions toward the OSI were sparked by a personal vendetta against Hadley. These feelings were strongly bipartisan. Republican Representative Norman F. Lent referred to Healy's behavior as "bizarre." Healy dismissed Dingell's charges as "preposterous," and stoutly maintained her actions "were based on careful and deliberate judgment" and were provoked by her grave concerns about the "due process, confidentiality, fairness, and objectivity" of the OSI. In the postmortems that followed, observers agreed Healy had steamrollered over the normally combative congressman, in one of the few confrontations he ever lost. It was truly a Pyrrhic victory, though—Healy may have won the battle but there was no doubt who would ultimately win the war—and her performance that day would haunt her tenure at the NIH. In Dingell, she had created an implacable foe who wouldn't hesitate to use his power—which was immense—to undermine her authority.

Less than two weeks after Healy's acrimonious confrontation with Dingell, an internal NIH memo was leaked to the press, which further undermined the government's staunch defense of its star scientist. The draft report was based upon the findings of an eighteen-month investigation into alleged improprieties in Robert Gallo's laboratory during the time when he developed the AIDS antibody test. The document reportedly outlined numerous instances where Gallo made "untrue and misleading statements" in sworn statements to support the patent application filed by NIH lawyers on his behalf, though it stopped short of asserting that he deliberately committed perjury. Stunned NIH officials moved quickly to control the damage. "This is based on speculation on the outcome of an ongoing NIH investigation," John Diggs, NIH deputy director for extramural research told *The Washington Post*. Lawyers for Gallo and Popovic said the memo's conclusions were flawed and the report contained numerous inaccuracies. But unfavorable perceptions about Gallo's conduct were crystallizing within the scientific community.[6]

Over the summer of 1991, Fred Richards, in a display of the dogged persistence that had made him a top scientist, finally got his wish. Along with the seven other members of his committee, he was escorted to a small conference room hidden in the basement of one of the NIH office buildings, where the group was allowed to read the draft OSI report. "This was a secret meeting," Dr. Richards recalls, to prevent any of the damaging press leaks that were endemic to Washington. "We weren't allowed to take in our briefcases or notebooks and there was no access that wasn't guarded by security guards. We spent about four or five hours reading the OSI report. Then Dr. Healy came in and we had a discussion with her that lasted about an hour."

Despite these draconian precautions, portions of the OSI draft report subsequently appeared in the *Chicago Tribune*. "The discussions we had were all known to Crewdson," says Richards, shaking his head in a mixture of admiration and disbelief. For most of the public, this was merely the latest skirmish in an arcane hairsplitting match. For the cognoscenti, however, who understood the implications, the draft OSI report was a watershed: it contained what appeared to be the first real hard evidence that Robert Gallo had lied.

For years, Gallo had indignantly dismissed charges that his lab had purloined the French virus as ludicrous since they were unable to grow the samples of AIDS virus Montagnier had sent them. How can you steal something you can't incubate in cell cultures? he would argue again and again. The OSI report directly contradicted this: Mikulas "Mika" Popovic, Gallo's assistant, *had* been able to grow the French virus. An analysis of Popovic's crucial lab notebooks from the fall of 1983—which Suzanne Hadley had to personally remove from the LTCB—indicated there were notes from October 1983 about experiments with the French virus in live cell lines. And what was even more incriminating is that Popovic willingly acknowledged the Pasteur's contribution when he wrote up the original *Science* paper reporting his findings. Gallo edited out references to Montagnier's virus in early drafts of the paper, and wrote in the margins, "Mika you are crazy," and "I just don't believe it. You are absolutely incredible."

In a bizarre twist to a story that already had enough labyrinthine turns to fill a John le Carré spy novel, Popovic, a Czechoslovakian refugee who was accustomed to dealing with tyrannical bosses, said he sent a copy of the original draft to his sister in Prague for safekeeping. In a lengthy memo to Suzanne Hadley described in the OSI draft report, Popovic wrote that he had done this to establish his own innocence in the event questions arose—as they now had. "Sometime in the future," he explained, "[I thought] I might need them as evidence to prove that I gave fair credit . . . to the Pasteur scientists."[7]

But, as Congressional investigators later noted, a veritable avalanche of other evidence was accumulating that pointed to only one thing—that Gallo's group had used the French virus to develop their AIDS-antibody test, and that American officials had covered up evidence of this to protect their patent. In the fall of 1991, Dingell's subcommittee received a damaging report from scientists at Roche Molecular Systems, a subsidiary of the giant Swiss drugmaker Hoffmann-La Roche. OSI investigators had asked the researchers to do a genetic analysis of virus samples from the LTCB and the Pasteur lab. Roche scientists discovered the American and French viruses were identical, and the chance they had come from different individuals was "essentially impossible."[8]

"Jules Hallum rightly discerned that those reports would soon be in the media," Hadley remembers. "So he wrote a press release saying that Gallo had all these other [viral] isolates, so he had no need to steal the French virus." Hallum apparently believed that this was the case, but Hadley, who was now unofficially assisting Dingell's committee, did not. "The myth that Gallo had other isolates that were useful for making the blood test at the time he was growing LAV, which implies he had no motive to misappropriate the French virus, is a big lie," Hadley told reporters.[9]

Hadley's honesty didn't win any kudos from her employer, the NIH. She was accused of disclosing confidential information to the media and became the target of an FBI inquiry, after Bernadine Healy lodged a complaint about Hadley's alleged "unauthorized" removal of investigative files from the NIH. In her trademark theatrical style, Dr. Healy wrote to the FBI that "the future of American biomedical and behavioral research . . . [is] directly at risk if the public and scientific trust in our ability to conduct fair investigations is violated."[10] Justice Department officials, however, unconvinced that the fate of the free world hinged upon recovery of these files, declined to prosecute Hadley.

In response to all these stunning revelations, French diplomats, who had long maintained a discreet silence, were ordered to "lean harder" on Washington to scuttle the 1987 agreement, and insist on reparations for past royalties and that the U.S. relinquish claims to all future royalties from the AIDS test. "As far as we are concerned there is now little doubt that the agreement is null and void and should be renegotiated," a top official at the French Ministry for Research and Technology told *Science*. "We are getting very impatient."[11]

An exasperated John Dingell, despairing that the NIH would ever do the right thing, started his own investigation into the patents. Almost immediately, Dingell's staffers ran into the same bureaucratic brick wall that had exhausted and finally defeated Suzanne Hadley. For months, the subcommittee had requested the files of Dr. Lowell Harmison, a former Assistant HHS Secretary, which they felt were pivotal to their probe. Harmison had orchestrated the U.S. government's patenting and licensing of Robert Gallo's AIDS test and had also coordinated the initial American response to the Pasteur Institute's 1986 legal challenge to these patents. Dingell's aides were desperately attempting to reconstruct a paper trail of exactly what had transpired in those critical months leading up to the settlement. They were getting absolutely zero cooperation from HHS, however.

Finally, Dingell peevishly wrote to HHS Secretary Louis Sullivan, noting that their inability to get these documents from HHS "is highly curious" since Harmison was "deeply and extensively involved in the Gallo patent dispute."[12] Several months later, Dingell received a sheepish response from Sullivan. "A number of cartons in Dr. Harmison's office, believed to contain records and other materials of Dr. Harmison's, were noted to be missing," the Secretary wrote. Harmison insisted, however, that he only took "personal items" and threw away "files containing trade secret, proprietary or confidential information." When Dingell's office pressed him, Harmison maintained that all the documents the subcommittee had asked for were "left in my office upon leaving" his job at HHS.

In the spring of 1992, a remarkably watered-down version of Hadley's original report managed to find its way into the press. The revised report exonerated Gallo of misconduct, and placed full blame on Popovic, who had exhibited, according to the new document, "a lack of respect for truth and accuracy in the conduct and reporting of scientific research."

Fred Richards, who had read the original draft report before it was leaked to the media, was outraged by what he saw as the OSI whitewash. "Suzanne's original report was much more in line with our thoughts," says Richards. "The strongest feeling we had—which never deviated—was we did not think they could distinguish between the guilt of Gallo and Popovic. If they thought one was guilty then they both were guilty." He fired off an angry letter to Bernadine Healy that condemned Gallo and his underlings in the strongest language the gentlemanly scientist could muster.

"The Gallo lab," he wrote, "'went to school' *with the French virus*, yet they later failed to mention they had propagated the French virus. . . . Given the quality of the information derived from propagation of the French virus, we believe this constitutes intellectual recklessness of a high degree—in essence, *intellectual appropriation* of the French viral isolate." The report itself neglected to address what Richards, echoing the sentiments of fellow panelists, believed was Gallo's cardinal sin: "a *pattern* of behavior on Dr. Gallo's part that repeatedly misrepresents, suppresses and distorts data and their interpretation in such a way as to enhance Dr. Gallo's claim to priority and primacy."[13]

Fred Richards's explosive missive didn't deter Dr. Healy, though. She forwarded the new draft report to her HHS superiors on March 27, noting that Gallo "had been absolved of allegations of scientific misconduct." Yes, he had exhibited some bad manners, she admitted, but a little tutoring in the fine points of scientific etiquette, she maintained, should dispense with any future problems. To those who had seen the original report, Healy's actions would have been laughably ludicrous if so many lives weren't at stake and millions of taxpayer dollars weren't being poured into a laboratory rife with more intrigue and corruption than the house of the Medicis.*

By that time, the OSI itself was history, having been merged with another agency and shifted outside of the NIH and renamed the Office of Research Integrity (ORI). Jules Hallum had the dubious distinction of being the tiny agency's first and last director. "I used to have a reputation before I worked for the government," the normally mild-mannered

---

*In July 1992, Gallo's principal deputy for nearly two decades was found guilty of embezzling laboratory funds and making false statements to the NIH. Two years earlier, another of Gallo's top aides pleaded guilty to charges of accepting illegal kickbacks. A congressional hearing into fraud in the LTCB, the NIH's largest and most well-funded laboratory, revealed that Gallo, who traveled frequently abroad for speaking engagements and conferences, had lost control of his laboratory. There was no clear-cut chain of command, and duties were so compartmentalized that no one took responsibility for decisions.

virologist said indignantly before he left Washington in the summer of 1992.[14] The final OSI report was released in May 1992. Then the Office of Research Integrity issued *its* report in December 1992. The ORI was not quite as charitable in its findings as the OSI; it concluded Gallo had appropriated credit for himself that really belonged to French scientists, and that Dr. Mikulas Popovic fudged data in a key 1984 scientific paper that described how he had cultured the HIV virus.

Gallo and Popovic's attorneys moved to get the ruling overturned by an appeals board of the Department of Health and Human Services. In November 1993, the appeals board exonerated Popovic. In the face of this defeat, the ORI decided to drop its case against Gallo. But Lyle Bivens, the head of ORI, was "dismayed by the panel pronouncements." He told reporters that "It is clear that the panel now applies different standards from those applied by ORI to review findings of 'scientific misconduct.'" Suzanne Hadley was now officially transferred to Capitol Hill, on loan from the NIH, where she worked with Dingell's aides, who were investigating whether Gallo was guilty of perjury and patent fraud when he filed the original patent application. It was only then, safely ensconced in an airy office with large windows and high ceilings tucked away in a corner of the congressional office building, that Suzanne Hadley began to grasp fully the enormity of what had actually happened: the battle over who discovered the virus first was almost beside the point. This was a patent dispute, pure and simple, and at stake was the protection of that lucrative license. "At the beginning, at the OSI, we were overwhelmed with documents, with issues, with people, and then we factor in a 'Fast Eddie' main character, who at every turn was trying to do a tap dance on our head, I'm amazed that we did as well as we did," Hadley recalls. "But we missed so much. And I fault myself because I was too naive to recognize what this case was about and what we were up against."

Using congressional oversight powers, Hadley, working with Dingell's top investigators, Peter Stockton and Bruce Chafin, was finally able to obtain long-suppressed documents. In combing through tens of thousands of pieces of paper, Hadley was shocked by what she read. "In each file, I'd find buried gems," says Hadley, with one smoking gun after another that would refute key elements of Gallo's story—until the entire rotten edifice started to crumble under the staggering weight of incriminating evidence.

"The first box I opened had the CDC data—a printout and a tally of the CDC data [comparing the efficacy of the American and French AIDS tests]," she recalls. "And I thought: 'Oh my God, they *did* have it. They had it all this time. There it is, right there.' And there was a transmittal memo from the Justice Department to HHS dated in the fall of 1986." This discovery was quite significant. In the patent application, under penalty of perjury, Robert Gallo and others at HHS had sworn that they had no knowledge of what is known in patent law as prior art. What this means is they claimed under oath that they knew of no other discoveries—in this case, another blood test or identification of an AIDS-causing virus—that paved the way for Gallo's invention of the AIDS-antibody blood test.

Now here was a cache of documents that seemed to prove that someone at HHS *did* know about the breakthroughs achieved by Pasteur scientists. And testimony by CDC officials indicated that Gallo himself was well aware of the Pasteur's discoveries. The CDC's Don Francis testified that in April 1984, on a visit to the Pasteur, he showed Gallo the CDC's data that indicated the French's LAV, like his HTLV-3, causes AIDS. It was during that trip, shortly before Heckler's fateful press conference, that an agreement was consummated for a collaboration between the two laboratories. Moreover, Gallo was apparently apprised of the efficacy of the French blood test at a meeting on March 12, 1984, in a Bethesda restaurant with the CDC's James Curran. There, Curran says, he told Gallo that the Pasteur's blood test results were virtually the same as Gallo's test in detecting viral antibodies in AIDS and pre-AIDS patients.

What was even more significant than what Gallo did or didn't know, however, was the institutional response, according to Suzanne Hadley. In court, the Justice Department and HHS argued that "the only available blood test was Gallo's," she recalls. "But here was proof that they had evidence to the contrary to what they stated in court." In fact, James Curran told subcommittee staffers, "We at CDC *never* tried to encourage the United States to support the Gallo patent. They had Don's [Francis] stuff—they had it all this time." And during the period leading up to the 1987 settlement, Curran testified, he met with HHS lawyers on at least two occasions and divulged everything he knew. This startling evidence suggested not only that the patent application contained misleading information but that the Justice

Department *knew it*—at least after the fact (but before the settlement). As the Staff Report noted, it was not possible to tell exactly what DOJ officials knew and when they knew it. What was clear to investigators, however, was that the considerable resources of the United States government were mobilized to defend, as Lowell Harmison put it, "the red, white, and blue," and to freeze out the French.

Then in November 1993, Suzanne Hadley uncovered even more shocking material. A package of documents was delivered to the subcommittee that included a lengthy memo written in August 1984 by Malcolm Martin, a lab chief at the National Institute of Allergy and Infectious Diseases, along with his data about his comparison of Gallo's HTLV-3 with Montagnier's LAV. In doing a genetic analysis of viral samples from the two labs, Martin discovered a unique genetic variant common to both, which meant they were the same virus. The genetic fingerprint, Martin wrote, was the "smoking gun." What so stunned Hadley was what had been written across Martin's memo. Dr. Peter Fischinger had scrawled a note to Robert Gallo: "This information was transmitted to us from Dr. Harmison OASH to help you formulate a precise answer. PJF."

The implications were staggering. Fischinger had been in charge of the internal NIH probe that was instigated after Pasteur director Raymond Dedonder had demanded a share of the patent royalties in August 1985. The three-week inquiry that ensued cleared Gallo and rejected the French's patent claims. Consequently, as the Dingell committee later concluded, there was only one way to interpret Fischinger's message: Gallo had been coached.

Dingell immediately wrote to Bernadine Healy, advising her of this discovery and demanding all the documents from Fischinger's initial probe in August 1985, which he now believed had been deliberately withheld. "What crippled us over and over again in the investigation was the niggardly production of documents from HHS and the NIH," says Hadley. This revelation also prompted HHS's Office of the Inspector General, the agency's internal FBI, to instigate an independent probe. And what both teams of investigators eventually unearthed was a chilling indictment of the role of public servants in the midst of a dire public health emergency. HHS officials "conducted a parody of an investigation," congressional staffers later noted.

"[T]hey did not seek the truth but rather sought to create an official record to support the claims of Gallo."

Hadley found perhaps the most damaging puzzle piece in December 1993—but not because the NIH willingly surrendered its files. A source outside the NIH told the subcommittee about the existence of what became known as the "Myers documents." In order to obtain them, however, Hadley had to march down to the NIH's Freedom of Information Office and search their files. Once she read the documents she had so laboriously retrieved, she understood why the NIH had resisted relinquishing them—they "had significant potential to demolish the settlement's underpinnings."[15]

The files documented research conducted by Dr. Gerald Myers, a leading geneticist and director of the Los Alamos HIV Sequence Data Base, during the early part of 1987. Myers shared the results of his research in what was described as a "remarkable exchange of correspondence" between Myers and several NIH scientists and senior administrators, including Robert Gallo, NCI director Samuel Broder, and Dr. Anthony Fauci, director of the NIAID and head of the NIH Office of AIDS Research.

The staff report noted that shortly after the settlement agreement was signed, in April 1987, Dr. Myers wrote to his superiors that "literally a 'double fraud' took place when [Gallo's isolates] were declared to be independent from LAV and derived from blood pooled from several patients. The probability of either account being true is very small by this analysis. . . . it is the astonishing and unforeseen variation of the virus which exposes the fraud. . . . I suggest that we have paid for this deception in more than the usual ways. Scientific fraudulence always costs humanity . . . but here we have been additionally misdirected with regard to the extent of variation of the virus, which we can ill afford during the dog days of an epidemic let alone during halcyon times."

In a subsequent memo sent in the spring of 1989 to Robert Gallo, Dr. Myers noted, "From our earliest tree analyses, it was patently evident that the LAV and HTLV-3 viruses had to have had a recent common ancestor. . . . *There is no doubt but that it shows [that] the LAV is the source of the HTLV-3 viruses.*" At this point, according to Dr. Myers, Dr. Gallo was prepared to "throw in the towel" and admit that HTLV-3 might have originated with LAV. Gallo readied a statement that acknowledged "the distinct possibility that HTLV-3 and LAV are the same isolate." At the eleventh hour, though, Gallo reneged. He supposedly told Myers he decided to withdraw the statement after he "discussed the matter with lawyers."[16] Gallo's lawyer disputes Myers' account.

Dr. Myers later told Dingell's aides that he had hoped that the issues raised by his data would be resolved "within the tradition" of the scientific process. That never happened, and Gallo's failure to honor his commitment to tell the truth demoralized Myers, who now said of Gallo, "I just do not trust the man."[17] And despite repeated document requests to the NIH, until the subcommittee searched the FOIA files, the Myers documents were *never* provided to the subcommittee, and their existence was never disclosed to the OSI or to the Inspector General—even though at least half a dozen top government officials knew about them. It was only an anonymous tip that alerted investigators to their existence.*

On July 10, 1994, NIH director Harold Varmus, who succeeded Bernadine Healy in 1993, met with French officials, ostensibly for the annual meeting of the French and American AIDS Foundation, which oversees disbursements of royalties from the two blood tests. Behind the scenes, however, the patent dispute had flared up again, provoked by the release of the final report of the HHS's Office of the Inspector General (OIG). The OIG's two-year probe echoed what had been uncovered by previous investigations, that Robert Gallo and Mikulas Popovic used the Pasteur's virus to devise the American blood test. The OIG sent on its findings to Maryland's U.S. Attorney's office, which considered charging the two scientists with a number of criminal offenses, including perjury, obstruction of justice, mail fraud, and conspiracy to defraud the government. After some deliberation, the U.S. Attorney decided not to prosecute Gallo and Popovic. The five-year statute of limitations had expired on some of the alleged crimes, and because of the complexity of the science, it would be hard to sway a jury beyond reasonable doubt that either one had "acted with requisite criminal intent."

The patent, however, was an entirely different matter. After Gallo

---

*Even James Watson jumped into the fray. At one point, the Nobel laureate, who apparently had seen too many cop shows, met with Peter Stockton and, according to Stockton, attempted to negotiate a plea bargain for Gallo based on temporary insanity.

finally admitted in 1991 that, due to what he called "an accidental contamination," he had used the French virus for his AIDS test, Maxime Schwartz, who succeeded the distinguished Raymond Dedonder as director of the Pasteur Institute, pressed the Bush administration for a bigger royalty share—but he was turned down flat. Pasteur officials hoped for better treatment from the Clinton White House, and dispatched to Harold Varmus a thick file of information detailing their case, along with a twenty-six-page memo from Pasteur's New York attorneys. "The Clinton administration need not perpetuate a lie," the memo said. If the Pasteur didn't receive a more equitable royalty share, the memo further warned, the United States would be sending "a frightful message to the international scientific community: Don't cooperate and don't collaborate."[18]

Varmus, who was no Gallo apologist, was curiously unresponsive, even after repeated requests from the French, who threatened to sue if a new agreement was not reached. During a series of meetings with Dingell's aides in February 1994, he was presented with ample evidence conclusively demonstrating that Gallo had used the French virus to create his AIDS test. Yet he refused to take action, impatiently dismissing their charges as "old stuff," and allowed Gallo to continue to helm a lab budgeted at more than $15 million a year and to collect annual royalties of $100,000, the maximum permitted to federal employees.*

Finally, in a June 8 letter to Maxime Schwartz, Varmus reluctantly admitted, in what ranks as one of the great understatements of the twentieth century, "the acknowledgment of the role of the Institute Pasteur in isolating the AIDS-causing virus was very slow to occur." Nevertheless, Varmus insisted the contributions of the Americans were equally important: "Both hands, as it were, were necessary to grip the problem."[19] Consequently, he saw no reason to renegotiate. His rather haughty attitude underwent a remarkable sea change when John Crewdson, who had switched long ago from being a journalistic observer into a key player in this long-running soap opera, publicized the confidential OIG report in a June 19 story in the *Chicago Tribune*.

---

*Since 1986, Gallo, as well as Popovic, has received more than $1 million in royalties, which he will continue to accrue until the year 2002; in addition, he's been the recipient of nearly a million dollars more for winning such awards as the prestigious General Motors Cancer Prize and the Japan Prize.

After a decade of shooting at each other across the Atlantic, the board of the French and American AIDS Foundation—which included Gallo, Montagnier, Varmus, and Schwartz—did, in fact, renegotiate the patent arrangement when they convened on July 11 at the NIH. The French were awarded the lion's share of the proceeds, in what was widely viewed as a tacit admission that the Americans probably had no right to the royalties in the first place (in the preceding seven years, the U.S. collected $20 million in royalties while the French received $14 million). The new agreement was aimed at "normalizing the sometimes rocky relations" between the two top research centers, Dr. Varmus told reporters. And for the first time, Varmus said, the United States openly admitted that "scientists at the NIH used a virus provided to them by Institut Pasteur to invent the American HIV test kit." Varmus hailed the new deal as "fair and equitable" and hoped that it would finally put "this distraction behind us."[20]*

This seemingly casual announcement, which trivialized nearly a decade of bitter acrimony and costly litigation as a mere "distraction," was almost anticlimactic. There was one more scene in this lengthy melodrama that had yet to be played: the official release of the results of Dingell's three-year probe. Yet once again, providence intervened, and fortuitous timing enabled Gallo to escape the harsh judgment of his inquisitors. The mammoth 267-page report, with the heft and breadth of the Manhattan phone book, was culled from thousands of pages of long-buried documents and extensive interviews with more than fifty of the pivotal players in this scientific drama. It was being readied for release by the end of the year. In November, however, the Democrats were unexpectedly trounced at the polls. For the first time in forty years, they no longer had the majority in either house of Congress—and when the new Congress was sworn in John Dingell was forced to relinquish his chairmanship of the powerful House Energy and Commerce Committee and its subcommittee on investigations.

---

*According to Onek, the French weren't awarded the lion's share of the royalties. "The French were given exactly what they thought they had gotten in the first place— everyone thought the proceeds of the royalties were split in half in the original [1987] agreement," he says. "Each side kept 20 percent of the royalties from its own blood test. But in the end, nobody bought the French blood test. So the re-negotiations were just to make sure they actually got half. There was a lot of posturing for various purposes. But once they got a little more money they went home."

Republicans chose to pursue their own agenda under the newly formed House Commerce Committee and, as a consequence, Dingell's exhaustive report was never officially released.

The unofficial draft, however, was widely circulated, like a subversive manifesto greedily read and distributed by the dissident underground in the heyday of the Soviet Union. The painstakingly prepared document contained a shocking indictment of the behavior of one of the nation's top scientists, and of the participation of the guardians of governmental science in hiding his actions—even in the face of an overwhelming onslaught of incriminating evidence. "Error or fraud in science is probably to be expected. . . . But to foster distrust of science itself by treating its self-corrective mechanisms with contempt is intolerable, especially for an agency like the NIH," wrote the *Chicago Tribune* in a blistering editorial. "It is a species of corruption roughly on a par with lawbreaking by the FBI or contempt for the presumption of innocence by the Department of Justice."[21] As the Dingell subcommittee report itself soberly concluded: "One of the most remarkable and regrettable aspects of the institutional response to the defense of Gallo et al. is how readily public service and science apparently were subverted into defending the indefensible. The fraud became self-perpetuating. Defending the indefensible became a reflex, until ultimately, the cover-up was so burdened with falsehoods that its collapse was inevitable."

Robert Gallo, as usual, landed on his feet. In May 1995, he announced he was leaving the NIH after thirty years to start the Institute for Human Virology (IVH), which would be affiliated with the University of Maryland in Baltimore. Gallo boasted to reporters he'd been courted by several states before Maryland's governor made him an offer he couldn't refuse.

The state of Maryland committed $20 million to finance this venture, which is expected to be self-sufficient within five years. State officials, who didn't seem bothered by the controversies that dogged Gallo for more than a decade, maintained this was just good business. After all, noted state finance analyst William Ratchford, Gallo's patent on the AIDS-antibody test has generated more than $20 million in royalties for the NIH, and his presence should attract hundreds of AIDS researchers and patients from around the world. Ratchford added that Gallo "has expressed confidence that the institute will generate research findings not unlike his previous efforts at NIH."[22]

The devastating irony of all this was not lost on Suzanne Hadley, who was all too familiar with Gallo's "previous efforts at the NIH." At state legislative hearings, she tried to torpedo the plan, but Gallo condemned her remarks as "innuendos and allegations" and "a frightening aspect of political intervention in science."[23] The diminutive Hadley found herself crushed in the stampede by state officials to get on the Gallo bandwagon, which they believed would produce big bucks for Maryland and yield a rich harvest of political capital for them. "No information," said one key lawmaker, "has been forthcoming that would justify us not going ahead."[24]

After the changing of the guard in Congress, Suzanne Hadley went on leave from the NIH and spent her days working in a small room of her cozy town house in a wooded suburb of Maryland near Bethesda. Subsequently, she was assigned to be a visiting associate professor in the department of psychiatry at George Washington University. The once idealistic psychologist is deeply disillusioned. "With Dingell out of the picture, there's no accountability now, no pressure in any quarter," she says disconsolately, leaning back in a dark walnut rocking chair in her living room, which is decorated like an English country house, with burnished woods, Laura Ashley furnishings, and an overstuffed couch. "I shudder to think what's going on in the NIH now that nobody's watching."

One of last times Suzanne Hadley saw Robert Gallo up close and personal was when she attended his tenth annual lab meeting, which was held in September 1994. Gallo's week-long lab meetings, which draw more than 800 top AIDS investigators and virologists from around the world, have been dubbed a scientific "folk festival," with an intimate atmosphere that's more conducive to real scientific exchange than the circuslike extravaganzas the international AIDS conferences are now. And no matter what troubles may have engulfed him, Gallo's lab meetings place him squarely in the spotlight. "He's a very hands-on operator at these meetings," says Hadley. "I always tried to come early and leave late, because I didn't want to be intrusive. One morning we ran into each other in the hall and he was going very fast, coming at me. I quietly said, 'Hi, Bob.' He was actually quite pleasant. 'Oh, Suzanne,' he said, patting my arm. 'Glad to see you here.' It was surreal."

247

*　　　*　　　*

By 1994, the news from the AIDS front was bleak. In fact, medical science's war on AIDS was such an unmitigated disaster that one of America's most eminent scientists felt compelled to voice his criticisms in public, normally a mortal sin among the clubby dons of science, who adhere to a stricter code of silence than the Mafia. In a widely publicized commentary that rocked the AIDS research establishment, Harvard's Bernard Fields called for profound changes in the research strategy. Billions have been squandered, he wrote, on "narrow" and "counterproductive" approaches to conquering this plague.

The "ultimate goals of preventing and treating this epidemic have not been achieved," Fields continued in *Nature,* the prestigious British science journal. A "large bureaucracy and infrastructure may make it difficult to implement a real change. . . . [But] we need to alter substantially the way we set priorities and fund AIDS research. The real challenge is to put aside easy answers so that we can concentrate on studies that offer a real possibility of working. AIDS is a novel disease requiring new paradigms and a new conceptual framework. We must give serendipity (and reasoned scientific redirection) a chance to join the war on AIDS."[25]

Fields's brutal evaluation was a damning admission of what scientists already knew: fifteen years, 22 billion taxpayer dollars, and a quarter of a million American lives later, we're no closer to a cure, to a vaccine, or even to effective treatments than when the epidemic began.

Bernard Fields's words were quickly seconded by NIH director Harold Varmus in what appeared to be a carefully choreographed public relations Kabuki dance. This was no doubt part of a major, but very much behind-the-scenes, housecleaning in the AIDS establishment by the respected Varmus. Earlier, Varmus had put William Paul in charge of the NIH's AIDS office, replacing Anthony Fauci, the de facto AIDS czar since the epidemic's earliest stages. Then NCI director Samuel Broder, who had championed approval of AZT for treating AIDS, resigned to take a job in industry, prompted, some say, by an "escalating personal enmity between Varmus and Broder."[26] Soon after, Robert Gallo announced his imminent departure.

What went wrong? AIDS research was riven by rampant self-interest, high-stakes turf wars, patent disputes, and probes into misconduct, fraud, and corruption. This had spawned total anarchy in the research effort and become an embarrassment to scientific bluebloods like Harold Varmus and Bernard Fields, himself fatally stricken with pancreatic cancer. In the discussion following Fields's stunning declaration, though, no one would go on record with the real reason why science's war on AIDS was such a fiasco. But everyone knew the dirty secret unuttered by Fields: the poisonous atmosphere around AIDS research was a direct result of the money involved. Whoever finds a cure for this dread disease won't just win Nobels—He'll make millions.

"Of the many compelling questions raised by the Gallo affair," noted John Crewdson, from his singular vantage point in observing the AIDS research establishment, "among the most disturbing is whether the now universal practice of patenting biomedical discoveries—particularly by the NIH—advances, or impedes, the progress of life-saving knowledge."[27] In the Robert Gallo case, there *never* would have been the long-running controversy that tied up the resources of two key labs—and required the pricey services of a battalion of attorneys—if there wasn't a patent worth millions at stake.

The NIH and Robert Gallo weren't the only ones who profited from the epidemic. Many other scientists in the AIDS inner circle had extensive ties to industry, which placed them in a unique position to benefit financially—through patent royalties, corporate consulting contracts from drugmakers, and equity shares in biotech firms. So it's probably not surprising that the fortunes of these companies have paralleled those of medicine's war on AIDS. By 1994, many of them had fallen on hard times as well.

Stock prices in Immune Response, the company founded by polio pioneer Jonas Salk, plunged when tests of its flagship drug, Remune, a therapeutic vaccine to boost the immune systems of AIDS patients, showed no clear benefit. A report at the 1993 International Conference on AIDS in Berlin was hopeful. "It is safe [and] it enhances immune response," Dr. Alexandra Levine, a University of Southern California researcher who conducted the trials, told her colleagues. "But it is far too short a time to say whether these individuals will be well."[28] Other scientists weren't impressed, and didn't think Remune provoked enough of an immune response to do any good. The investment community was even more dubious, and reacted to the news by hammering the price of the stock down to $16 from a high of $27 the month before. After Salk's death in 1995, however, the Carlsbad-based company, which has spent more than $70 million to develop Remune, continued to forge ahead. It instituted a new study of Remune involving about 2,500 patients at more than fifty U.S. medical centers, which should be completed by the year 2000. Skeptical Wall Street analysts say the outcome of this clinical trial will determine the fate not only of the drug but of the company as well.

Cambridge BioScience, which grew up alongside the AIDS epidemic, has fared even worse. (The company merged with Biotech Research Laboratories in 1990 to become Cambridge Biotech). On March 31, 1994, in a move that stunned Wall Street, accountants from Deloitte & Touche took the highly unusual step of walking out on an audit of the company. Amid allegations of possible fraud, bribery, and financial improprieties, shares in the Boston-based firm dropped by half. On June 29, the firm filed for Chapter 11.

Cambridge Biotech's spectacular crash was a surprising twist for a company that had vaulted into the stratosphere on the basis of breakthroughs made by its founders, Harvard's William Haseltine and Max Essex. In 1985, Essex discovered gp 120, a protein on the surface of the HIV virus. Cambridge Biotech held the rights to gp 120, which was used to devise a fast, cheap doctor's office procedure to test for the presence of the virus in the blood, and was also licensed to more than a dozen drug companies involved in the development of an AIDS vaccine. Sales of the AIDS tests fell far short of the company's optimistic projections, however, and corporate balance sheets were swamped in a sea of red ink.

The company bounced back from this setback in 1990 by merging with Biotech Research Laboratories. The Rockville, Maryland, company did extensive contracting work for Robert Gallo's laboratory and was started by his longtime mentor and friend, Robert Ting (who also founded another of Gallo's chief contractors, Litton Bionetics; Biotech Research Laboratories and Litton Bionetics were two of the five companies that were awarded lucrative licensing rights to Robert Gallo's AIDS-antibody test). A 1991 public offering raised $27 million, which the company used to buy a trio of small foreign diagnostic concerns. The hybrid company, Cambridge Biotech, was a Wall Street favorite; its stock price rose to $16, based upon revenues that climbed to $38 million by 1992 and a steady diet of multimillion-dollar government subcontracts, courtesy of the LTCB.

Ironically, many scientists questioned the real value of the company's breakthroughs. In 1987, Max Essex discovered what he thought was a new variant of the AIDS virus, which he dubbed HIV-2, and organized a costly government-sponsored expedition to Africa—with a *Washington Post* reporter on board to record their trek for posterity—to verify his findings. He never could, though; it emerged that the "new" virus came from lab samples contaminated with monkey viruses from the nearby New England Primate Laboratory. Then, a 1988 study revealed that Cambridge Biotech's HIV tests were the least accurate of all HIV tests. However, a 1990 study conducted by Essex, among others, found that Cambridge BioScience tests were as effective as other commercial tests. And in 1994, trials of vaccines using the gp 120 protein were halted due to fears the vaccine may have actually accelerated the onset of AIDS in one participant and infection with HIV in four others.

Worse yet, mounting losses at their foreign subsidiaries prompted company insiders to inflate revenues artificially—until sharp-eyed auditors spotted the bookkeeping irregularities. "It was a case of an autocratic chief executive, and a board that was somewhat passive, spending too freely and getting overextended," a former Cambridge Biotech vice president told *The Wall Street Journal*.[29] By October 1996, the company had emerged from Chapter 11, but it was a shadow of its former high-flying self. The SEC dropped its investigation of the company and various divisions were sold off; the therapeutics assets—including their vaccine research program—were transferred to Aquilla Biopharmaceuticals, which is strictly a research and development company. Cambridge Biotech itself is now a privately held subsidiary of a French company, Biomerieux.

In May 1993, Cambridge Biotech's founder, William Haseltine, announced plans to take a leave of absence from Harvard to head up Human Genome Sciences, a Maryland-based biotech. He told reporters his decision to leave Boston stemmed in part from a growing frustration about the prospects of beating HIV. Haseltine used to line his office with empty champagne bottles, each commemorating a discovery related to AIDS. Those halcyon days are over, though, he admitted: "The immediate future of AIDS research is one based more on hope than knowledge." If he had any insights into the role that his or other AIDS researchers' commercial ties may have played in creating this impasse, he didn't share it with his audience.

251

*   *   *

One afternoon, I met Michael Callen for lunch at a popular West Hollywood sidewalk café, where the rap and dance tracks throbbing in the background provided a pulsating beat for the vibrant street life passing by. Elfin and delicate, with enormous, upturned green eyes that made him resemble a gentle alien, Callen seemed incongruous in the sea of muscular men in cutoffs and tank tops romping in the picture-perfect southern California weather.

Callen was a twenty-five-year-old musician when he was diagnosed with AIDS in 1982, an illness which transformed him into a high-profile AIDS activist. He had nimbly defied death for over a decade, one of the longest of the long-term survivors, a battle chronicled in his best-selling book, *Surviving AIDS*. On that cloudless afternoon, however, we both knew time was running out. His right leg was elephantine, swollen to several times its normal size by Kaposi's lesions. He had lesions all over his lungs as well, and the pain was unremitting. It was an effort for him to talk, and he hardly touched his lunch. But as we were leaving the restaurant, he grabbed my arm with a surprising strength.

"I have managed to survive for eleven years with full-blown AIDS and we're still nowhere," he said, his kind face contorting in anger. "While they were frittering away billions of dollars with all this intrigue and scandal, while they were dallying with AZT, they were not pursuing treatments that could have saved my life. And I will pay for their stupidity with my life."

His words echoed in my head when I read his obituary in the newspaper less than a year later. And percolating in the back of my mind was another thought that would come to me many more times as I researched this book.

What would Max think?

CHAPTER 12

MONEY CHANGES EVERYTHING

Kirk Raab's tumultuous reign at the helm of Genentech came to an abrupt end in July 1995. Genentech officials discovered that the hard-charging CEO had secretly sought a $2 million personal loan guarantee from Roche Holdings, a Swiss pharmaceutical giant that had purchased 66 percent of Genentech's stock in a controversial 1990 merger. Inside a stack of Raab's files, a junior employee accidentally found a letter Raab had written to Roche asking for the loan guarantee. Top-level executives were "stunned" when they learned of Raab's request, which came in the midst of sensitive negotiations with Roche to buy the balance of Genentech's stock. Apparently, the debt-swamped Raab needed the money to settle a sizable IRS bill.

Raab's actions were the last straw for Genentech's top brass. It crystallized their growing embarrassment over his aggressive stewardship, during which the company had faced probes by Congress, the FDA, and the FTC, and indictments on bribery charges of his top sales executive—not to mention the hefty $162,400 fine levied on his wife, Mollie, by the Securities and Exchange Commission in 1990 for insider trading because she tipped a family member about the impending Roche deal. After conducting an internal investigation, Genentech executives demanded Raab's resignation and named Arthur D. Levinson, one of the original whiz kids hired on in 1980 and Genentech's chief scientist, as his successor. It was quite a comedown for Raab, who less than three years earlier had been one of only two pharmaceutical company executives—the other was Dr. Roy Vagelos, then head of Merck, long considered the Tiffany's of the industry—invited to attend

Bill Clinton's 1992 postelection economic summit in Little Rock. And whatever his personal failings, Raab left the company in excellent shape, with a peerless research department and several promising drugs in the pipeline.

In the wake of Raab's sudden departure, Levinson, a well-liked forty-five-year-old biochemist, who is regarded by colleagues as a model of rectitude, moved swiftly to restore flagging morale. "My aspiration is to make sure Genentech is a place where we have fun, we're excited about what we're doing, and where we are proud to work," Levinson told employees the morning after Raab's sudden departure. "We have always had fun, but we haven't always been proud to work here," he added, in a thinly veiled allusion to the ethical dilemmas that plagued Raab's tenure.[1] Levinson's appointment was clearly aimed at rehabilitating Genentech's tarnished reputation, reassuring its stellar scientific staff of its commitment to top-flight research, and stemming the exodus of scientific talent that had occurred since the union with Roche.

Levinson's elevation to the top slot sent quite a different message to Wall Street, however, which viewed him as a corporate neophyte with no experience running a major company. In 1990, Raab engineered the $2.1 billion Roche merger to assure that Genentech, whose earnings had stalled, could remain a scientific pioneer; the infusion of money allowed the company to continue to plow one-third of its revenues—more than double the industry average—into research and development of the costly genetically engineered proteins. At the time, honchos at Roche promised to "protect Genentech from a stifling embrace."[2] With Raab's dismissal, however, that now seemed less likely and Genentech's survival as an autonomous drugmaker was doubtful. "For a marketing organization, one as swashbuckling as Genentech, to have a scientist out in front is quite striking," said one industry observer. "It's a pretty strong signal that this is going to be a research-driven organization, rather than a marketing organization from here out."[3] Levinson himself admitted as much, though he insisted it was in Genentech's best interests to let Roche take over sales and marketing. "What we are good at," he maintained, "is discovering and developing drugs."[4]

All the upbeat rhetoric, though, couldn't hide what was painfully obvious to veteran analysts: after two decades of generous patronage from the U.S. government, the nation's pioneering biotech was now little more than a giant contract lab for a foreign pharmaceutical.

Genentech, which was conceived and nurtured into a sturdy adolescence in Herbert Boyer's UCSF laboratory, has come full circle—except that the American taxpayer won't derive any financial benefit from advances that emanate from the company's estimable scientific staff. "In 1976, it was not clear how to translate the new technology [of recombinant DNA] into its useful roles," observed Phillip A. Sharp, a Nobel laureate at MIT. "But Genentech provided the model for attracting venture capital, reaching agreements with pharmaceutical companies, and securing Wall Street funding. Over the past two decades, this has remained the paradigm for transferring biotechnology advances from university labs to the commercial world."[5] And once again, Genentech's fate mirrors that of the industry it helped found. Of the several hundred biotechnology companies in the United States, only a small number are profitable, and even fewer are not controlled by large corporations. Biotechnology, once relentlessly hyped as the salvation of a discovery-driven industry that was hitting one dry well after another, never fulfilled its promise. Billions of dollars later, only a handful of genetically engineered drugs have come to market and few qualify as real breakthroughs.

What's more, these medications are very expensive to manufacture. And many observers wonder if their benefits justify their exorbitantly high production costs. Even t-PA, which is arguably the most successful drug to emerge from the laboratories of the nation's biotechs, is only marginally more effective than rivals—and a new generation of clot-busting agents is poised potentially to blow t-PA out of contention. Of course, the argument is: How much of a price tag should we put on a human life? Containing our skyrocketing medical bill, however, has moved to the top of the nation's agenda. Perhaps the more practical question is: How long can the United States, which is hobbled competitively by the highest health-care costs in the world, afford astronomically expensive drugs whose superiority is questionable?

Genentech, like virtually all other biotech companies, had only one drug—t-PA—that was a potential blockbuster. Its other products, such as human growth hormone or Pulmozyme, which eases symptoms of cystic fibrosis, are fine medications but they are used by only a small patient population—and efforts to broaden their market have met with decidedly mixed results. Consequently, the company resorted to hardball marketing tactics to maintain sales of t-PA. If biotechnology was truly viable as a business—and not built on empty promises—would this be necessary? The larger drug companies, which hardly qualify as candidates for canonization, rarely stoop to dubious sales practices because they have several products to boost bottom lines. Tellingly, the more conservative Europeans didn't embrace the biotech business with the same fervor as the Americans, and there's been only a handful of start-ups across the Atlantic.

The truth is that most biotech companies' revenues are generated either by selling other biotechs reagents to do experiments, in a never-ending, self-perpetuating process of parasitic renewal, or from sales of diagnostic tests for incurable ills like AIDS or for genetic predispositions to ailments like Huntington's disease or breast cancer that medical science has made little or no headway in combating. And despite the blizzard of media attention given to the discovery of genes responsible for these deadly ills, most people are understandably reluctant to find out whether they've won or lost life's genetic lottery. In a recent survey of patients with a strong familial history of breast and ovarian cancer, for example, less than half of the study's subjects opted to be tested for the presence of the BRCA1 gene, which significantly boosts risks of developing these cancers. Many feared a positive result would jeopardize their health and life insurance coverage, or provoke needless anxiety and surgery.[6]

"So where is all this leading?" wonders Sheldon Krimsky of Tufts University, a longtime observer of the commercialization of academic research. "Clearly the fastest way to make money is if companies can convince insurance companies to pay for these tests. But these are not cures. They don't involve improving the quality of life. They involve in most cases creating an enormous body of information. There's a tremendous gap, however, between getting information and creating therapeutics—but we're constantly being sold a bill of goods about the wonders." Was this phenomenally expensive excursion into devising genetically engineered therapeutics—which has burned through *billions* of taxpayer and investor dollars—worth the trip? Or could these treatments have been formulated by big drugmakers for far less money using conventional methods—which would have left the integrity of basic research intact? The unholy marriage between science and business that we've witnessed over the last decade has made researchers rich, but it's highly debatable whether this union has benefited public health.

Nor is Genentech's merger with Roche all that unusual. After the technology transfer revolution touched off by the formation of Genentech and the passage of the Bayh-Dole Act, academic institutions figured it was open season on forging corporate ties—"especially during the Reagan giveaway years," consumer activist Ralph Nader acridly observed. Even elite nonprofit research centers saw nothing wrong with entering into lucrative liaisons with foreign companies. In 1992, for example, the Scripps Research Institute inked a ten-year $300 million agreement granting Sandoz, another Swiss pharmaceutical, the right to commercialize breakthroughs made by Scripps scientists. When Dr. Bernadine Healy, then director of the NIH, got wind of this arrangement, she went ballistic. This is "against the spirit of science and possibly against the law," Dr. Healy fumed at a congressional hearing convened to examine this alliance. This will transform Scripps, which receives $100 million annually in federal funding, into what Healy called a "subsidiary of a foreign drug company." Since the deal covers a ten-year period, this arrangement would allow Sandoz to achieve a leveraged buyout of a $1 billion research effort—*and* the exclusive rights to drugs formulated with American taxpayer dollars.

These agreements are "nothing unique," countered Scripps officials, who refused to furnish government investigators with copies of their contracts, which they said were confidential. They insisted there was nothing wrong with selling the rights to taxpayer-supported research to a European company for a fraction of their cost. They became conciliatory only when Dr. Healy threatened to cut off their grants. For the La Jolla-based Scripps, though, these arrangements aren't unusual. In the years since forging their controversial 1982 alliance with Johnson & Johnson, which expires in 1997 when the Sandoz deal goes into effect, Scripps has established a myriad of other commercial connections with major corporations like PP&G and several San Diego–based biotechs. These arrangements, augmented by substantial grants from the NIH, enabled Scripps to double the size of its senior faculty and recruit topflight researchers at a time when other facilities were forced to cut back because of dwindling financial resources. On the strength of its industrial ties, the Scripps Research Institute eclipsed its longtime rival, the Mayo Clinic, to become America's preeminent private biomedical research facility. However, the Institute's director, Richard Lerner, downplays charges that Scripps's commercial agreements shape its research agenda. "We would like to do something practical," he said. "We're not unaware of the fact that there could be financial gains. Who's kidding whom? But we never make decisions on that basis."[7]

These are certainly lofty sentiments, but the available evidence indicates that corporate ties *do* influence research decisions. And where do the interests of American taxpayers fit into this cozy equation? The fact that foreign firms are quietly taking over America's flagship labs is worrisome, and HHS officials throughout the last three administrations have consistently abdicated their watchdog role. In fact, one of the key oversight provisions of the Bayh-Dole Act was that the government retained "march-in rights" over the patents of products that were devised with input from federally funded scientists. So if a licensee declined to develop the product, the government had the legal clout to rectify the situation. Later on, a fair-pricing clause was added, so if a drug was outrageously overpriced—as was the case with the AIDS drug AZT, which had been devised originally as a chemotherapy by taxpayer-supported researchers—pressure could be applied to companies to cut costs. Yet in the probusiness, antiregulatory atmosphere of the Reagan-Bush White House, this option was hardly ever exercised. And the Clinton administration has backed off completely from imposing price controls on products devised using public money. "Industry maintains that if we impose these controls, it will stymie innovation—and the government, in its inimitable wisdom, has bought the industry line," says Peter Arno, a health-care economist at the Albert Einstein Medical School in New York. "But it's another rip-off of the American taxpayer whose dollars are used to support research," added Representative Ron Wyden, "and then when the products come on-line, they're priced excessively high even though the taxpayer did the heavy lifting."[8]

Compounding this problem was the fact that the contributions of the federally funded scientists were rarely acknowledged, thus depriving the government of the legal basis for stepping in. When the House Small Business Subcommittee on Regulation investigated Scripps, for example, it uncovered flagrant abuses. Congressional probers discovered that over a ten-year period Scripps had filed for about 130 patents, many of which were later licensed to Johnson & Johnson. "We wanted to know how many of these patents acknowledge the federal support they have received," says Steve Jenning, a subcommittee staffer. "And how many of these have been developed into commercial products—or was J&J just sitting on these, but denying the license to somebody else? Scripps said we'll get back to you."

Representative Ron Wyden, who was then chair of the subcommittee, had no intention of waiting around for a response from Scripps and asked the HHS Inspector General (IG) to conduct an independent audit. What the IG uncovered was shocking. The NIH Technology Transfer Office was aware of only five Scripps patents which listed any federal involvement. After the IG exerted some pressure, Scripps officials suddenly discovered that out of 130 patents, about 50 had some federal involvement. Considering that nearly three-quarters of Scripps's funding comes from federal coffers, the IG thought this number was still quite low. After an eighteen-month audit of all of Scripps patents, the IG determined 94 patents resulted from federally sponsored research. Scripps officials maintained that their failure to credit federal involvement on all of these discoveries was merely an oversight.

Scripps, however, was merely "a microcosm of a much larger problem afflicting the entire NIH research community," said Ron Wyden. He ordered his committee to broaden its investigations to include five randomly selected institutions, which receive $6 billion out of a total of $8 billion in federal funds dispensed each year to the research community. What they discovered was significant underreporting, though none approached the staggering level of Scripps, and the NIH had no mechanism to ensure compliance. "The NIH was not being a good taskmaster," says Steve Jenning. "If universities fail to report, there is not a fail-safe program at the NIH to do the backup—there's only one person in the NIH's Technology Transfer Office to track 2,000 patents. And the NIH should be in a proactive posture rather than sitting in the basement waiting for the mail to arrive." After the skirmish with Scripps, the NIH convened a task force to devise more stringent rules for these collaborative alliances, but most believe these deals have become so pervasive that it is far too late to exert controls.

Since Harold Varmus replaced Bernadine Healy, the NIH's record has improved somewhat. "Varmus came in after the train wreck," says Steve Jenning. In fact, the agency was downright aggressive when

Myriad Genetics, a Salt Lake City biotech, and the University of Utah filed a patent application in October 1994 for the BRCA1 breast cancer gene—and excluded their NIH collaborators. The discovery of a gene that was a marker for breast cancer made headlines. The University of Utah team was led by Mark Skolnick, a former NIH researcher who migrated to the largely Mormon state because it was the perfect laboratory for genetic studies. It had a relatively homogeneous population, and elders of the Mormon Church kept meticulous genealogy records dating back more than ten generations. So it made immeasurably easier the job of tracking clusters of familial breast cancer and then zeroing in on the common aberrant gene.

The normally unflappable Harold Varmus was angry, however, about the disregard of the significant role played by the NIH in identifying this gene. "This discovery is the result of the arduous and scientifically challenging work of over 40 researchers at several institutions," he wrote in a scathing letter to Ron Wyden. Varmus went on to warn that "omission from a patent application of a true inventor could render" the patent invalid. The patent on a test for a predisposition to a cancer that strikes one in nine American women could be worth millions. This bitter dispute was settled in February 1995 when the University of Utah–Myriad Genetics team added the NIH's researchers to the patent application, and awarded the government 25 percent of potential royalties.

Nevertheless, this is a small victory in a war we can't afford to lose: these patents are worth millions. To cite just a few notable examples, the three patents on gene-splicing technology that UCSF shares with Stanford University have generated royalties in excess of $150 million (Boyer and Cohen, who initially refused their royalties, collected $4.4 million in patent income in 1995); royalties on the hepatitis B vaccine, which was devised by UCSF scientists, have totaled $66.2 million, while human growth hormone has yielded nearly $20 million in royalties.[9]

In addition to the very real concerns as to who actually owns the rights to inventions created with taxpayer funds is the issue of how scientists themselves behave when there is a potential for astounding windfalls. And Scripps's president, Richard Lerner, for one, has profited quite handsomely from these arrangements, dating back to the early 1980s, when he negotiated a $60,000-a-year consulting contract with Johnson & Johnson. Later on, an enterprising reporter discovered Dr. Lerner was a shareholder and board member of Cytel Corporation, a joint venture between Scripps and Sequel Therapeutics, a small San Diego biotechnology firm. Lerner had also bought shares in a Cytel subsidiary for $900 and sold them back to the company nine months later for $71,000. Then, on July 27, 1992, just a few months before the Scripps-Sandoz deal was consummated, Lerner sold 10,000 of his 125,000 shares in Cytel for $92,800. And to close this cozy little circle, Cytel is a subsidiary of—you guessed it—Sandoz.

Lerner didn't do anything illegal, though he certainly can be faulted for suspiciously bad timing. But if Kirk Raab was forced out by angry Genentech stockholders for stepping over the line in his dealings with Roche, then where does Richard Lerner register on the scale of moral opaqueness? After all, how strongly can he defend the public's interest in negotiations with a company that's made him nearly $200,000 richer? Lerner distanced himself from charges of impropriety by recusing himself from negotiations on the Cytel deal. "We have a situation where the lab and the drug companies romance one another, cut sweetheart agreements, and the taxpayer gets jilted," Ron Wyden remarked during his subcommittee's hearings. "In addition, the federal government has turned a blind eye toward conflict-of-interest risks involving key administrators or researchers at these tax-exempt, federally subsidized institutions. Drug companies may reward these individuals with consulting contracts and equity ownership incentives. Clearly, these sweetheart deals can bias decisions made by these key lab personnel regarding the research direction taken by the federally subsidized labs, and who gets to market the results."

In fairness, what compels many researchers to form alliances with industry is that government funding sources are dwindling. Nobel laureate physicist Leon Lederman, the former president of the American Association for the Advancement of Science (AAAS) conducted a recent survey of researchers at fifty universities. He calculated that 1990 federal funding for scientific research at these institutions was only 20 percent higher than in 1968, while the number of scientists has doubled. In light of these sharp cutbacks, researchers now face the same conundrum as athletes do over whether to take steroids. They may not want to hook up with industry, but they believe they have no other choice if they want to remain competitive. "We're just concessionaires—little more than hucksters renting a booth at a baseball game," says one leading scientist, referring to the fact that scientists must pay a portion of their grants to their respective universities for overhead costs. "Biotech saved us," he insists. But at what cost?

Many believe the fevered race to cut lucrative business deals has perverted the scientific process: it promotes secrecy, which dangerously retards research, spawns a culture of credit that undermines the traditions of cooperation and sharing, and sacrifices the ethics of science on the altar of profits. Top scientists must now also be adept salespeople who seize upon every find and magnify it into a major advance to keep federal money flowing and woo investor dollars. Competitive pressures have been amplified to insane levels, tempting scientists to cut corners, to round off numbers so that results appear more impressive, to overlook anomalous findings that would put the data in a less favorable light—or to just cheat. In fact, incidents of misconduct, manipulation or faking of data, and outright criminal behavior have made front-page news with alarming regularity. In a November 1991 survey of 1,500 scientists conducted by the AAAS, more than a quarter of respondents said they had witnessed faking, falsifying, or outright theft of research in the past decade. "There's no hard evidence, but my gut feeling is the problem has gotten much worse in the past five years," says Walter Stewart, an NIH scientist who's participated in several fraud investigations. "There's been a collapse of the professional consensus that you have to behave correctly. But the consequences of failing to face up to ethical necessities are devastating and profound. Science is about discovering the truth—if dishonesty is condoned in one sphere, it spreads like a disease and infects the whole process."

All of these disparate strands when pieced together point to one inescapable conclusion: commercialism has tainted basic science to the point where it now jeopardizes public health. The Gallo affair, for instance, *never* would have gone on as long as it did, consuming the precious time and resources of key scientists who should have been waging war on a fatal pathogen, if so much money wasn't at stake. And the lengthy controversy over who discovered the AIDS virus was merely a smoke screen—the real battle was over who would get tens of millions of dollars in patent royalties from the use of the AIDS virus. According to one report, Gallo himself was ready "to throw in the towel" as far back as 1989 (though his own lawyer denies this) but buckled under pressure from attorneys, so this acrimonious dispute continued for another five years. The Gallo case was certainly a dark chapter in the annals of science, but the whole episode could have been chalked up to the lapses of a scientist who wanted to win at any cost. What elevated this above the ordinary—and what was truly morally indefensible—was the fact that public servants allowed money to shackle AIDS research in the midst of a deadly epidemic.

This scandalous episode, though, is merely a high-profile instance of what happens when the Darwinian laws of the marketplace, not the genteel etiquette of science, rule research. A 1996 Harvard survey of 210 U.S. companies that fund academic scientists reached some disturbing conclusions. The study revealed that the ethical dilemmas and practical problems sparked by industrial intrusions on campus a decade or so ago were now endemic and magnified a thousandfold: corporate funding creates profound conflicts of interest, and promotes a secrecy in science which undermines medical progress. And contrary to the stout protests by people like Richard Lerner, the evidence was overwhelming that companies did, in fact, dictate what research was conducted by government-supported scientists. "Whoever pays the piper calls the tune," says David Blumenthal, chief of health policy research at Harvard's Massachusetts General Hospital, who led the study. "It's very hard to imagine industry supporting research if it gets nothing out of it."

In the vast majority of instances, the Harvard study revealed, companies paid for applied research that resulted in immediate payoffs rather than supporting the ambitious fishing expeditions of basic research. And for industry, these collaborations were very good business; 60 percent of the time, the research generated patents, products, and sales. In fact, according to one estimate, industry has earned about $9 billion from sales of products devised in partnerships with universities. However, the long-term consequences of the switch from basic to applied research could be disastrous. It is science's unfettered exploration of the body's deepest truths that adds to our understanding of the underlying biological mechanisms of disease. Without this knowledge, we cannot devise effective therapies. Laboratories doing basic studies are, in essence, the very beginning of the drug development pipeline. And despite all the hoopla about the great discoveries emanating from biotechnology, the real innovations still stem from the research at the bench in the ivy-covered halls of academia.

The numbers tell the story. The federal government, along with states, institutions, and private foundations, doles out more than $20 billion each year to support biomedical research. This is roughly four times what the entire biotechnology industry invests in discovery research; although the pharmaceutical companies spend about $10 billion on R&D, most of that money is directed into product development, not basic research. So it's no wonder that only 12 of the 348 drugs introduced by the twenty-five largest pharmaceuticals between 1981 and 1991 were considered therapeutic advances by the FDA. The vast majority—84 percent—were viewed as having little or no potential for advances in treatment. Research in corporate labs was directed primarily at concocting "copycat" or "me too" drugs to compete with rivals that had already established a market niche, rather than gambling on developing genuinely new drugs that advance medical treatment. In stark contrast, 70 percent of the drugs that have substantial therapeutic gain are produced with government involvement, and up to half of the most promising AIDS and cancer drugs are concocted in government or university labs. In 1991 alone, the NIH, or researchers supported through extramural grants, had 121 drugs under development—more than any single drug company. In that same year, the FDA approved 327 new drugs and products, yet only 5 of them were considered a significant advance, 9 were targeted to "severely debilitating or life-threatening illness," and 2 were for the treatment of AIDS. *All* 5 of the therapies deemed an important therapeutic gain, 6 of the 9 drugs for treatment of serious ills, and both AIDS drugs were devised with federal funds.

Consequently, the corporate takeover of the nation's laboratories threatens the future of the risky basic research that industry is loath to fund. By definition, this change weakens science's crusade to formulate effective treatments to eradicate disease. "Universities would be unwise to depend heavily on industry to sustain their capabilities in the life sciences," Blumenthal and his colleagues at Harvard warned, because "such support may not generally be conducive to maintaining the level of excellence of fundamental academic research."[10] This was a harsh assessment of the impact of commercial ties on academia, especially considering that Blumenthal's group could not, by any stretch of the imagination, be considered partisan zealots.

Dr. Steven A. Rosenberg, chief surgeon at the National Cancer

264

Institute, agreed with the Harvard researcher's findings. Rosenberg, who headed the surgical team that operated on President Reagan for colon cancer, was one of the first prominent scientists to go public with his frustrations. He charged that companies' insistence that scientists sign confidentiality agreements, and not reveal the results of their research until the findings can be commercialized, stifles the free exchange of information that is the bedrock of the scientific process. "It is an insidious problem," Dr. Rosenberg wrote, in a scathing commentary that accompanied the publication of the Harvard study in *The New England Journal of Medicine,* one that "has escalated dramatically in the past decade and is impeding the progress of medical research." He believes these restrictions delay development of crucial new therapies and lives could be needlessly lost. "Concealing information to protect future patent rights or to prevent competing companies from obtaining information is often considered essential to preserve the financial holdings of the company's investors," noted Rosenberg, who advocates boycotting these agreements. "The impact of this behavior can be profound. . . . Deliberately withholding useful information or reagents is a violation of the principle[s of medical research]. If secrecy slows progress, then human suffering may be prolonged and unnecessary deaths may occur . . . [this is the] logical consequence of such secrecy."[11]

What can be done? In 1989, HHS Secretary Louis Sullivan proposed conflict-of-interest guidelines, but they were squelched by the Bush White House. A watered-down version of these regulations were later adopted but even these rules are rarely enforced. The NIH must take its watchdog role of monitoring these arrangements more seriously, and be given the power to ensure compliance so that conflicts of interest don't infect the research process. Their current system is "paper-driven with one person to track these deals, which is just doomed to failure," says Steve Jenning. "They need to do something as simple as install an electronic computerized system—it's not a feat of technological legerdemain—and make the system provide a proactive fail-safe to cover for those institutions that don't voluntarily do a good job."

Moreover, at a time when we are staggering under the weight of a nearly $5 trillion debt, American taxpayers can no longer be expected to support our vast research infrastructure. Instead of prowling around for lucrative contracts with biotechs or with pharmaceutical companies, scientists must learn "to live on a more modest research budget," says Dr. Sheldon Krimsky. "There's a certain kind of self-righteousness every scientist has about the importance of their work. But 95 percent of all biomedical research leads nowhere." And there simply aren't enough resources to go around. Since World War II, scientists have replicated themselves exponentially—each scientist may train a dozen or more scientists, who, in turn, churn out a dozen or so more. This expansion couldn't go on forever. The twenty years of growth, from 1950 to 1970, are considered the Golden Age of American science and the achievements of our celebrated research enterprise during that era are breathtaking. By the mid-1970s, however, when Genentech was founded, the system could no longer absorb all the Ph.D.s produced by our nation's graduate schools.

For years, savvy scientists who understood what was happening urged their underlings to find work in allied professions, rather than procuring an endless round of postdoctoral holding-tank appointments in the futile hope a faculty position will open up. This must become a matter of national policy. "The leaders of American science today are from a generation that came of age during the Golden Age," observed David Goodstein, a physicist and vice provost at Caltech. "We think of those as normal times and wait wistfully for them to return. . . . But the future will not be—cannot be—like the past. . . . That's the real dilemma of American science. It needs to be reorganized from the ground up, but we who are its leaders still refuse to believe that we can't go on as we have always done before."[12]

ENDNOTES

Unless otherwise noted, all quotes are from interviews I conducted in the past four years while I researched this book and for the series of articles that led to the writing of this book.

CHAPTER 1

1. Horace Freeland Judson, *The Eighth Day of Creation: Makers of the Revolution in Biology* (Simon & Schuster: New York, 1979), p. 19.
2. Barry Werth, *The Billion Dollar Molecule: One Company's Quest for the Perfect Drug* (Simon & Schuster: New York, 1994), p. 122.
3. The Kitasato Institute, *The Life of Max Tishler* (Shirokane Minato-Ku: Tokyo, 1984).
4. David Masters, *Miracle Drug: The Inner History of Penicillin* (Eyre & Spottiswoode: London, 1946), pp. 104–8.
5. Ibid., p. 111.
6. John C. Sheehan, *The Enchanted Ring: The Untold Story of Penicillin* (MIT Press: Cambridge, Mass., 1982), p. 42.
7. Ibid., pp. 44–60.
8. *Billion Dollar Molecule*, p. 121.
9. *The Enchanted Ring*, pp. 40–43.
10. Ibid., p. 65.
11. Stephen P. Strickland, *Politics, Science, and Dread Disease: A Short History of United States Medical Research Policy* (Harvard University Press: Cambridge, Mass., 1972), p. 35.
12. David Dickson, *The New Politics of Science* (Pantheon Books: New York, 1984), p. 90.
13. Paul Starr, *The Social Transformation of Medicine* (Basic Books: New York, 1983), p. 343.
14. Vannevar Bush, *Science: The Endless Frontier* (Natural Science Foundation: Washington, D.C., 1960), p. 19.
15. *Billion Dollar Molecule*, p. 125.
16. Susan Wright, *Molecular Politics* (University of Chicago Press: Chicago, 1994), p. 21.

17. Robert Teitelman, *Profits of Science: The American Marriage of Business and Technology* (Basic Books: New York, 1994), p. 48.
18. *The New Politics of Science*, p. 26.
19. David F. Nobel, "The Selling of the University," *The Nation*, February 6, 1982.
20. *Molecular Politics*, p. 22.
21. Laurie Garrett, *The Coming Plague* (Farrar, Straus and Giroux: New York, 1994), p. 30.
22. *Molecular Politics*, pp. 27, 69.

CHAPTER 2

For background on this chapter, I used the Recombinant DNA Controversy History Collection (MC 100), which is part of the Institute Archive and Special Collections, MIT Libraries, Cambridge, Mass.

1. *The Eighth Day of Creation*, p. 41.
2. *Profits of Science*, p. 181.
3. Joshua Lederberg, "Fifty Years of DNA," *The Scientist*, February 21, 1994, p. 11.
4. *The Eighth Day of Creation*, p. 41.
5. Ibid., p. 41.
6. James D. Watson, "Salvador E. Luria (Obituary)," *Nature*, March 14, 1991, p. 113.
7. John Cairns, Gunther S. Stent, and James D. Watson, *Phage and the Origins of Molecular Biology* (Cold Spring Harbor Laboratory Press: 1992), p. 6.
8. *The Eighth Day of Creation*, p. 65.
9. Robert Olby, *The Path to the Double Helix* (University of Washington Press: Seattle, 1974), p. 306.
10. Dennis L. Breo, "The Double Helix—Watson & Crick's 'Freak Find' of How Like Begets Like," *Journal of the American Medical Association*, February 24, 1993, p. 1046.
11. Stephen S. Hall, "James Watson and the Search for Biology's Holy Grail," *Smithsonian*, February 1990, p. 44.
12. *The Eighth Day of Creation*, p. 581.
13. Stephen S. Hall, "Old School Ties: Watson, Crick and 40 Years of DNA," *Science*, March 12, 1993, p. 1532.
14. "The Double Helix," p. 1046.
15. Ibid., p. 1047.
16. *Phage and the Origins of Molecular Biology*, p. 6.
17. *Molecular Politics*, p. 68.
18. Norbert Weiner, "Science: The Megabuck Era," *The New Republic*, January 27, 1958, p. 10.
19. Merle A. Tune, "Is Science Too Big for the Scientists?" *Saturday Review*, June 6, 1959, p. 49.
20. David Jackson, MIT Archives interview, pp. 9–10.
21. *The Eighth Day of Creation*, p. 487.
22. Leslie Roberts, "Cold Spring Harbor Turns 100," *Science*, October 20, 1990, p. 497.
23. Paul Berg, MIT Archives interview, May 17, 1975, p. 17.
24. Bryan J. Ellison and Peter H. Duesberg, *Why We Will Never Win the War on AIDS* (Inside Story Communications: El Cerrito, Calif., 1994), p. 66.

25. Daniel S. Greenberg, "Whatever Happened to the War on Cancer?" *Discover,* March 1986, p. 58.
26. *Molecular Politics,* p. 25.
27. Robert Teitelman, *Gene Dreams: Wall Street, Academia, and the Rise of Biotechnology* (Basic Books: New York, 1987), pp. 51–52.

CHAPTER 3

For background on this chapter, I used *Invisible Frontiers: The Race to Synthesize a Human Gene* by Stephen S. Hall (Atlantic Monthly Press: New York, 1987).

1. William Boly, "The Gene Merchants," *California Magazine,* September 1982, p. 179.
2. Ibid., p. 179.
3. Herbert Boyer, MIT Archives interview, May 20, 1975.
4. *Molecular Politics,* p. 74.
5. Ibid., p. 131.
6. *Profits of Science,* p. 168.
7. Michael Rogers, "The Pandora's Box Congress," *Rolling Stone,* June 19, 1975, p. 38.
8. Janet L. Hopson, "Recombinant Lab for DNA and My 95 Days in It," *Smithsonian,* August 1976, p. 55.
9. Roy Curtiss III, MIT Archives interview, pp. 110–12.
10. "How Two Genies at Stanford and Cal Evoked Science of Recombinant DNA," *The Wall Street Journal,* December 30, 1980, p. 12.
11. Sydney Brenner, MIT Archives interview, p. 46.
12. "The Pandora's Box Congress," p. 41.
13. *Molecular Politics,* p. 152.
14. Ibid., p. 153.
15. "The Pandora's Box Congress," p. 82.

CHAPTER 4

For background on this chapter, I used "The Great AIDS Quest" by John Crewdson, which was published as a special section in the *Chicago Tribune* on November 19, 1989, and *And the Band Played On* by Randy Shilts (St. Martin's Press: New York, 1987).

1. Malcolm Gladwell, "Rights to Life: Are Scientists Wrong to Patent Genes?" *The New Yorker,* November 13, 1995, p. 122.
2. Robert Gallo, *Virus Hunting, AIDS, Cancer & the Human Retrovirus: A Story of Scientific Discovery* (Basic Books: New York, 1991), p. 18.
3. Ibid., p. 38.
4. Vincent Coppola, "Robert Gallo Wants to Fight," *Worth,* June 1996, p. 114.
5. *Virus Hunting,* p. 76.
6. Ibid., 77.

7. Ibid., p. 86.
8. Ibid., p. 36.
9. Zinder Report.
10. "Whatever Happened to the War on Cancer?" pp. 62–63.
11. Seth Roberts, "Lab Rat," *Spy*, July 1990, p. 74.

CHAPTER 5

For background on this chapter, I used *Invisible Frontiers,* and *Gene Dreams.*

1. Herbert Boyer, MIT Archives interview.
2. Randall Rothenberg, "Robert A. Swanson, Chief Genetic Officer," *Esquire,* December 1984, p. 370.
3. Ibid., p. 372.
4. *Gene Dreams,* p. 25.
5. "Robert A. Swanson," p. 374.
6. *Invisible Frontiers,* p. 87.
7. "The Gene Merchants," p. 171.
8. *Invisible Frontiers,* p. 175.
9. "The Gene Merchants," p. 171.
10. Ibid.
11. "Insulin Research Raises Debate on DNA Guidelines," *The New York Times,* June 29, 1979, p. A18.
12. *Molecular Politics,* pp. 343–44.
13. Interview with Susan Wright.
14. *Molecular Politics,* p. 52.
15. Testimony of Philip M. Klutznick, Secretary of Commerce, on September 16, 1980, before the Subcommittee on Legislation and National Security of the Committee on Government Operations in the U.S. Congress; Hearings on HR 6933 to Amend the Patent and Trademark Laws, 96th Congress, 2nd Session, pp. 72–73.
16. Ibid., Testimony of Admiral Rickover, p. 77.
17. Interview with David Nobel.
18. Harold Schmeck, Jr., "Justices' Ruling Recognizes Gains in the Manipulation of Life Forms," *The New York Times,* June 1, 1980, p. 1.
19. Interview with Jeremy Rifkin.
20. Kathryn Christensen, "Gene Splicers Develop a Product: New Breed of Scientist-Tycoons," *The Wall Street Journal,* November 24, 1980, p. 27.
21. "The Gene Merchants," p. 179.
22. *The New Politics of Science,* p. 78.
23. Ibid., p. 75.
24. "The Gene Merchants," p. 179.

CHAPTER 6

For background on this chapter, I used "The Gene Kings" by John Carey, Joan O'C. Hamilton, et al., which appeared in *BusinessWeek,* May 8, 1995, "The Great AIDS

Windfall" by Barry Werth, which appeared in the *New England Monthly* in June 1988, and Randy Shilts's *And the Band Played On.*

1. Cambridge BioScience offering prospectus.
2. Seth Rolbein, "Peptide T and the AIDS Establishment," *Boston Magazine*, June 1990, p. 129.
3. Institutional Response to the HIV Blood Test Patent Dispute and Related Matters, Staff Report of the Subcommittee on Oversight and Investigations of the Committee on Energy and Commerce, U.S. House of Representatives, p. 8.
4. Ibid., pp. 67–69.
5. Office of the Inspector General, Investigative Memorandum; Dr. Robert Gallo, Chief, Laboratory of Tumor Cell Biology; Dr. Mikulas Popovic, former researcher, Laboratory of Tumor Cell Biology; Re: Alleged Scientific Fraud, Fraud Against the Government, False Statements; File Number: W-90-00066-4; June 10, 1994, p. 5.
6. Staff Report, p. 91.
7. Ibid., p. 88.
8. Ibid., p. 89.
9. Ibid., p. 14.
10. "The Great AIDS Quest," Section 5, p. 7.

CHAPTER 7

1. Testimony of Donald Kennedy on June 8, 1981, before the Subcommittee on Oversight and Investigations and the Subcommittee on Science, Research, and Technology in the U.S. Congress, House Committee on Science and Technology, Hearings on the Commercialization of Academic Research, 97th Congress, 1st Session, pp. 6–28.
2. "The Gene Merchants," p. 176.
3. *The New Politics of Science*, p. 77.
4. Jeffrey L. Fox, "Can Academia Adapt to Biotechnology's Lure?" *Chemical and Engineering News*, October 12, 1981, p. 44.
5. Derek Bok, "Balancing Responsibility and Innovation," *Change*, September 1982, p. 22.
6. *The New Politics of Science*, p. 77.
7. Nicholas Wade, "La Jolla Biologists Troubled by the Midas Factor," *Science*, August 7, 1981, p. 624.
8. Ibid., p. 624.
9. Ibid.
10. Hearings on the Commercialization of Academic Research, p. 25.
11. Interview with Leon Wofsy.
12. Hearings on the Commercialization of Academic Research, pp. 27–28.
13. Robert Reinhold, "Government Scrutinizes Link Between Genetics Industry and Universities," *The New York Times*, June 16, 1981, p. 15.
14. Sheldon Krimsky, *Biotechnics and Society: The Rise of Industrial Genetics* (Praeger: New York, 1991), pp. 78–79.
15. Katherine Bouton, "Academic Research and Big Business: A Delicate Balance," *The New York Times Magazine*, September 11, 1983, pp. 119–20.

CHAPTER 8

1. Sol Sherry, *Reflections and Reminiscences of an Academic Physician* (Lea & Febiger: Philadelphia, 1993), p. 206.
2. Ibid., p. 208.
3. Burton E. Sobel, Désiré Collen, and Elliott B. Grossbard, *Tissue Plasminogen Activator in Thrombolytic Therapy* (Marcel Dekker: New York, 1987), p. 76.
4. Minutes of the Fifty-first Meeting of the Cardiovascular and Renal Drugs Advisory Committee, May 28, 1987, p. 459.
5. Marilyn Chase, "Genentech Drug to Treat Heart Attacks Receives High Marks in Federal Study," *The Wall Street Journal*, March 15, 1985, p. 10.
6. Marilyn Chase, "Genentech Gears Up to Enter the Marketplace: Gene-Splicer's Strategy Emphasizes Manufacturing, Sales," *The Wall Street Journal*, October 15, 1985, p. 6.
7. Brenton R. Schlender and Michael Waldholz, "Genentech's Missteps and FDA Policy Shift Led to TPA Setback," *The Wall Street Journal*, June 17, 1987, p. 22.
8. Ibid.
9. *Reflections*, p. 211.
10. Robert Bazell, "Dying for Drugs," *The New Republic*, November 9, 1987, p. 18.
11. "Are Scientific Misconduct and Conflicts of Interest Hazardous to Our Health?" Nineteenth Report by the Committee on Government Operations, U.S. House of Representatives, September 10, 1990, p. 23.

CHAPTER 9

1. R. E. Lapp, *The New Priesthood: The Scientific Elite and the Uses of Power* (New York: Harper & Row, 1965), pp. 39–40.
2. Anthony Liversidge, "AIDS: Words from the Front," *Spin*, February 1988, p. 67.
3. Nicholas Regush, "AIDS Risks Limited, Studies Suggest," *Montreal Gazette*, August 15, 1987, pp. B1, B4.
4. John Lauritsen, "Kangaroo Court Etiology," *New York Native*, May 9, 1988, p. 16.
5. Ibid., p. 18.
6. Ibid.
7. "Peptide T and the AIDS Establishment," p. 126.
8. Morton Hunt, "Teaming Up Against AIDS," *The New York Times Magazine*, March 2, 1986, p. 51.
9. Ibid., p. 83.
10. Ibid., p. 81.
11. "Peptide T and the AIDS Establishment," p. 30.
12. Staff Report, p. 126.
13. Ibid., p. 130.
14. Ibid., p. 120.
15. Ibid.
16. Ibid.
17. John Crewdson, "The Great AIDS Quest," *Chicago Tribune*, November 19, 1989, Section 5, p. 11.

18. Steven Benn, et al., "Genomic Heterogeneity of AIDS Retroviral Isolates from North America in Zaire." November 22, 1985, pp. 949–51.

19. O. Sattaur, "How Gallo Got Credit for AIDS Discovery," *New Scientist*, February 7, 1985, p. 3.

20. David Marsh, "French Evaluate AIDS Tests as Patent Row Continues," *The Financial Times*, February 28, 1985, p. 8.

21. Memorandum from the HHS's Executive Secretariat's Tim Miller to McClain Haddow, HHS Secretary Margaret Heckler's Chief of Staff; dated August 7, 1985.

22. Staff Report, p. 153.

23. Ibid., pp. 107–8.

24. Investigative Memorandum, Department of Health and Human Services, Office of the Inspector General, File Number: w-90-00066-4, p. 7.

25. Staff Report, p. 156.

26. Ibid., p. 169.

27. Ibid., pp. 172–73.

28. Ibid., p. 227.

29. Ibid., p. 261.

CHAPTER 10

1. Gene Bylinsky, "Genentech Has a Golden Goose," *Fortune*, May 9, 1988, p. 54.

2. *Reflections*, p. 210.

3. Robert Teitelman, "Genentech: A Fractured Fairy Tale," *Financial World*, November 15, 1988, p. 14.

4. "Genentech Has a Golden Goose," p. 62.

5. Barry Werth, "How Short Is Too Short?" *The New York Times Magazine*, June 16, 1991, p. 15.

6. Ibid., p. 19.

7. Ibid., p. 29.

8. Marilyn Chase, "Battle of Heart Attack Drugs Heats Up as SmithKline Decries Genentech Tactics," *The Wall Street Journal*, March 8, 1990, p. B8.

9. Pat Holobaugh, "Results of Investigations into the Activities of Genentech Sales Representatives with Respect to the ISIS-3 Study," Department of Health and Human Services, Investigative Memorandum, November 7, 1991.

10. Carl T. Hall, "Questions Remain After FDA Ruling," *San Francisco Chronicle*, May 5, 1995, pp. D1, D3.

11. "Battle of Heart Attack Drugs," p. B1.

12. Andrew Purvis, "Cheaper Can Be Better," *Time*, March 18, 1991, p. 70.

13. Gary Slustsker, "Patenting Mother Nature," *Forbes*, January 7, 1991, p. 90.

14. Michael Waldholz, "Genentech, Inc., Pressed by Data on Clot Drugs," *The Wall Street Journal*, March 27, 1992, p. B3.

15. Ralph T. King, Jr., "In Marketing of Drugs, Genentech Tests Limits of What Is Acceptable," *The Wall Street Journal*, January 10, 1995, p. A14.

16. Kathleen Day, "Two Drugs, Two Prices Spark a Battle," *The Washington Post*, September 16, 1994, pp. D1, D3.

17. Ibid., p. D3.

18. "Questions Remain After FDA Ruling," p. D3.
19. "In Marketing of Drugs," p. A14.

CHAPTER 11

1. Barry Werth, "By AIDS Obsessed," *Gentlemen's Quarterly*, August 1991.
2. John Crewdson, "Burden of Proof," *Chicago Tribune*, December 6, 1992, Section 4, p. 1.
3. "The Fraud Case That Evaporated," Editorial, *The New York Times*, June 25, 1996, p. A10.
4. "TechnoPolitics," Program No. 119; August 9, 1991, p. 9.
5. Benjamin Weiser, "Derailing or Due Process?" *The Washington Post*, August 14, 1991, p. A19.
6. Malcolm Gladwell, "NIH Memo Cites Possible Inaccuracies in AIDS Researchers' Patent Application," *The Washington Post*, August 12, 1991, p. A4.
7. Staff Report, p. 77.
8. John Crewdson, "Scientific Panel Accuses Gallo of 'Recklessness,'" *Chicago Tribune*, March 27, 1992, p. 1.
9. Pamela Zurer, "NIH Clears Gallo: Patent Probes Go On," *Chemical & Engineering News*, May 11, 1992, p. 37.
10. Daniel S. Greenberg, "The Gallo Case: Is This Really Happening?" *The Lancet*, June 27, 1992, p. 1594.
11. Peter Coles, "France Set to Reopen AIDS Pact?" *Science*, September 27, 1991, p. 1479.
12. John Crewdson, "U.S. Agency Admits Aide Destroyed AIDS Test File," *Chicago Tribune*, June 26, 1992, pp. 1, 10.
13. Frederic Richards letter to Bernadine Healy, February 19, 1992.
14. "Burden of Proof," p. 4.
15. Staff Report, p. 262.
16. Ibid., pp. 262–65
17. John Dingell memorandum to Harold Varmus, February 23, 1994.
18. Jon Cohen, "U.S.-French Patent Dispute Heads for a Showdown," *Science*, July 1, 1994, p. 25.
19. Ibid.
20. Edwin Chen, "U.S. Admits French Role in HIV Test Kit," *Los Angeles Times*, July 12, 1994.
21. "The Way to End a Scientific Scandal," Editorial, *Chicago Tribune*, December 12, 1992.
22. Eliot Marshall, "Gallo's Institute at the Last Hurdle," *Science*, March 8, 1996, p. 1359.
23. Ibid.
24. Ibid.
25. *Nature*, May 1994.
26. Rick Weiss, "Leaving an Unhappy Ship," *The Washington Post National Weekly Edition*, January 2–8, 1995, p. 34.
27. "Burden of Proof," p. 1.
28. Marilyn Chase, "Investors Hammer Immune Response After Update on Testing of AIDS Drug," *The Wall Street Journal*, June 10, 1993, p. B7.

29. David Stipp, "Ex-Insider at Cambridge Biotech Tells How Firm Allegedly Used Bogus Sales," *The Wall Street Journal,* July 26, 1994, p. B8.

CHAPTER 12

1. Charles McCoy, "Genentech's New CEO Seeks Clean Slate," *The Wall Street Journal,* July 12, 1995, p. B6.
2. Joan O'C. Hamilton, "A Star Drug Is Born," *BusinessWeek,* August 23, 1993, p. 68.
3. Lawrence M. Fisher, "With New Genentech Chief, Science Takes Center Stage," *The New York Times,* July 12, 1995, p. C2.
4. Ibid.
5. Phillip A. Sharp, "Biotech in the 1990's: What's in Store?" *The Scientist,* May 2, 1994, p. 4.
6. Terence Monmaney, "Many Don't Want to Know Genetic Risk of Cancer," *Los Angeles Times,* June 26, 1996, p. 1.
7. Yvonne Baskin, "Manifest Destiny at the Scripps Research Institute," *Science,* July 12, 1991, p. 142.
8. Philip J. Hilts, "U.S. Seeks to Protect Fruits of Tax-Supported Research," *The New York Times,* June 17, 1992, p. 38.
9. Paul Jacobs, "UC Relishes Power of the Patent," *Los Angeles Times,* February 14, 1996, pp. A1, A23.
10. David Blumenthal, NancyAnne Causino, Eric Campbell, and Karen Seashore Louis, "Relationships Between Academic Institutions and Industry in the Life Sciences—An Industry Survey," *The New England Journal of Medicine,* February 8, 1996, p. 368.
11. Steven A. Rosenberg, "Secrecy in Medical Research," *The New England Journal of Medicine,* February 8, 1996, pp. 393–94.
12. David Goodstein, "The Coming Dark Age of U.S. Research," *Los Angeles Times,* August 31, 1994, p. B7.

SECURITIES AND EXCHANGE
COMMISSION DOCUMENTS

Systemix, Inc. Offering Prospectus, June 19, 1991. Securities and Exchange Commission Registration Number 33-4118.

Cambridge BioScience Corporation. Offering Prospectus, April 5, 1983. Securities and Exchange Commission Registration Number 2-82032.

Biotech Research Laboratories, Inc. Offering Protectus, March 11, 1981. Securities and Exchange Commission Registration Number 2-70509.

Human Genome Sciences, Inc. Offering Prospectus, October 27, 1993. Securities and Exchange Commission Registration Number 33-6950.

Genentech, Inc. Offering Prospectus, October 23, 1980. Securities and Exchange Commission Registration Number 2-68864.

Biogen, N.V. Offering Prospectus, March 22, 1983. Securities and Exchange Commission Registration Number 2-81689.

Cytel Corporation. Offering Prospectus, November 22, 1991. Securities and Exchange Commission Number 33-43356.

Cytel Corporation. Corporate Insider Transactions; 7-1992-5-1994.

GOVERNMENT DOCUMENTS

Department of Human Health and Human Services. Investigative Memorandum on Alleged Scientific Fraud Against the Government. June 10, 1994.

Hearings Before a Committee of the Committee on Government Operations, House of Representatives.

"Prices: Are We Getting our Money's Worth?" 101st Congress, 1st Session. August 1989.

————. "Federal Response to Misconduct in Science: Are Conflicts of Interest Hazardous to Our Health?" 100th Congress, 2nd Session. September 29, 1988.

Human Resources and Intergovernmental Relations Subcommittee of the Committee on Government Operations, House of Representatives. Hearings on Drugs for Opportunistic Infections in Persons with HIV Disease. 101st Congress, 2nd Session. August 1, 1990.

Minutes of the Fifty-first Meeting, Cardiovascular and Renal Drugs Advisory Committee. May 28, 1987.

National Institutes of Health. Forum on Cooperative Research and Development Agreements (CRADAs). July 21, 1994.

Nineteenth Report by the Committee on Government Operations. "Are Scientific Misconduct and Conflicts of Interest Hazardous to Our Health?" September 10, 1990.

Office of Technology Assessment. "Pharmaceutical R&D: Costs, Risks, and Rewards." February 1993.

Subcommittee on Oversight and Investigations of the Committee on Energy and Commerce, House of Representatives. Hearings on Scientific Fraud. 102nd Congress, 1st Session. March 6 and August 1, 1991.

Subcommittee of the Committee on Government Operations, House of Representatives. Hearings on the Patent and Trademark Law Amendments of 1980. 96th Congress, 2nd Session. September 16, 17, 1980.

————. Hearings on Testing and Availability. 100th Congress, 2nd Session. April 28, 29, 1988.

Subcommittee on Oversight and Investigations and the Subcommittee on Science, Research, and Technology of the Committee on Science and Technology, House of Representatives. Hearings on University/Industry Cooperation in Biotechnology. 97th Congress, 2nd Session. June 16, 17, 1982.

————. Hearings on the Commercialization of Academic Research. 97th Congress, 1st Session. June 8, 9, 1981.

Subcommittee on Oversight and Investigations of the Committee on Energy and Commerce, House of Representatives. Investigation of the Institutional Response to the HIV Blood Test Patent Dispute and Related Matters.

————. House of Representatives. Hearings on Scientific Fraud (Part 2). 101st Congress, 2nd Session. April 30 and May 14, 1990.

Subcommittee on Regulation, Business Opportunities, and Technology. Hearings on Conflicts of Interest, Protection of Public Ownership, in Drug Development Deals Between Tax-Exempt, Federally Supported Labs and the Pharmaceutical Industry. 103rd Congress, 1st Session. June 17, 1993.

Subcommittee on Science, Technology, and Space of the Committee on Commerce, Science, and Transportation, Senate. Hearings on the National Technology Innovation Act. 96th Congress, 1st Session. June 21, 27, and November 21, 1979.

Subcommittee on the Courts, Civil Liberties, and the Administration of Justice of the Committee on the Judiciary, House of Representatives. Hearings on the Industrial Innovation and Patent and Copyright Law Amendments. 96th Congress, 2nd Session. April 3, 15, 17, 22, 24, May 8, and June 9, 1980.

SELECTED BIBLIOGRAPHY

"Abbott Lab's Raab Resigns as President and Operations Chief." *The Wall Street Journal*, January 7, 1983.

"Allegation of Insider Dealing." *Nature*, May 10, 1990, p. 102.

"Asilomar Conference on DNA Recombinant Molecules." *Nature*, June 5, 1975, pp. 442–44.

"Business and Universities: A New Partnership: Colleges get funds, industry gets talent. But academic freedom may suffer." *BusinessWeek*, December 20, 1982, pp. 58–62.

"FDA Doesn't Need 'Fixing.'" Letters. *The Wall Street Journal*, June 2, 1987.

"For a New Deal on AIDS Royalties." *Chicago Tribune*, September 18, 1992, p. 18.

"The Fraud Case That Evaporated." Editorial, *The New York Times*, June 25, 1996, p. A10.

"Genentech, Biotechnology Stocks Tumble After Ruling on t-PA Drug for Blood Clots." *The Wall Street Journal*, June 2, 1987, pp. 3, 18.

"Genentech Gets Shot at the Big Time." *Science & Technology*, October 28, 1985, p. 108.

"Genentech Says Enzyme Will Dissolve Blood Clots." *The Wall Street Journal*, June 11, 1982.

"Heart-Drug Survey Sees Little Difference in Patient Death Rate." *The Wall Street Journal*, March 4, 1991.

"How Two Genies at Stanford and Cal Evoked Science of Recombinant DNA." *The Wall Street Journal*, December 31, 1980, p. 12.

"Human Sacrifice." Editorial. *The Wall Street Journal*, June 2, 1987, p. 30.

"John Crewdson: Science Journalist as Investigator." *The Wall Street Journal*, November 15, 1991, pp. 946–47.

"New Approach in War on a Tenacious Plague: Return to Basic Science Is Urged in Seeking an AIDS Cure." Editorial. *Los Angeles Times*, May 31, 1994, p. B4.

"Patent Decision Fuels Genetic Research Debate." *Lawscope*, August 1980, pp. 943–44.

"Proxy Statement," Genentech, Inc., December 31 1992.

"Report from the Commissioners." Editorial. *The Wall Street Journal*, June 25, 1987.

"Robert C. Gallo Looks Beyond NIH and Defends the Past." *The Scientist*, November 14, 1994, p. 12.

"The AIDS Feud: A Truce Offer Spurned." *Newsweek*, June 10, 1991, p. 22.

"The Big Bucks of Biology." *Education*, April 5, 1982, pp. 69–70.

"The Decision Against a Heart Drug." Editorial. *The Wall Street Journal*, July 13, 1987.

"The Flat Earth Committee." Editorial. *The Wall Street Journal*, July 13, 1987.

"The One True Virus." *The Economist*, June 8, 1991, pp. 83–84.

"The People Behind Some of the Bright Ideas." *The New York Times*, December 27, 1987, p. 10.

"The Way to End a Scientific Scandal." Editorial. *Chicago Tribune*, December 6, 1992.

"Universities, Profit and Research." *Nature*, March 4, 1982, p. 1.

Aldhous, Peter. "Healy and Dingell Lock Horns." *Nature*, August 8, 1991, p. 461.

———. "Trouble for Healy over Misconduct Office." *Nature*, August 1, 1991, p. 361.

Altman, Lawrence K. "A Surprise in War Between Heart Drugs." *The New York Times*, May 1, 1993, p. 6.

———. "Crucial Study on AIDS Treatment Is Found to Have a Serious Flaw." *The New York Times*, July 22, 1993, p. A1.

———. "Panel Offers Sharp Criticism of AIDS Research Programs." *The New York Times*, March 14, 1996, pp. A1, A9.

Anderson, Christopher. "The Aftermath of the Gallo Case." *Science*, January 7, 1994, pp. 20–22.

Angier, Natalie. "AIDS Research Chief Awaits Key Report on Propriety Questions." *The New York Times*, August 7, 1990, p. C3.

———. "Ideas & Trends: Seeking After the Truth in Times of Scarcity." *The New York Times*, November 28, 1993, p. 4.

Baltimore, David, and Sheldon Krimsky. "The Ties That Bind or Benefit." *Nature*, January 10, 1980, pp. 130–31.

Barinaga, Marcia. "Confusion on the Cutting Edge." *Science*, July 31, 1992, pp. 616–19.

Baskin, Yvonne. "Manifest Destiny at the Scripps Research Institute." *Science*, July 12, 1991, pp. 140–42.

Bazell, Robert. "Dying for Drugs." *The New Republic*, November 9, 1987, pp. 17–19.

Bell, Robert. *Impure Science: Fraud, Compromise, and Political Influence in Scientific Research.* John Wiley & Sons: New York, 1992.

Berg, Paul, David Baltimore, Herbert W. Boyer, et al. "Potential Biohazards of Recombinant DNA Molecules." Letters. *Nature*, July 1974, p. 303.

Biddle, Wayne. "A Patent on Knowledge." *Harper's*, March 5, 1984, pp. 22–26.

Bishop, Jerry E. "Genentech Says Blood Clot Dissolver Is Successful at Stopping Heart Attacks." *The Wall Street Journal*, November 13, 1984.

Blumenthal, David. "Growing Pains for New Academic/Industry Relationships," *People to People Health Foundation*, Vol. 13, No. 3 (Summer 1994).

Blumenthal, David, Michael Gluck, Karen Seashore Louis, and David Wise. "Industrial Support of University Research in Biotechnology." *Science*, January 17, 1986, pp. 242–46.

Blumenthal, David, Michael Gluck, Karen Seashore Louis, Michael A. Stoto, and David Wise. "University-Industry Research Relationships in Biotechnology: Implications for the University." *Science*, June 13, 1986, pp. 1361–66.

Boly, William. "The Gene Merchants." *California Magazine*, September 1982, pp. 76–79, 170–79.

Bouton, Katherine. "Academic Research and Big Business: A Delicate Balance." *The New York Times Magazine*, September 11, 1983, pp. 63, 126, 151–53.

Breo, Dennis L. "The Double Helix—Watson & Crick's 'Freak Find' of How Like

Begets Like." *Journal of the American Medical Association*, February 24, 1993, pp. 1040–46.

Burton, Thomas M. "Caremark Faces Heat for Paying Doctors Who Sent It Patients." *The Wall Street Journal*, November 11, 1994.

———. "Caremark Probe Seen Resulting in Indictments." *The Wall Street Journal*, August 4, 1994, pp. A4–A5.

———. "Doctor Is Charged with Kickbacks from Caremark." *The Wall Street Journal*, August 22, 1994.

Bush, Vannevar. "The Kilgore Bill 1." *Science*, December 31, 1943, pp. 571–77.

———. *Science: The Endless Frontier.* Natural Science Foundation: Washington, D.C., 1960.

Bylinsky, Gene, "Genentech Has a Golden Goose." *Fortune*, May 9, 1988, pp. 53–62.

Cairns, John, Gunther S. Stent, and James D. Watson. *Phage and the Origins of Molecular Biology.* Cold Spring Harbor Laboratory Press, 1992.

Carey, John. "'NIH Is Not the Institution It Was.'" *BusinessWeek*, November 5, 1990, pp. 145, 148.

———."How Many Times Must a Patient Pay?" *BusinessWeek*, February 1, 1993, pp. 30–31.

Carey, John. Joan O'C. Hamilton, Julia Flynn, and Geoffrey Smith. "The Gene Kings." *BusinessWeek*, May 8, 1995, pp. 72–78.

Chase, Marilyn. "Battle of Heart-Attack Drugs Heats Up As SmithKline Decries Genentech Tactics." *The Wall Street Journal*, March 8, 1990, pp. B1, B8.

———. "Genentech Drug to Treat Heart Attacks Receives High Marks in Federal Study." *The Wall Street Journal*, March 15, 1985, p. 10.

———. "Genentech Facing Lawsuits Related to Drop in Stock." *The Wall Street Journal*, October 17, 1988.

———. "Genentech Gears Up to Enter the Marketplace: Gene-Splicer's Strategy Emphasizes Manufacturing, Sales." *The Wall Street Journal*, October 15, 1985, pp. 6–7.

———. "Genentech's Insulin Excites Doctors Less Than It Did Brokers." *The Wall Street Journal*, November 2, 1982, p. 21.

———. "Investors Hammer Immune Response After Update on Testing of AIDS Drug." *The Wall Street Journal*, June 10, 1993, p. B7.

———. "Little Difference Is Found Between TPA and Rival in Small Study of Heart Drugs." *The Wall Street Journal*, November 11, 1988.

———. "Old Heart Drug Works as Well as Costly TPA in Study." *The Wall Street Journal*, March 9, 1990, pp. B1, B4.

———. "Trade in Stock of Genentech Is Focus of Inquiry." *The Wall Street Journal*, March 4, 1990.

———. "Universities to Wield Power in DNA Field via Patent on Processes." *The Wall Street Journal*, December 31, 1980, pp. 1, 12.

———. "Wider Uses Seen for Heart Drug, But Side Effects Pose a Challenge." *The Wall Street Journal*, March 23, 1987.

Chen, Edwin, "U.S. Admits French Role in HIV Test Kit." *Los Angeles Times*, July 12, 1994.

Christensen, Kathryn. "Gene Splicers Develop a Product: New Breed of Scientist-Tycoons." *The Wall Street Journal*, November 11, 1980.

Clark, Don. "Two Months After Genentech Ouster." *The Wall Street Journal*, September 14, 1993.

Cohen, Jon. "The Culture of Credit." *Science,* June 23, 1995, pp. 1706–18.

———. "Shalala Backs Reorganization." *Science,* February 12, 1993, p. 889.

———. "Stormy Weather Ahead for OSI's Gallo Report." *Science,* February 21, 1992, pp. 914–15.

———. "U.S.-French Patent Dispute Heads for a Showdown." *Science,* July 1, 1994, pp. 23–25.

Cohn, Victor. "Max Essex." *The Washington Post,* June 19, 1990, p. 7.

Colburn, Don. "Tracking the 'Other' AIDS Virus HIV-2." *The Washington Post,* October 27, 1987, pp. 14, 15–21.

Coles, Peter. "France Set to Reopen AIDS Pact?" *Science,* September 27, 1991, p. 1479.

Cook-Deegan, Robert. *The Gene Wars: Science, Politics, and the Human Genome.* W. W. Norton: New York, 1994.

Coppola, Vincent. "Robert Gallo Wants to Fight." *Worth,* June 1996, pp. 111–18, 154–56.

Corner, George W. *A History of the Rockefeller Institute, 1901–1953: Origins and Growth.* Rockefeller Institute Press: New York, 1964.

Crane, Johana. "Chemistry Professor Max Tishler Dies at 82." *The Wesleyan Argus,* March 31, 1989.

Crewdson, John. "Burden of Proof: Gallo Case Spotlights Key Question: Can U.S. Science Be Believed?" *Chicago Tribune,* December 6, 1992, pp. 1, 4–5.

———. "Ex-Gallo Aide Guilty of Pocketing $25,000." *Chicago Tribune,* July 8, 1992, p. 4.

———. "The Great AIDS Quest," *Chicago Tribune,* November 19, 1989, Section 5.

———. "Inquiry Concludes Data in AIDS Article Falsified." *Chicago Tribune,* February 9, 1992, pp. 1, 17–18.

———. "Inquiry Hid Facts on AIDS Research." *Chicago Tribune,* March 18, 1990, pp. 1, 16–17.

———. "Probe Finds Fraud in AIDS Studies," *Chicago Tribune,* August 11, 1991, Section 1, pp. 1, 15.

———. "Scientific Panel Accuses Gallo of 'Recklessness.'" *Chicago Tribune,* March 27, 1992, p. 1.

———. "U.S. Agency Admits Aide Destroyed AIDS Test Files." *Chicago Tribune,* June 26, 1992, pp. 1, 10.

———. "U.S. Rebuffs France in AIDS Test Dispute." *Chicago Tribune,* September 17, 1992, p. 12.

Culliton, Barbara J. "The Hoechst Department at Mass. General." *Science,* June 1982, pp. 1200–3.

Day, Kathleen. "Two Drugs, Two Prices Spark a Battle." *The Washington Post,* September 16, 1994, pp. D1, D3.

Dembart, Lee. "Industry, Academics Consider Profits of Biotechnology." *Los Angeles Times,* March 26, 1982, p. 3.

Dickson, David. "Clouds on Biotechnology Horizon." *Nature,* March 4, 1982, p. 3.

———. *The New Politics of Science.* Pantheon Books: New York, 1984.

Duesberg, Peter H. *Inventing the AIDS Virus.* Regnery: Washington, D.C., 1996.

Dye, Lee. "The Ph.D. Glut: New Scientists Outnumber Jobs in Many Fields." *Los Angeles Times,* February 15, 1995, p. D5.

Ellison, Bryon J., and Peter H. Duesberg. *Why We Will Never Win the War on AIDS.* Inside Story Communications: El Cerrito, Calif., 1994.

Essex, Myron. "Africa and the Biology of Human Immunodeficiency Virus." *Journal of the American Medical Association,* May 15, 1987.

———. "Comparison of Immunofluorescence, Particle Agglutination, and Enzyme Immunoassays for Detection of Human T-Cell Leukemia Virus Type I Antibody in African Sera." *Journal of Clinical Microbiology,* September 28, 1990.

———. "Molecular Mimicry Between the Human Immunodeficiency Virus Type 1 GP 120 V3 Loop and Human Brain Proteins." *Journal of Virology,* December, 1993.

———. "U.S. Policy Threatens Boston AIDS Meeting." *The Washington Post,* July 23, 1991, p. 6.

Ezzell, Carol. "First U.S. patent on TPA for Oxford University." *Nature,* June 2, 1988, p. 383.

Fettner, Ann Guidici. *Viruses: Agents of Change.* McGraw-Hill: New York, 1990.

Finn, Robert. "Corporate Board Membership: Enriching in More Ways Than One." *The Scientist,* January 10, 1994, pp. 21–22.

———. "Layoffs in Biotechnology Signify Growing Pains for an Industry in Transition, Analysts Contend." *The Scientist,* May 1, 1995, pp. 1, 4–5.

Fisher, Lawrence M. "Rehabilitation of a Biotech Pioneer." *The New York Times,* May 8, 1994.

———. "With New Genentech Chief, Science Takes Center Stage." *The New York Times,* July 12, 1995, p. C2.

Freudenheim, Milt. "F.T.C. Seeks Data on Caremark Alliances." *The New York Times,* November 24, 1994.

Gabor, Andrea. "How a Blockbuster Went Awry." *BusinessWeek,* November 14, 1988.

Gallo, Robert. *Virus Hunting, AIDS, Cancer & the Human Retrovirus: A Story of Scientific Discovery.* Basic Books: New York, 1991.

Garrett, Laurie. *The Coming Plague.* Farrar, Straus and Giroux: New York, 1994.

Giamatti, A. Bartlett. "The University, Industry, and Cooperative Research." *Science,* December 24, 1982, pp. 1278–80.

Gibson, G. Thomas. "Research for Sale." *Venture,* March 1984, pp. 79–80, 82, 86.

Gladwell, Malcolm. "NIH Fraud Procedures Under Attack." *The Washington Post,* August 2, 1991, p. A23.

———. "NIH Memo Cites Possible Inaccuracies in AIDS Researchers' Patent Application." *The Washington Post,* August 12, 1991, p. A4.

———. "Rights to Life: Are Scientists Wrong to Patent Genes?" *The New Yorker,* November 13, 1995.

Goodman, David. "The Coming Dark Age of U.S. Research." *Los Angeles Times,* August 31, 1994, p. B7.

Green, Jesse. "Who Put the Lid on gp 120?" *The New York Times Magazine,* March 26, 1995, pp. 50–57, 74, 82.

Greenberg, Daniel S. "The Gallo Case: Is This Really Happening?" *The Lancet,* June 27, 1992, p. 1594.

———. "Whatever Happened to the War on Cancer?" *Discover,* March 1986, pp. 47–64.

Gurin, Joel, and Nancy E. Pfund. "Genetic Engineering Bonanza in the Bio Lab." *The Nation,* November 22, 1980, pp. 543–48.

Hall, Carl T. "Questions Remain After FDA Ruling: Genentech Now Allowed to Aggressively Tout Favorable Results of Its Heart Attack Drug." *San Francisco Chronicle,* May 5, 1995, pp. D1, D3.

285

Hall, Stephen S. "Gadfly in the Ointment." *Hippocrates,* September–October, 1988, pp. 76–77, 79, 81.

———. *Invisible Frontiers: The Race to Synthesize a Human Gene.* Atlantic Monthly Press: New York, 1987.

———. "James Watson and the Search for Biology's 'Holy Grail.'" *Smithsonian,* February 1990.

———. "Old School Ties: Watson, Crick, and 40 Years of DNA." *Science,* March 12, 1993, pp. 1532–33.

Hamilton, David. "In the Trenches, Doubts About Scientific Integrity." *Science,* March 27, 1992, p. 1636.

———. "Can OSI Withstand a Scientific Backlash." *Science,* September 6, 1991, pp. 1084–86.

———. "Did OSI Rewrite History?" *Science,* May 15, 1992, p. 959.

———. "OSI Investigator 'Reined In.'" *Science,* July 26, 1991, p. 372.

———. "The Richards Panel Tosses a Curve." *Science,* April 3, 1992, p. 23.

Hamilton, Joan O'C. "A Star Drug Is Born." *BusinessWeek,* August 23, 1993, pp. 66–68.

———. "Biotech: An Industry Crowded with Players Faces an Ugly Reckoning." *BusinessWeek,* September 26, 1994, pp. 84–88, 90, 92.

———. "Genentech: A Textbook Case of Medical Marketing." *BusinessWeek,* August 13, 1990, pp. 96–97.

Hilts, Philip J. "A New Assertiveness at the U.S. Health Institutes." *The New York Times,* September 9, 1991, pp. A13–A14.

———. "American Scientist Who Found H.I.V. Is Investigated Anew." *The New York Times,* March 2, 1992, pp. A1, A10–A11.

———. "Health Official Concedes Mishandling of Inquiry." *The New York Times,* August 2, 1991, p. B6.

———. "Key Patent on AIDS to Favor the French." *The New York Times,* July 12, 1994, p. B6.

———. "New Questions in Scientific Misconduct Cases Prompt Withdrawal of Health Official." *The New York Times,* August 1, 1991, pp. B6–B7.

———. "U.S. Seeks to Protect Fruits of Tax-Supported Research." *The New York Times,* June 17, 1993.

Hoke, Franklin. "AIDS Research Progress Stymied by Narrow Focus, Critics Charge." *The Scientist,* July 11, 1994, pp. 1, 4–5, 11.

———. "Gallo's Meeting: A Scientific 'Folk Festival.'" *The Scientist,* November 14, 1994, pp. 1, 4–5.

———. "NIH Chief Varmus, in His Second Year, Credited with Reinvigorating Agency." *The Scientist,* February 20, 1995, pp. 1, 6–7.

———. "In Letter to Congress, Corporate Leaders Call Campus Science Crucial to Progress." *The Scientist,* May 1, 1995, pp. 1, 6–7.

———. "Universities Reassess Social Role As Tech Transfer Activity Mounts." *The Scientist,* September 20, 1993, pp. 1, 6, 21.

Holden, Constance. "Haseltine Moves to Biotech Firm." *Science,* May 28, 1993, p. 1238.

Holobaugh, Pat. "Results of Investigations into the Activities of Genentech Sales Representatives with Respect to the ISIS-3 Study." U.S. Department of Health and Human Services. Investigative Memorandum, November 7, 1991.

Hood, Leroy, and Daniel J. Kevles. *The Code of Codes.* Harvard University Press: Cambridge, Mass., 1992.

Hopson, Janet. "Recombinant Lab for DNA and My 95 days in It." *Smithsonian,* August 1976, pp. 55–62.

Hubbard, Ruth, and Elijah Wald. *Exploding the Gene Myth.* Beacon Press: Boston, 1993.

Hudson, Richard. "Genentech's Heart Drug TPA Appears Only to Equal Its Rivals, Report Says." *The Wall Street Journal,* September 2, 1988.

Hunt, Morton. "Teaming Up Against AIDS." *The New York Times Magazine,* March 2, 1986, pp. 42–44, 51, 78–83.

Jacobs, Paul. "UC Relishes Power of the Patent." *Los Angeles Times,* February 14, 1996, pp. A1, A23.

Jaroff, Leon. "Crisis in the Labs." *Time,* August 26, 1991, pp. 44–51.

———. "A Few Words from the Pioneers." *Time,* March 15, 1993, pp. 58–60.

———. "Happy Birthday, Double Helix." *Time,* March 15, 1993, pp. 56–60.

Judson, Horace Freeland. *The Eighth Day of Creation: Makers of the Revolution in Biology.* Simon & Schuster: New York, 1979.

Kefalide, Paul. "Apathy, Outrage Accompany Leak of Unofficial Report on Gallo Case." *The Scientist,* April 3, 1995, pp. 1, 4–5.

Kenney, Martin. *Bio-technology: The University-Industrial Complex.* Yale University Press: New Haven, Conn., 1986.

Kevles, Daniel J. "The Assault on David Baltimore." *The New Yorker,* May 27, 1996, pp. 94–109.

Keysworth, G. A., II. "Federal R&D and Industrial Policy." *Science,* June 10, 1983, pp. 1122–25.

Kilgore, Senator H. M. "Science and the Government." *Science,* December 21, 1945, pp. 630–38.

King, Ralph T., Jr. "FDA Widens Marketing Probe of Genentech." *The Wall Street Journal,* November 10, 1994, p. A3.

———. "Genentech's 2nd-Period Net Rose 11%; Raab Departs with $6.4 Million to Come." *The Wall Street Journal,* July 19, 1995, p. B4.

———. "In Marketing of Drugs, Genentech Tests Limits of What Is Acceptable." *The Wall Street Journal,* January 10, 1995, pp. A1, A14.

Kitasato Institute. *The Life of Max Tishler.* Shirokane Minato-Ku: Tokyo, 1984.

Kolata, Gina. "Fraud Inquiry Aims at a Home Health Care Giant." *The New York Times,* August 26, 1994, p. A20.

———. "Top Official Says AIDS Fight Is Inefficient." *The New York Times,* February 3, 1995.

Krimsky, Sheldon. *Biotechnics and Society: The Rise of Industrial Genetics.* Praeger: New York, 1991.

Lauritsen, John. "Kangaroo Court Etiology." *New York Native,* May 9, 1988, pp. 14–16, 18–19.

Leary, Warren E. "On the Trail of Research Misconduct, 'Science Police' Take the Limelight." *The New York Times,* March 25, 1991.

Lee, Kerry L., Robert M. Califf, John Simes, Frans Van de Werf, and Eric J. Topol. "Holding GUSTO Up to the Light." *American College of Physicians,* 1994, pp. 876–81.

Lewis, Anthony. "Tale of a Bully." *The New York Times,* June 24, 1996, p. A11.

Marranto, Gina. "Genetic Engineering: Hype, Hubris, and Haste." *Discover,* June 1986, pp. 50–64.

Marsh, David, "French Evaluate AIDS Tests As Patent Row Continues," *The Financial Times,* February 28, 1985, p. 8.

Marshall, Eliot. "A New Phase in the War on Cancer." *Science*, March 10, 1995, pp. 1412–15.

———. "Gallo's Institute at the Last Hurdle." *Science*, March 8, 1996, p. 1359.

———. "NIH Gets a Share of BRCA1 Patent." *Science*, February 24, 1995, p. 1086.

———. "R&D Policy That Emphasizes the 'D.'" *Science*, March 26, 1993, pp. 1816–19.

———. "Scripps Backs Down on Controversial Sandoz Deal." *Science*, June 25, 1993, pp. 1872–73.

———. "Suit Alleges Misuse of Peer Review." *Science*, December 22, 1995, pp. 1912–14.

———. "Varmus Orders Up a Review of the Science of Gene Therapy." *Science*, March 17, 1995, p. 1588.

Massachusetts Biomedical Research Corporation, Massachusetts General Hospital Committee on Research. Conference on Conflicts of Interests in Biomedical and Biotechnology Research, October 15–16, 1990.

Masters, David. *Miracle Drug: The Inner History of Penicillin.* Eyre & Spottiswoode: London, 1946.

McCoy, Charles. "Genentech's New CEO Seeks Clean Slate." *The Wall Street Journal,* July 12, 1995, p. B6.

McKenna, M. A. J. "The Big Picture." *Boston Magazine,* February 1995, pp. 54–57, 100–2.

Meyerhoff, Albert H. "UC Research Ties: A Secret Needing a Dose of Sunshine." *Los Angeles Times,* February 2, 1982.

Miller, Jeff. "AIDS Heresy." *Discover,* June 1988, pp. 62–68.

Mitchell, M. "Companies Vie over New Heart Drug." *Science,* July 10, 1987, pp. 120–22.

Monmaney, Terence. "Many Don't Want to Know Genetic Risk of Cancer." *Los Angeles Times,* June 26, 1996, pp. A1, A13.

Monmaney, Terence, Ruth Marshall, and Mary Hagar. "Another AIDS Virus Appears." *Newsweek,* January 4, 1988, pp. 60–61.

Negin, Elliott. "Why College Tuitions Are So High." *The Atlantic Monthly,* March 1993, pp. 32, 34, 43–44.

News Transcripts, Inc. "TechnoPolitics." Program No. 119, August 9, 1991.

Noble, David F. "The Selling of the University." *The Nation,* February 6, 1982, Cover, pp. 143–48.

Olby, Robert. *The Path to the Double Helix.* University of Washington Press: Seattle, 1974.

Olmos, David R. "Genentech Ousts CEO over Conflict Question." *Los Angeles Times,* pp. D1, D7.

Palca, Joseph. "Bernadine Healy: A New Leadership Style at NIH." *Science,* September 6, 1991, pp. 1087–89.

———. "Gallo Concedes Contamination (Again)." *Science,* June 7, 1991, p. 1369.

———. "NIH Grapples with Conflict of Interest." *Science,* July 7, 1989, p. 23.

———. "Scientists Get Mad at OSI." *Science,* June 21, 1991, pp. 1606–7.

———. "The Genome Project: Life After Watson." *Science,* May 15, 1992, pp. 956–58.

———. "'Verdicts' Are in on the Gallo Probe." Science, May 8, 1992, pp. 735–38.

Piller, Charles, and Keith R. Yamamoto. *Gene Wars: Military Control of the New Genetic Technologies.* Beech Tree Books: New York.

Purvis, Andrew. "Cheaper Can Be Better." *Time,* March 18, 1991, p. 70.

Queenan, Joe, and William M. Alpert. "Scientists and Stock Pushers: They Make Strange and Embarrassing Bedfellows." *Barron's,* March 21, 1988, pp. 8–9, 40–41, 44–48.

Ready, Tinker. "Market Research or Scientific Research? Study Raises Questions." *Charlotte News & Observer,* April 16, 1995.

———. "The Doctor and His Implants." *Charlotte News & Observer,* March 31, 1994, pp. 7–9.

Regush, Nicholas, "AIDS Risks Limited, Studies Suggest." *Montreal Gazette,* August 15, 1987, pp. B1, B4.

Reinhold, Robert, "Government Scrutinizes Link Between Genetics Industry and Universities." *The New York Times,* June 16, 1981, p. 15.

Rentrop, Peter K. "Restoration of Anterograde Flow in Acute Myocardial Infarction: The First 15 Years." *American College of Cardiology,* June 1995, pp. 1S–2S.

Rhein, Reginald. "NIH Finds Scripps-Sandoz Deal Unusual for Sponsored Research Agreement." McGraw Hill Biotechnology Newswatch, February 7, 1994.

Richards, A. N. "Production of Penicillin in the United States (1941–1946)." *Nature,* February 1, 1964, pp. 441–45.

Ridker, Paul M., Christopher O'Donnell, Victor J. Marder, and Charles H. Hennekens. "A Response to 'Holding GUSTO Up to the Light.'" *American College of Physicians,* 1994, pp. 882–85.

———. "Large-Scale Trials of Thrombolytic Therapy for Acute Myocardial Infarction: GISSI-2, ISIS-3, and GUSTO-1." *Annals of Internal Medicine,* September 15, 1993, pp. 530–32.

Riengold, Nathan. *Science, American Style.* Rutgers University Press: New Brunswick, N.J..

Rigdon, Joan E. "Genentech CEO, a Man Used to Pushing Limits, Exceeds It and Is Out." *The Wall Street Journal,* July 11, 1995.

Roberts, Leslie. "Cold Spring Harbor Turns 100." *Science,* October 26, 1990, pp. 496–98.

Roberts, Seth. "Lab Rat." *Spy,* July 1990, pp. 70–79.

Rogers, Michael. "The Pandora's Box Congress." *Rolling Stone,* June 19, 1975, pp. 36–42, 74, 77, 78, 82.

Rolbein, Seth. "Peptide T and the AIDS Establishment." *Boston Magazine,* June 1990, pp. 79–80, 126–34.

Roman, Mark B. "When Good Scientists Turn Bad." *Discover,* April 1988, pp. 50–58.

Root-Bernstein, Robert S. "Agenda for U.S. AIDS Research Is Due for a Complete Overhaul." *The Scientist,* April 4, 1994, pp. 1, 11, 14.

Rose, Craig D. "4 Area Institutes Targeted on Sales." *San Diego Union-Tribune,* February 13, 1993, pp. A1, A19.

———. "Time for NIH to Take a Good Look at Funds." *San Diego Union-Tribune,* February 1, 1993.

Rosenberg, Steven A., "Secrecy in Medical Research," *The New England Journal of Medicine,* February 8, 1996, pp. 393–94.

Rothenberg, Randall. "Robert A. Swanson, Chief Genetic Officer." *Esquire,* December 1984.

Rothman, Matt. "Genentech, Inc.: Marriage of Great Convenience." *California Business,* January 1991, p. 18.

Rubinstein, Ellis. "The Gallo Factor: Questions Remain." *Science,* August 16, 1991, p. 732.

Salwen, Kevin G. "Genentech, Inc., Chief Executive's Wife Settles SEC Charges of Insider Trading." *The Wall Street Journal,* November 12, 1990.

Sankaran, Neeraja. "Growth in Federal Scientific Work Force in 1989–1993 May Be Offset by Recent Cuts." *The Scientist,* May 1, 1995, pp. 1, 8.

————. "Pharmaceutical Companies Stress Innovative Research for Success." *The Scientist*, December 12, 1994, pp. 1, 11.

Sattaur, Omar, "How Gallo Got Credit for AIDS Discovery," *New Scientist*, February 7, 1985, p. 3.

Schlender, Brenton R., and Michael Waldholz. "Genentech's Missteps and FDA Policy Shift Led to TPA Setback." *The Wall Street Journal*, June 16, 1987.

Schmeck, Harold M., Jr. "Justices' Ruling Recognizes Gains in the Manipulation of Life Forms." *The New York Times*, June 1, 1980, p. 1.

Seligman, Daniel. "Who Has the Next Wonder Drug?" *Fortune*, September 28, 1987.

Sharp, Phillip A. "Biotech in the 1990's: What's in Store?" *The Scientist*, May 2, 1994, p. 4.

————. "The Test Tube Wars." *The New York Times*, November 28, 1993.

Sheehan, John C. *The Enchanted Ring: The Untold Story of Penicillin.* MIT Press: Cambridge, Mass., 1982.

Sherry, Sol. *Fibrinolysis, Thrombosis, and Hemostasis: Concepts, Perspectives, and Clinical Applications.* Lea & Febiger: Philadelphia, 1992.

————. *Reflections and Reminiscences of an Academic Physician.* Lea & Febiger: Philadelphia, 1993.

Sherry, Sol and Victor J. Marder. "Creation of the Recombinant Tissue Plasminogen Activator (rt-PA) Image and Its Influence on Practice Habits." *American College of Cardiology*, November 15, 1991, pp. 1579–82.

Shilts, Randy. *And the Band Played On.* St. Martin's Press: New York, 1987.

Shogreen, Elizibeth. "FDA Approves New Drug for Cystic Fibrosis." *Los Angeles Times*, December 31, 1993, p. A24.

Shuit, Douglas. "Panel Studies UC Conflict Issue." *Los Angeles Times*, October 6, 1981, pp. 3, 16.

Sia, Richard H. P. "A Prescription for Trouble." *San Jose Mercury News*, December 18, 1994, pp. 1D–3D.

Silverman, Milton, Mia Lydecker, and Philip R. Lee. *Bad Medicine.* Stanford University Press: Stanford, Calif., 1992.

Slutsker, Gary. "Patenting Mother Nature." *Forbes*, January 7, 1991.

Sobel, Burton E., Désiré Collen, and Elliott B. Grossbard. *Tissue Plasminogen Activator in Thrombolytic Therapy.* Marcel Dekker: New York, 1987.

Starr, Paul. *The Social Transformation of American Medicine.* Basic Books: New York, 1982.

Steinbrook, Robert. "Harvard Scientists Admit Error in AIDS Virus Report." *Los Angeles Times*, February 18, 1988, pp. 3, 22.

————. "Two Variant AIDS Viruses—a Windfall for Researchers." *Los Angeles Times*, November 19, 1986, pp. 3, 26.

Stent, Gunther S. *The Coming of the Golden Age: A View of the End of Progress.* Natural History Press: Garden City, N.Y., 1969.

————. "DNA's Stroke of Genius." *New Scientist*, April 24, 1993, pp. 21–26.

Stiff, David. "A Clot-Dissolving Drug Proves Effective in Federal Tests of Heart-Attack Patients." *The Wall Street Journal*, March 10, 1988.

Stolberg, Sheryl. "Seeking a Cure: Faith, Frustration." *Los Angeles Times*, August 7, 1994, pp. A1, A12, A19.

Stone, I. F. "The Cancer Cartel." *The Nation*, February 12, 1944, pp. 178–79.

290

Strickland, Stephen P. *Politics, Science, and Dread Disease: A Short History of United States Medical Research Policy.* Harvard University Press: Cambridge, Mass., 1972.

Swann, John P. *Academic Scientists and the Pharmaceutical Industry: Cooperative Research in Twentieth-Century America.* John Hopkins University Press: Baltimore, 1988.

Swazey, Judith P., Melissa S. Anderson, and Karen Seashore Louis. "Ethical Problems in Academic Research." *Omni*, November–December, 1993, pp. 542–53.

Sylvester, Edward J., and Lynn C. Klotz. *The Gene Age: Genetic Engineering and the Next Industrial Revolution.* Charles Scribner's Sons: New York, 1983.

Taubes, Gary. "Misconduct: Views from the Trenches." *Science*, August 27, 1993, pp. 1108–11.

Teitelman, Robert. *Gene Dreams: Wall Street, Academia, and the Rise of Biotechnology.* Basic Books: New York, 1989.

——— "Genentech: A Fractured Fairy Tale." *Financial World*, November 15, 1988, pp. 14, 16.

———. "Get a Second Opinion." *Financial World*, December 23, 1986, pp. 106–7.

———. *Profits of Science: The American Marriage of Business and Technology.* Basic Books: New York, 1994.

———. *Gene Dreams: Wall Street, Academia, and the Rise of Biotechnology.* Basic Books: New York, 1989.

Tishler, Max. "The Siege of the House of Reason." *Science*, October 10, 1969, pp. 192–94.

Topol, Eric J., William R. Bell, and Myron L. Weisfeldt. "Coronary Thrombosis with Recombinant Tissue-Type Plasminogen Activator." *American College of Physicians*, 1985, pp. 837–43.

Wade, Nicholas. "Georges Koehler, 48, Medicine Nobel Winner." *The New York Times*, March 4, 1995, p. 13.

———. "La Jolla Biologists Troubled by the Midas Factor." *Science*, August 7, 1981, pp. 623–26, 628.

Waldholz, Michael. "Genentech Heart Drug Dealt Critical Blow." *The Wall Street Journal*, March 30, 1989.

———. "Genentech, Inc., Pressed by Data on Clot Drugs." *The Wall Street Journal*, March 27, 1992.

Watson, James D. "Salvador E. Luria (Obituary)." *Nature*, March 14, 1991, p. 113.

———. *The Double Helix.* Atheneum: New York, 1968.

Weiner, Charles, "Universities, Professors, and Patents: A Continuing Controversy," *Technology Review*, February/March, 1986, pp. 33–43.

Weiser, Benjamin. "Derailing or Due Process?" *The Washington Post*, August 14, 1991, pp. A19–A20.

Weiss, Rick. "Leaving an Unhappy Ship." *The Washington Post Weekly Edition*, January 28, 1995, p. 34.

Werth, Barry. "By AIDS Obsessed." *Gentlemen's Quarterly*, August 1991, pp. 144–51, 205–8.

———. "How Short Is Too Short?" *The New York Times Magazine*, June 16, 1991, pp. 15, 17, 28–29, 47.

———. *The Billion Dollar Molecule: One Company's Quest for the Perfect Drug.* Simon & Schuster: New York, 1994.

———. "The Great AIDS Windfall," *New England Monthly,* June 1988.

Wright, Susan. *Molecular Politics.* University of Chicago Press: Chicago, 1994.

Zinman, David. "Doctors as Stock Holders: A Question of Ethics When Researchers Invest in Drugs They're Testing." *Newsday,* September 29, 1987, p. 1.

INDEX

293

Morrow, John, 61
Mount Sinai Hospital, 153, 159
Murphy, Frederick, 187
Murrow, Edward R., 50
Mycosis fungeoides, 78, 80–81
Myers, Gerald, 242–43
Myocardial infarction, 126, 153
  National Registry of, 210
  See also Heart attacks
Myriad Genetics, 260

Nader, Ralph, 141, 257
National Academy of Sciences, 60, 63,
  90, 185
  Richards Committee of, 229–30, 232,
  234–35
National Cancer Institute (NCI), 27, 242
  DeVita as head of, 71, 111, 195, 196
  See also Gallo, Robert
National Cooperative Growth Study, 208
National Heart, Lung, and Blood Insti-
  tute (NHLBI), 153, 159, 160
National Institute of Mental Health
  (NIMH), 228
National Institutes of Health (NIH)
  in AIDS patent case, 192, 196, 197,
  225–34
  bids for AIDS test sought by, 191
  Gallo at, 71–82, 105, 110–20
  genetic engineering mandates of, 92,
  94
  growth hormone study by, 209
  Healy as head of, 149, 230–35, 243,
  257, 259
  hierarchical organization of, 28
  history and description of, 27–29,
  69–71
  Office of AIDS research, 242, 248
  Shannon as head of, 28–29
  Technology Transfer Office, 259
  t-PA testing and, 155–57
  Varmus as head of, 243–45, 248, 249,
  259–60
  See also Office of Research Integrity
  (ORI); Office of Scientific Integrity
  (OSI)
National Institute of Allergy and Infec-
  tious Diseases (NIAID), 8, 111,
  178, 190, 241, 242
National Registry of Myocardial Infarc-
  tion, 210
National Resources Defense Council
  (NRDC), 131

Nature, 37–38, 62, 174, 196, 248
NCI. *See* National Cancer Institute
New England Journal of Medicine, The,
  151–52, 158, 203, 265
Newsday, 201
New York Times, The, 61, 94, 117–18,
  182, 183, 195, 196, 226
NHLBI. *See* National Heart, Lung, and
  Blood Institute
NIAID. *See* National Institute of Allergy
  and Infectious Diseases
NIH. *See* National Institutes of Health
NIMH (National Institute of Mental
  Health), 228
Nirenberg, Marshall, 41, 59, 69
Nixon, Richard M.
  academic scientists distrusted by, 96
  War on Cancer of, 8, 46–48, 51, 70, 76,
  83, 173
Nobel, David, 99, 138
Nottingham University Medical Center,
  203
NRDC (National Resources Defense
  Council), 131
Nucleic acids, 32, 58
Nucleotides, 38–39, 41
Nurses, on Genentech's promotional
  staff, 209–10, 212

Ochoa, Severo, 41
Office of Research Integrity (ORI), in
  Gallo case, 10, 238–39
Office of Science and Technology Policy,
  96
Office of Scientific Integrity (OSI)
  abolition of, 238–39
  creation of, 225
  due process allegedly denied by,
  231–32
  in Gallo case, 113, 227–33,, 235–37
Office of Scientific Research and Devel-
  opment (OSRD), 19–20
Oil spill, no noncommercial scientist
  available for advice on, 142
Oncogenes, 46, 75, 175, 176–77
O'Neill, William, 211
Onek, Joseph, 10, 187, 189, 232, 245n
Oppenheimer, Robert, 25
ORI. *See* Office of Research Integrity
Ortho, 191
OSI. *See* Office of Scientific Integrity
OSRD (Office of Scientific Research and
  Development), 19–20